Instructor's Resource Manual

PLAZAS

LUGAR DE ENCUENTROS

Second Edition

Sandra Schreffler
Appalachian State University

Deborah Mistron
Middle Tennessee State University

Guadalupe López-Cox
Austin Community College

THOMSON

HEINLE

Australia   Canada   Mexico   Singapore   Spain   United Kingdom   United States

Contents

Printed in the United States of America by Thomson/West.
1 2 3 4 5 6 7 8 9 10   08 07 06 05 04

For permission to use material from this text or product, submit a request online at http://www.thomsonrights.com. Any additional questions about permissions can be submitted by email to thomsonrights@thomson.com.

ISBN: 0-8384-0956-3 (Instructor's Resource Manual)
ISBN: 0-8384-1015-4 (Instructor's Resource Manual + Test Bank CD-ROM)

Introduction

Plazas: Lugar de encuentros is a beginning Spanish language text that encourages the development of all four language skills—listening, speaking, reading, and writing—plus the fifth skill—understanding culture—using a communicative approach to second language acquisition. The theme of the "plaza," a meeting place for interactive activities in Spanish within a Spanish-speaking culture, is an emblem for the focus of the text. The presentation of the vocabulary, grammatical structures, readings, and cultural information, together with a wide variety of practice activities, are intended as tools for attaining proficiency in Spanish in all five skill areas.

Plazas is uniquely suited to instructors and programs whose goals for students include the development of second language proficiency along with an understanding of the cultures in which Spanish is spoken. This ***Instructor's Resource Manual*** presents pedagogical material, classroom recommendations, and practical teaching ideas and exercises that allow you to effectively utilize the program to address and satisfy the needs of your learners as well as your second language program. This *Manual* contains materials and ideas to aid you in effectively teaching beginning Spanish, including:

• Teaching the four + one skills—listening, speaking, reading, writing, and culture
• Teaching the five Cs—communication, cultures, connections, comparisons, and communities
• Teaching grammar
• Classroom management
• Lesson and syllabus planning guide
• Sample lesson plans and sample syllabi
• Professional development resource material

The ***Plazas*** program and the ***Instructor's Resource Manual*** are flexible and provide you with ample opportunities for individual creativity in teaching and learning. The suggestions presented can be used, adapted, or even ignored, if you wish, according to your requirements and the needs and proficiency of your students. Although a textbook or instructor's manual cannot consider or solve all of the problems that may occur in the classroom, these recommendations are intended to guide the instructor and are consistent with current theory and methodology in the field of second language acquisition and teaching. While additional readings are not required, the bibliographical references are provided as a starting point for further independent investigation.

It is extremely important to keep in mind that there are many different learning styles. However, practice and application must be part of the acquisition process, regardless of the method used in teaching and the learning style of students. To this end, *Plazas* provides a wide variety of activities to make learning a second language as interesting and rewarding as possible for both you and your students. Nonetheless, one of the most important elements in successful second language acquisition—flexibility—remains with the instructor. The instructor's enthusiasm and expertise will yield the best results if she/he remains open-minded, flexible, and able to adapt to the needs and interests of her/his students. *Plazas* is designed for optimum flexibility in order to ensure maximum adaptability for instructors.

CHAPTER ORGANIZATION

WHAT IS *PLAZAS*?

Plazas is an introductory Spanish program that, much like a Hispanic plaza, focuses on meeting and connecting and goes to the "heart" of the Spanish language. The text was designed to bring students and teachers together to communicate and interact. The organization of each chapter reflects what instructors really do in class, and is aimed at the development and practice of all five skills involved in the successful acquisition and usage of a second language.

Plazas' fifteen-chapter format, plus a **Capítulo preliminar,** makes it flexible enough to use over two, three, or even four semesters. Consistent chapter structure includes:

CHAPTER OPENER

Each chapter opener features:

- a photo of a major plaza in the profiled country(ies)
- demographic information for said country(ies)
- the communicative goals and the grammar and cultural topics of the chapter
- a brief activity to accompany the new **Bienvenidos a...** video, which introduces the geographic area of focus

VOCABULARIO

- Instead of dry lists, the **Vocabulario** sections present active terms through illustrations or photos.
- All words listed in the comprehensive end-of-chapter **Vocabulario esencial** also appear on the text audio CD.

EN CONTEXTO

This section contains dialogs illustrating the vocabulary students have just learned and foreshadows the grammar **(Estructuras)** to come.

- Dialogs always take place in the profiled country, and the speakers' language and mannerisms reflect the uniqueness of each region.
- All dialogs appear on the Text Audio CD.

Just as discussion with friends prepares you for what you will hear later in the day, the dialogs also serve as advance organizers for the video to come in the **Síntesis** section, exposing the students to situations they will encounter in the video, so that their experience watching the video is more fruitful and satisfying.

ESTRUCTURAS

Reflecting the struggles students have today with grammar, the **Estructuras** sections seek to teach students the essential forms that will allow them to use the Spanish language as comfortably, comprehensibly, and accurately as possible. These sections feature:

- clear and complete grammar explanations in plain English
- contextualized examples to further illustrate the grammar point
- plenty of practice exercises to apply the new forms

ASÍ SE DICE

These brief sections cover certain grammar points lexically (for example, **tener** idioms) at a level appropriate for first-year students. Some points, such as **hay** and **gustar,** are treated in **Así se dice** early in the book so that students can use them to communicate. Students then are given a fuller explanation, including rules and exceptions, later in the book.

ENCUENTRO CULTURAL

Plazas seeks to expose students to the richness and diversity of Spanish-speaking cultures. The **Encuentro cultural** sections offer:

- real cultural encounters, where students are asked to think critically about the topic and compare it to their own experiences
- all-Spanish presentations of culture (except for the *Capítulo Preliminar*)
- diverse, high-interest topics from the use of herbal remedies in Latin America to the architecture of Gaudí in Spain

¿NOS ENTENDEMOS?

In keeping with *Plazas'* focus on cultural and linguistic authenticity, each chapter includes a selection of notes that highlight regional variations in language use.

ACTIVITIES

A consistent pattern of activities reinforces each **Vocabulario, Estructura,** and **Así se dice** presentation.

- The two-tiered activity chain offers controlled practice (**¡A practicar!**) and open-ended application (**En voz alta**). This activity progression is replicated in the workbook.
- All activities are personalized and culturally relevant, and offer a variety of individual, pair, group, whole-class, and role-play options.
- Activities recycle material learned earlier in the chapter and earlier in the book.

SÍNTESIS: FOUR + ONE SKILLS PRACTICE

Whether you choose to use the **Síntesis** materials in the textbook, or the completely different online **Síntesis** activities, your students will be pulling together all the material they have studied in the chapter in creative and effective ways.

- **¡A ver!** sections correspond to the all new story line video and contain comprehension and communicative activities. The video follows the lives of five students as they come together in a Spanish-speaking culture, modeling the vocabulary, structures, and communicative goals of the respective chapter. A video transcript is available separately for instructors.
- **¡A leer!** develops reading skills through authentic documents, literary readings, and reading strategies that can be carried over to other disciplines.
- **¡A escribir!** features step-by-step writing strategies. Activities based on the chapter's theme recycle both the strategies of the current chapter and those of earlier chapters. This section guides students through the writing process, from organizing ideas to sequencing paragraphs to writing for different genres. All activities are supported by the *Atajo 4.0 Writing Assistant for Spanish.*
- **¡A conversar!** encourages students to use the target language through pair and group activities and roleplays. Each section now has a pronunciation focus as well.

PLAZAS REVISTA

Appearing every three chapters, the *Plazas* cultural magazine provides a fresh look at culture and an opportunity for students to make connections and comparisons with high-interest topics. Its approach is rooted in the five Cs: Communication, Culture, Connections, Comparisons, and Communities. It offers abundant photos, authentic materials, and activities that creatively integrate the themes, functions, and cultures of the preceding chapters.

THE *PLAZAS* PROGRAM: INTEGRATING THE SUPPLEMENTS

The *Plazas* text is accompanied by a wide range of supplementary materials that support student learning and are fully integrated with the material presented in the main text.

The Student Text, along with the Student Text Audio CDs, the Workbook/Lab Manual, the Lab Audio Program, and the video program, form the core of the *Plazas* program. These integrated components offer ample in-class, lab, and homework activities.

- The Student Text Audio CDs are packaged with the Student Text, and present oral material from each chapter. They are designed to enhance students' listening comprehension and pronunciation skills. The **En contexto** dialogs are recorded to model pronunciation, vocabulary, and linguistic functions. These dialogs may be played in class or assigned as homework. The **Vocabulario esencial** is pronounced by native speakers of the language. Students may listen to this section as often as necessary or desired outside of class to perfect their pronunciation of active vocabulary items.
- The Workbook, coordinated with the Student Text, offers additional practice of the vocabulary, grammar, reading, writing, and culture presented and practiced in class. These exercises may be assigned as homework and corrected at home with the aid of a separate answer key, which may be purchased or packaged with the Workbook/Lab Manual. The Workbook also includes **Auto-pruebas** *(self-tests),* to assist students with diagnosing areas for additional practice and to prepare for exams. The Lab Manual portion of the Workbook/Lab Manual provides abundant listening comprehension practice for students, using dialogs, simulated conversations, and pronunciation practice. These exercises, which can be used in the language lab or at home, offer students additional practice in listening comprehension beyond the usual classroom contact hours. The Lab Audio Program consists of eight audio CDs that correspond to the material in the Lab Manual. They feature thirty minutes of core audio exercises per chapter, recorded in the accent of the country of focus, plus ten to fifteen additional minutes of expansion audio activities. The Audio Program remains an invaluable resource for improving pronunciation and listening comprehension, as well as for getting a feel for the sound of Spanish in different Spanish-speaking countries. As an alternative to the Workbook/Lab Manual and Lab Audio Program package, the ⬭ Online Workbook/Lab Manual may be used. **QUIA** offers expanded content in an electronic format. These exercises are complemented by audio recordings, are self-correcting, and may be sent directly to the instructor and recorded automatically in the online grade book.

- The new video program contains two videos: **Bienvenidos a... ,** which corresponds to the chapter opener, takes students to the chapter's country or region of focus, and provides background information on geography and climate, history and culture, and people and places all over the Spanish-speaking world, and **¡A ver!,** which corresponds to the chapter-ending **Síntesis,** and follows the lives of five students as they come together in a Spanish-speaking culture, modeling the vocabulary, structures, and communicative goals of the respective chapters. The video program offers additional practice in listening comprehension and enhances students' cultural understanding of Spanish-speaking countries.

In addition to these core materials, the *Plazas* Web site offers additional activities to enhance student learning:

- **ⓘLrn** quizzes offer self-scoring grammar and vocabulary drills to reinforce what students have studied in the chapters. These quizzes may be used daily or as a pre-testing review.
- The **Síntesis** section provides students with additional practice in reading, writing, and listening, within the context of an unfolding story. In completing these exercises, students will visit pertinent Web sites and/or pages, which allows for additional cultural exploration. These activities may be printed out or emailed to the instructor.

The *Plazas* program also offers an interactive Multimedia CD-ROM. Within the context of a work-study program, students build a résumé in Spanish by completing real-world tasks. The CD-ROM allows students to practice vocabulary, grammar, reading, writing, listening, and speaking in a virtual environment that boasts of illustrations, photos, videos, and audio recordings. Although this component is integrated with the entire program, its use is optional. It can be done in the lab, as homework, or as a pre-test review.

For instructors, the *Plazas* program offers many additional resources: the annotated edition of the text with tips for in-class activities, a resource manual with sample lesson plans and syllabi, Power-Point presentations or overhead transparencies for use in class to introduce or practice vocabulary and grammar, an activity file with lesson-specific worksheets, a complete Test Bank on CD-ROM with multiple versions of chapter tests and exams for two- and three-semester programs, and the *Atajo 4.0 Writing Assistant for Spanish*, for use with ¡**A escribir!** activities in the **Síntesis** section of the text. The new edition of *Plazas* also boasts of a WebTutor Toolbox, which provides instructors with the course management capabilities of WebCT or Blackboard.

As indicated, along with the core materials, the *Plazas* program offers instructors a wide variety of support materials that will enhance their courses and facilitate student study. All components tie seamlessly to the lessons taught in the main text.

TEACHING TO THE NATIONAL STANDARDS

The *Plazas* program emphasizes a communicative, interactive approach to the teaching of language and culture and follows the principles outlined in ACTFL's National Standards for Foreign Language Learning. The main principles are often called the five Cs: Communication, Culture, Connections, Comparisons, and Communities. The five Cs symbolize the primary goals of language teaching—to provide the linguistic and cultural foundations for students to interact in the real world, to allow students to engage in interdisciplinary studies, to explore new cultures, and, in so doing, to learn more about our own language and culture. *Plazas* assists you in integrating the 5 Cs into your course in ways that are feasible for beginning students.

The sections that follow explain how to implement the standards and offer practical advice for teaching each section.

TEACHING THE FOUR + ONE SKILLS AND THE FIRST "C": COMMUNICATION

Communication includes the Four + One Skills—listening, speaking, reading, writing, plus culture.

As a communicative, proficiency-oriented program, *Plazas* seeks to bring students to the intermediate level on the ACTFL scale and to teach the foundational skills that will allow for more advanced levels of proficiency. With this goal in mind, the core materials of *Plazas* emphasize ACTFL's communication standard. This standard is often thought of as "four skills plus culture." The National Standards document stresses that both linguistic and cultural knowledge are essential for communication and that it is important to provide students with many opportunities to use the target language in meaningful situations. The National Standards use the traditional "four skills plus culture" as a point of departure to lead teachers and students to a new way of thinking about communication.

The communication standard stresses the four language skills of listening, speaking, reading, and writing, within three communicative modes: interpersonal, interpretive, and presentational. The *Plazas* program presents each of the skills individually, but the culminating activities of each chapter, especially in the **Síntesis** section, combine the four skills much as people do in the real world.

Interpersonal Mode: Direct oral or written communication between individuals in personal contact and involving the negotiation of meaning, such as face-to-face or telephone conversations, emails, and letters.

The Chapter Opener, **Vocabulario, Estructuras, Así se dice, ¡A practicar!,** and **En voz alta** sections provide the vocabulary, pronunciation information, grammatical structures, and speaking strategies necessary for basic conversation. Some sections of **¡A escribir!** focus on the comprehension and writing of letters and email messages. *Plazas* contains many interpersonal exercises that allow students to interact and exchange information, feelings, and opinions.

Interpretive Mode: Listening to oral or reading written messages when there is little or no opportunity to negotiate meaning with the speaker or writer, such as listening to speeches or broadcasts, reading articles, watching film, video, or TV.

The **En contexto** sections, the Lab Program, and the Video program, as well as the Web site and the Student Multimedia CD-ROM, provide students with ample opportunities to understand and interpret spoken language. The **Encuentro cultural** and **¡A leer!** sections, in addition to the *Plazas* magazines, allow students many opportunities to practice and improve their reading skills.

Presentational Mode: One-way communication in which a spoken, recorded, or written message is created and then presented to others with whom there is little or no direct contact, and thus little or no opportunity for the negotiation of meaning. This mode is used for giving a speech or writing a report, a composition, or an article.

The **¡A escribir!** sections, the Workbook/Lab Manual, the Student Multimedia CD-ROM, and the Web site provide ample opportunities for practice in the presentational mode.

Teaching Listening (Interpersonal and Interpretive Modes)

Listening plays an essential role in real-life communication, whether it is engaging in conversation, attending lectures in the classroom, or listening to the radio or television. Successful listening requires active participation on the part of the listener, drawing on a variety of mental processes and knowledge sources, including guessing, predicting, inferring, anticipating, and integrating meaning(s). You can make classroom listening more relevant and more similar to situations in the outside world, by encouraging your students to employ information they have previously heard, in order to understand what they are hearing during the many and varied activities in which they will participate in the classroom. One goal of the *Plazas* program is to prepare learners for listening situations outside the classroom setting. Listening activities in *Plazas* reflect real-life listening experiences.

The **Vocabulario** sections introduce students to new words and phrases using illustrations in which the vocabulary is clearly identified, as well as contextualized dialogs that offer a framework of template-type phrases that model specific linguistic functions, such as asking for information.

The **¡A practicar!** and **En voz alta** sections contain activities that guide students in true communication through contextualized oral activities, always attempting to recreate situations encountered outside the classroom and in the cultures of the Spanish-speaking world.

The **En contexto** sections feature dialogs that illustrate the chapter vocabulary and structures. Since all dialogs in this section appear on the Text Audio CD, students can listen to and practice the dialogs both inside and outside of the classroom.

The **Síntesis** section in the final part of each chapter contains video, with pre- and post-viewing activities that enhance students' listening skills. While it may be assigned as homework, it may also be used as in-class listening practice to reinforce the importance of this skill. The **Síntesis** section also contains important cultural information that can be discussed more fully in class.

The laboratory section of the Workbook/Lab Manual contains numerous listening activities to be assigned as homework. Instructors may check answers in class or provide an answer key.

Here are some suggestions that may help you to maximize class time while developing your students' listening skills:

- From the first day of class, demonstrate to your students that they are able to comprehend much more of the target language by paying careful attention to context, listening for cognates, and focusing on extra-linguistic cues such as gestures, facial expressions, and visual aids.
- Strive to use only the target language in the classroom, especially in conducting classroom business such as making announcements, giving instructions, assigning homework, or sharing information to be included on a test. Students are more likely to signal their lack of understanding if they have a personal reason for precisely understanding the information you are conveying.
- Try not to repeat questions or statements several times in Spanish or follow the Spanish phrase with an English translation, so that students can be encouraged to remain alert and give their full attention to the Spanish.
- Speak at a level appropriate for beginning Spanish learners, while at the same time trying to keep the language as natural as possible. Students should be reminded that they are able to understand much more than they are able to produce. Keep in mind that spoken Spanish has built-in redundancies, pauses, and lexical repetitions and circumlocutions that help people understand each other. Provide students with comprehensible input and ask for confirmation and repetition.
- Personalize the classroom activities so that students are encouraged to share their own lives and interests.
- Use pre-listening activities to orient students when they are to engage in extended listening activities. Provide them with opportunities to anticipate content and to reflect on and share their previous knowledge of the topic or related topics.

Teaching Speaking (Interpersonal and Presentational Modes)

The development of oral skills is essential to any program that encourages learners to express themselves and is based on the communicative approach. According to many language learners, speaking remains the skill that they most desire to master, yet it also remains one of the most stressful. As an instructor, one should try to create a positive classroom atmosphere, which encourages students to speak without fear of errors. Students should be reminded that errors are part of the linguistic system.

Here are some suggestions that may help you to maximize class time while developing your students' speaking skills:

- Be selective when it comes to error correction; only those errors that interfere with comprehension should be addressed. Always maintain the focus on the meaning of the utterance rather than the form it takes. If students are participating in a communicative activity, simply paraphrase or use the incorrect form in its proper manner; however, during exercises that focus on form, students should expect correction.
- Encourage natural speech patterns in class. Ask for complete sentences where appropriate and accept words or short phrases when they would normally occur.
- Allow students extra time to respond to a question before rephrasing or redirecting. A general rule of thumb is to wait three to five seconds to give students time to process the question and form a response.
- Try to include a variety of discourse structures when you practice speaking skills with your students, and use plenty of pair and group work. These techniques decrease inhibitions and allow everyone the opportunity to talk in a limited amount of time. Be sure to monitor the use of English and keep the students on task.
- Encourage students to present information to the class after conducting surveys or polls, or after conducting research on cultural topics. Try forming "presentation" groups of four or five students, and encourage those groups to give brief presentations in class.

The *Plazas* program is designed to bring students to the intermediate level on the ACTFL scale, which includes the ability to engage in conversations about oneself, friends and family, everyday life and interests, and to handle simple transactions (for example, making a purchase, ordering a meal, or asking for directions). A quick review of *Plazas'* chapter titles shows that these topics remain the thematic focus of a few chapters. The activities in **En voz alta** and **¡A conversar!** create opportunities for students to practice speaking in situations similar to those encountered in Spanish-speaking cultures. By providing students with situations and scenes centered on the chapter theme(s), creative use of the language is encouraged and students are provided an opportunity to stretch their speaking skills.

Teaching Reading (Interpretive Mode)

Reading plays an important role in the development of language skills in the *Plazas* program. Presenting students with authentic texts from the very beginning reinforces the Spanish they already know and gives them additional exposure to contextualized language. These texts provide both context and purpose for additional activities, and may later have an application in daily life (such as travel, business, pleasure, the study of literary or scientific texts). Although at first glance the texts may seem challenging for the elementary level, they remain accessible thanks to the exercises, tasks, and support materials that accompany them. These materials have been designed especially for beginning learners.

Authentic realia, such as menus, schedules, and ads, are integrated into the reading activities, especially those that emphasize transactions students may encounter in their travels, such as shopping, ordering food, or making travel arrangements. The **Encuentro cultural** offers reading practice, as does the **¡A leer!** portion of the chapter-ending **Síntesis** section. In the **¡A leer!** section, students can practice their reading skills and learn what it means to be an "active" or "participatory" reader. By providing students with specific tasks to which to apply the information gleaned from their readings, they are given goals similar to those found in their daily lives. In this section, we strive to create a classroom counterpart to the real-world setting.

Here are some suggestions that may help you to maximize class time while developing your students' reading skills:

- You may place your students in pairs or groups when completing reading activities, since it has been shown (Lee and Van Patten 1995) that reading is not a private, solitary activity but a social and public one. In this way, students are able to interact with one another and with you as they read, thus enriching their experience.
- Divide the reading process into pre-reading, reading, and post-reading tasks, so that even elementary learners can profit from authentic texts.

Plazas provides activities that facilitate the institution of this process. The pre-reading tasks activate background knowledge and familiarize students with the texts they are about to read: for example, looking at the title, subheadings or photos, brainstorming about the topic, or familiarizing themselves with new vocabulary words. The reading tasks promote a more complete understanding of the reading, and include skimming for the main ideas, scanning for specific information, verifying predictions, reading section by section, and summarizing. The post-reading activities help students to integrate the new material into their existing knowledge base. They consist of responding to true/false statements, putting events in chronological order, and using questions to guide group discussions.

More suggestions that may help you to maximize class time while developing your students' reading skills:

- Remind students that they are not expected to understand every word of the reading. Encourage them to go over each reading several times, and to follow the instructions in the exercises.
- When assigning a reading activity, take time to preview the content.
- When asking questions about content, focus on the basic information (*who, what, where, when, why*) before asking about the details.

Teaching Writing (Interpretive and Interpersonal Modes)

Many writing activities in *Plazas* reflect real-life tasks, such as taking notes, making lists, writing résumés, letters, or email messages. In the **¡A escribir!** section, students are exposed to a process writing approach. They learn to compose compositions that focus on the chapters' themes, as well as to recycle the strategies of previous chapters. The activities guide the students through the writing process, beginning with organizing ideas through writing the final draft. All of the writing activities are integrated with the *Atajo 4.0 Writing Assistant for Spanish.*

Here are some suggestions that may help you to maximize class time while developing your students' writing skills:

- In the process approach to writing of **¡A escribir!,** students work through a series of steps, such as generating ideas, organizing ideas, composing and revising drafts, and proofreading. Instructors may wish to evaluate various steps in the process rather than only the final piece.
- Try to maintain a balance between content and form in your evaluation of students' writing. Although it is important to correct errors when grading, instructors should also keep in mind that the purpose of writing is to communicate ideas. Give more attention to form when checking workbook exercises. One should focus corrections on points from the current lessons and/or forms that are important to the elementary level, such as word order, noun-adjective agreement, subject-verb agreement, the present tense (and other tenses, as studied).
- Encourage students to share their writing with one another by such techniques as peer editing or having groups of students create advertisements or other such projects.

THE SECOND "C": CULTURE

Plazas, as suggested by its title, is designed to weave cultural information throughout each lesson. Culture remains embedded in every facet of presentation and practice; it is featured in the **¿Nos entendemos?** and in the **Encuentro cultural** sections as well as in the *Plazas* cultural magazines. In these sections, students learn about the various Spanish-speaking countries and their social customs and values. Here are some suggestions that may help you introduce your students to the Spanish-speaking world and expand their curiosity about its peoples and cultures.

- Encourage students to figure out information from the data they have before them, whether it is vocabulary from the text, reading selections, or photographs. Use the data as points of departure for further discussion and discovery.
- Be certain to point out that cultural practices and societal norms vary among Spanish-speaking countries. You may wish to include activities that draw from authentic sources: the World Wide Web (See Moeller and Lafford 1997), films (with or without subtitles), and other realia, such as restaurant menus, maps, posters, or advertisements. These authentic materials may be used to compare and contrast elements of students' native culture with aspects of those being studied.
- Share your own experiences with your students. The more personal and diverse the experiences, the more students will be apt to consider the topics presented as relevant.
- Initially, you may wish to use English during discussions of complex cultural points rather than oversimplify in Spanish. As your students become more proficient in Spanish, the amount of English may be decreased and difficult or unknown terms may be provided in order to facilitate the discussion.
- Bear in mind that students do not always react positively when presented with unfamiliar, and sometimes objectionable, concepts, behaviors, or cultural patterns. Your students may also have preconceptions and stereotypes that must be examined and analyzed. Help them to develop awareness of cultural biases that may be influencing their opinions and encourage them to further investigate the topic. Cultural curiosity should be lauded.

Upon evaluation of the *Plazas* program, one quickly realizes that the connection between culture and language remains central to the program. The **¿Nos entendemos?** sections stress the cultural aspect of language by providing students with insights into regional variations and different ways of expressing the same sentiment. The *Plazas* program strives to convey that, although Spanish-speakers may share a common language and may have similar customs or traditions, they differ in many ways as well. As an instructor, one must attempt to offer students the opportunity to become not only bilingual but bi- and multi-cultural as well.

THE THIRD "C": CONNECTIONS

The study of languages also includes the exploration of related academic disciplines. The *Plazas* program is designed to aid beginning students in exploring such disciplines as literature, history, fine arts, political science, and business in a manner that remains appropriate for their proficiency level. Many of the culturally focused sections, such as **Encuentro cultural** and the *Plazas* **Revista,** also offer information related to other academic disciplines. Information about pre-Columbian cultures, celebrated Hispanic artists, or famous Hispanic authors, for example, can add to students' knowledge of anthropology, history, art, or literature.

THE FOURTH "C": COMPARISONS

The comparisons standard seeks to improve students' understanding of the nature of language—its structure and use—and of culture.

Language comparisons lie principally in the **Vocabulario, Estructuras,** and **¿Nos entendemos?** sections. Instructors may help students expand their comparisons beyond mere word differences to the linguistic task being performed. For example, the perfect tenses in Spanish, whose auxiliary verb translates as "have" in English, do not use the verb **tener** as the auxiliary verb but rather the verb **haber.** As such, a direct, "word-for-word" translation does not help; students need to focus on the primary linguistic task in order to negotiate the phrase's meaning.

Cultural comparisons are also integral to the *Plazas* program. This remains especially apparent in the **Encuentro cultural** and **Revista** sections. The notes, readings, and other authentic materials provide interesting information, and the activities require students to analyze with an eye to similarities and differences in customs, routines, and values.

THE FIFTH "C": COMMUNITIES

The communities goal consists of two parts. The first part focuses on having students use the target language in school and the community; the second focuses on using the language for personal enrichment and enjoyment. In order to meet this standard, instructors must strive independently in the classroom and cooperatively outside the classroom to create a Spanish-speaking environment. Instructors may also encourage students to initiate or participate in a Spanish club. Club activities could include Spanish-language films, community-service activities, parties on Hispanic holidays, dances or concerts with Hispanic music, or conversation hours (**tertulias**). Students should also be encouraged to search out information about Spanish-speaking communities and resources, such as restaurants, newspapers, TV and radio programs, and stores in their area.

TEACHING GRAMMAR

In this edition of *Plazas,* the section title **Gramática** has been changed to **Estructuras.** This change signals that students are not being presented with dry facts to memorize, but rather with the essential structures that will enable them to use the language. Each **Estructuras** section offers clear, concise linguistic information, followed by two types of practice activities. The first activity, **¡A practicar!,** offers contexualized practice of the structures, while **En voz alta** offers open-ended, communicative activities that build upon the previous exercises.

The *Plazas* scope and sequence works to bring students to the intermediate level—according to the ACTFL scale—introducing important structures early and reinforcing them consistently in succeeding chapters. Instructors should try to foster students' study, reminding them that the structures presented in one chapter will reappear in later chapters. As students practice using the structures, they will become internalized; that is, through repetition, the structures will begin to feel natural.

CLASSROOM MANAGEMENT

Every instructor has a unique presence and management style. The *Plazas* program is designed to accommodate a wide variety of teaching styles. The following suggestions are offered in the spirit of assisting each instructor to structure the class in the manner that best suits his or her style.

LESSON PLANNING

A successful language lesson usually revolves around a thematic center and has smooth transitions from one activity to the next. Each lesson should incorporate a wide variety of activity types that involve different kinds of responses—question and answer, dialogues, or writing sentences— or different kinds of interaction—individual, small group, or whole class activities—, board work, dictation, or active listening practice with follow-up questions to check comprehension. Novice teachers, especially, need to plan everything they expect to do in class. One should write down lesson objectives and how to achieve them, the materials needed, an approximate time for each activity, and how to assess student mastery of that objective. Make sure you are very familiar with the lesson you plan to teach by reading all the explanations in the text, as well as the exercises, so that you can anticipate students' possible problems with the activities. The better the instructor knows the lesson, the smoother the class will be. One should also plan extra activities or a variation on existing activities at a more challenging level, in case the class completes activities more quickly than expected.

Most lessons contain four sections:

• *Warm-up* Arrive early and set up so you can actively use every minute of class time. Begin promptly with a warm-up that will prepare your students to speak in Spanish again. Begin by chatting briefly (in Spanish!) about real-world topics, such as events, the weather, students' plans. Then try to choose topics that will lend themselves to the vocabulary or grammar points that you have been working on recently. For example, in a chapter about food, you might ask what the students plan to eat for lunch. If they have studied the preterite, you might ask what they ate for dinner last night. To make the transition to the day's lesson, look for a way to make a connection between a remark and the topic of the day.
• *Review and development of previously studied material* During this section of the class, the instructor should refresh students' memories of the vocabulary and grammar studied in the previous lesson and do one or two activities focused on these topics at a more advanced level.
• *Introduction and practice of new material* After the warm-up and review, the instructor should introduce one or two new topics for the lesson. Try to relate the new material to already familiar material. Any explanations of new material should be brief but contain lots of examples. Plan a variety of activities, in increasing order of difficulty, to practice the new material.
• *Wrap-up and preview of next lesson* During this portion of the class, the instructor may wish to do one culminating activity or review the most important points of the day's lesson. Most instructors also go over the homework assignment and mention the topic of the next lesson before dismissing the class.

USING SPANISH IN THE CLASSROOM

After the first few days, instructors should strive to use Spanish as much as possible in the classroom. Reassure students that they will be able to understand most of what is going on through cognates, repetition, previous material, or pantomime. They should be encouraged to raise their hands and ask for clarification if necessary. Using Spanish gives students the extra oral practice they need, plus it motivates them to pay close attention and to prepare thoroughly at home. Most importantly, it provides students with an opportunity to hear and use the target language in a communicative context.

Instructors should use moderately paced, simplified Spanish that is geared to the students' level, or slightly beyond their current level. They should not use broken, incorrect, or unnatural Spanish. In order to facilitate comprehension, use simple questions and statements, speak slightly more slowly than normal, and use frequent pauses. Repeating and rephrasing when students look puzzled remains a sound practice. The use of gestures, visual aids, props, or pantomime may also increase student comprehension. Instructors should give instructions in Spanish, to encourage students to pay close attention, but should also be sure to model the response expected and complete one or two items together as a whole class before dividing the class into pairs or groups.

DOING PAIR OR GROUP WORK

Pair or small-group work is a pleasant and efficient way to practice material in the language classroom; it aids in individualizing the lesson, involving more students, and removing the performance pressure.

There remain a number of ways to form pairs in class: ask students to select a partner, ask students to work with a classmate with whom they have not worked before, or assign pairs, usually two students with slightly differing levels of ability. Another option is to have students sit in semicircles with one empty chair, in which they take turns sitting. For example, after the first activity, the person at one end can take the empty chair, and each student works with the person on the other side, from right to left or left to right. To form groups, you can have students count off and then have all the "one's" work together, all the "two's," etc. It is best to have groups of no more than three or four people, or some students may not have a chance to participate. In either pair or small-group work, it is preferable to have an odd-numbered group rather than to have the instructor participate as a group member.

Before beginning the activity, the instructor should give precise instructions and model the activity. Specify if the students should alternate responses or if both students should respond to every item. Indicate if students are to write down any responses or if they will be expected to communicate any results or examples to the class as a whole. While the pairs or groups are working, the instructor should circulate around the room observing students' work and answering questions. Have a brief extension activity ready for the groups that finish more quickly. Establish a reasonable time limit for the activity. After completing the task, conduct a brief review of the activity with the whole class by checking answers or sharing information.

HOW AND WHEN TO CORRECT ERRORS

Error correction depends on the type of activity that your students are working on. If the exercise is focused on producing accurate forms (such as verb practice), you should point out the error or have students self-correct whenever possible. If it is a pair or group activity focused on communication, it is usually better to postpone correction as long as the Spanish remains comprehensible. At the end of the activity, you may wish to point out one or two patterns of error and have students provide the correct responses. When conversing with students individually, first make it clear that you have understood them so that communication remains the focus. Then in your response, you may be able to model the proper phrasing. Upon hearing restatements, students will often recognize their own mistakes and self-correct.

HOW TO REDUCE ANXIETY IN CLASS
(FOR INSTRUCTORS AS WELL AS STUDENTS!)

Every class has a unique group of students that results in a unique classroom climate. Try to create a positive atmosphere and a sense of community by learning your students' names quickly and helping them to learn their classmates' names. Mention students' individual interests so that you can tailor exercises and activities to your particular class.

Keep a light tone, injecting humor whenever possible, and reassure students that if millions of Spanish-speakers can learn the language, so can they. You should also make sure your expectations are clear and that students know in advance when and how they will be evaluated. It is especially important that students recognize what vocabulary is "active" (that is, it will appear on exams) and what vocabulary is for recognition only. If you allow a few minutes at the end of class to answer any questions in English, especially at the beginning of the semester or when you sense confusion or frustration, students will be made to feel more comfortable.

Another way to reduce anxiety is to engage in pair and group work often so that students do not have to perform in front of a large audience. You should also encourage them to practice out loud at home, to seek out practice partners, and to use Spanish whenever and wherever possible. Consider having oral evaluations in pairs, using role plays or interviews, rather than individually, but always confirm that students understand exactly what lessons will appear on the tests and what recycled vocabulary and structures they will be expected to use. You may also consider having students correct their own assignments (using a different colored ink) with the help of the answer key, so that they get immediate feedback on their homework. They should also be encouraged to study nightly; for example, thirty minutes a day is better than three hours once a week!

The instructor should keep the classroom atmosphere light and the pace brisk by using lots of humor and a wide variety of activities. When asking a question, call a student's name in order to keep everyone alert, and then count to ten before calling on a different student in order to give the student time to formulate a response. Be sure to provide a lot of praise and encouragement (**maravilloso, fabuloso, fenomenal**), show interest in responses, and be dramatic. If one explanation, example, or activity does not seem to be working, try another. It is essential that the instructor be willing to experiment with activities until finding the types that work well.

Finally, remind students that communicating in another language can be fun—they should relax, enjoy themselves, and allow themselves to make mistakes—that's a natural part of the learning process. The same holds true for instructors: relax, enjoy yourself, allow yourself to make mistakes, and consider your teaching a natural part of the learning process!

BIBLIOGRAPHIC REFERENCES

Allwright, D. & K.M. Bailey. 1991. **Focus on the Language Classroom: An Introduction to Classroom Research for Language Teachers.** Cambridge: Cambridge UP.

Bernhardt, E.B. 1991. **Reading Development in a Second Language: Theoretical, Empirical & Classroom Perspectives.** Norwood, NJ: Ablex.

Celce-Murcia. 1985. "Making Informed Decisions about the Role of Grammar in Language Teaching." **Foreign Language Annals.** 18:297–301.

——. 1991. "Grammar Pedagogy in Second and Foreign Language Teaching." **TESOL Quarterly.** 25:459–479.

Commeau, Raymond F. 1987. "Interactive oral grammar exercises." In Wilga M. Rivers, ed., **Interactive Language Teaching.** Cambridge: Cambridge University Press. 57–69.

Higgs, Theodore. 1985a. "Teaching Grammar for Proficiency." **Foreign Language Annals.** 18.4:289–296.

——. 1985b. "Oral Proficiency Testing and Its Significance for Practice." **Theory Into Practice.** Volume XXVI.4:282–287.

Kramsch, Claire M. 1987. "Interactive discourse in small and large groups." In Wilga M. Rivers, ed., **Interactive Language Teaching.** Cambridge: Cambridge University Press. 17–30.

Krashen, Stephen D. 1995. "What is Intermediate Natural Approach?" In Hashemipour, Maldonado and Van Naerssen, eds., **Studies in Language Learning and Spanish Linguistics.** New York: McGraw-Hill, Inc. 92–102.

Lee, James F. & Bill Van Patten. 1995. **Making Communicative Language Teaching Happen.** New York: Mc-Graw-Hill.

Melvin, Bernice S. & David F. Stout. 1987. "Motivating language learners through authentic materials." In Wilga M. Rivers, ed., **Interactive Language Teaching.** Cambridge: Cambridge University Press. 44–56.

Moeller, Phillips and Lafford. 1997. "Learning Language and Culture with Internet Technologies." In M. Bush and R. Terry, eds., **Technology-Enhanced Language Learning.** Lincolnwood, IL: National Textbook Company. 215–262.

Rivers, Wilga M. 1987. "Interaction as the key to teaching language for communication." In Wilga M. Rivers, ed., **Interactive Language Teaching.** Cambridge: Cambridge University Press. 3–16.

Rogers, C. & F. Medley. 1988. "Language with a purpose: Using authentic materials in the FL classroom." **Foreign Language Annals.** 21:467–488.

Rosen, Lois Matz. 1993. "Developing Correctness in Student Writing: Alternatives to the Error-Hunt." In Cleary and Linn, eds., **Linguistics for Teachers.** New York: McGraw-Hill, Inc. 371–382.

Russo, Gloria M. 1987. "Writing: an interactive experience." In Wilga M. Rivers, ed., **Interactive Language Teaching.** Cambridge: Cambridge University Press. 83–92.

Selinker, Larry. 1972. Interlanguage. **International Review of Applied Linguistics.** 10:201–231.

Shook, David J. 1996. Teaching culture in a North American context: Reading authentic texts in Spanish. **Mosaic.** 3:9–12.

Terrell, Tracy D. 1991. "The Role of Grammar Instruction in a Communicative Approach." **The Modern Language Journal.** 75:52–63.

Young, Dolly J. 1999. **Affect in Foreign Language and Second Language Learning, A Practical Guide.** New York: McGraw-Hill.

LESSON AND SYLLABUS PLANNING

ORGANIZING A COURSE USING *PLAZAS*

Exactly how one chooses to organize a course depends on a variety of factors, such as the types of students enrolled in the course(s), the time available, the goals of the program and of the individual course, and one's own personal teaching philosophy and style. The *Plazas* text, composed of fifteen full chapters, plus a **Capítulo preliminar,** is easy to adapt to either a semester or quarter system. One may divide the materials in a variety of ways: 8-8 (counting the **Capítulo preliminar**) for schools/universities on the semester system, 6-5-5 for those on the trimester system, and 5-4-4-3 for institutions on the quarter system where the text will be used for one year. The program may also be taught over three semesters by dividing the material as done with institutions on the trimester system. These suggested divisions are the most common possibilities, although certainly not the only ones.

One should keep in mind that the material contained in the first few chapters is generally more easily acquired than that found in the later chapters. One reason for this is that later lessons depend on students having learned the material in earlier lessons, therefore, material is cumulative. In addition, many structural points found in later lessons increase in difficulty due to the level of the learning task(s) with which they're associated. For example, learning about direct and indirect object pronouns involves not only learning the forms of each group of clitics and the rules regarding their placement within the sentence, but also how coherent discourse employing them must be structured. Likewise, learning the preterite and the imperfect tenses requires more than simply the memorization of the appropriate verb forms and their meanings; it also involves knowing and understanding the functions of and the differences between narration and description in the past. Due to this fact, you may want to allow additional time for the later chapters in the program so as to give your students (and yourself) the time necessary to thoroughly present, assimilate, and adequately produce the required material.

Below are some suggestions for organizing courses using the *Plazas* program, taking into consideration the students and the time devoted to the study of Spanish.

If the majority of your students are true beginners, you may want to divide the material in *Plazas* as follows:

	Term #1	Term #2	Term #3	Term #4
Semesters:	P/1–7	8–15		
Trimesters:	P/1–5	6–10	11–15	
Quarters:	P/1–4	5–8	9–12	13–15

As a general guideline, you should allow at least four classes per lesson; however, you may find it necessary to eliminate some sections or assign them for study outside the classroom in order to follow the plan. If you wish to cover the five *Plazas* **Revistas,** be sure to reserve sufficient time for each. These sections may be included whenever you wish, and you may include any or all of them, depending on the structure and length of your basic language program.

The sample lesson plan that follows divides the chapter for class presentation, in-class activities, and homework assignments within a two-semester, five-day framework. Naturally, the more class meetings dedicated to each chapter, the fewer sections that will need to be covered during the class, and the more practice and creative activities that can be built into the curriculum.

SAMPLE LESSON PLANS

If you wish to complete one chapter per five or six class meetings, the following is a suggested way to organize the first week.

Day 1:

Introduction to the course can be in English
- Take roll; collect student information.
- Pass out syllabus; explain policies.
- Show materials and explain how they will be used.

Capítulo preliminar

- Go over Communicative Goals with students.
- Point out the functions and tools to help them master the objective.

Warm-up

- Introduce the **Chapter Opener** by describing the picture, using simple Spanish, redundancies, gestures, and indicating items in the picture so that students are able to follow along.
- Use cognates whenever possible to show students that they already know some Spanish.
- Point to pictures in the text: **Son dos personas: un hombre y una mujer. Ellos son estudiantes. Son hispanos. Se saludan, están en la plaza.**
- Explain that they do not have to understand everything they hear, but just listen and pick up what they can.
- Repeat words, phrases, or sentences to help students understand.
- Act out some of the phrases that you use so that they can more fully understand.

Vocabulario: Saludos y despedidas

- **Una situación formal: entre un profesor y una estudiante**
- Write your name on the board and introduce yourself in Spanish: **Buenos días (Buenas tardes, Buenas noches), clase. Soy el (la) profesor(a)... Me llamo... y soy el (la) profesor(a) de español.** Repeat: **Me llamo...** emphasizing your name, then turn to a student and ask her/him: **¿Y usted? ¿Cómo se llama?**
- Ask students to identify others: **Y, ¿cómo se llama él/ella?**
- Ask students to turn to their classmates and introduce themselves. **Buenos días (Buenas tardes). Me llamo... ¿Y usted? ¿Cómo se llama?**
- Use gestures to indicate how you are feeling: **Yo estoy bien (mal).** Continue by asking: **¿Cómo está usted? ¿bien? ¿muy bien? ¿así, así? ¿mal?**
- Model your feelings when responding: **¡Qué bueno! / Lo siento.** Repeat with several students.
- **Una situación informal:** Repeat the same process. Point out differences between formal and informal situations and when each is used. Example: **¡Hola! ¿Qué tal? ¿Cómo estás? ¿Cómo te llamas?** versus **Buenos días. ¿Cómo está usted? ¿Cómo se llama usted?**

Note: It is recommended that you address the students with the **tú** form and have them address you with the **usted** form.

- Break students into groups to greet at least five new classmates for three to four minutes.
- Encourage students to use both formal and informal greetings.

Comprehension Check

- Students introduce you to their new classmates. The following will suffice for now: **Él se llama. / Ella se llama.**
- Model your responses by using **encantado(a) / mucho gusto.**

Wind-down and Preview

- Utilize the **¿Nos entendemos?** sections: **adiós** versus **hasta luego,** and **nos vemos** versus **chao (ciao)** to explain the social meanings when ending an encounter.
- Use the text to show the titles and pages of the assignments for next class.
- Ask students to study: **¡A practicar! P-1** and **P-2; En voz alta P-3** and **P-4; En contexto; Así se dice:** *Identifying quantities:* **hay** *and numbers 0–30;* **Vocabulario: Palabras interrogativas.** Also have them prepare: **Encuentro cultural: El lugar de encuentro: Las plazas;** and **Estructura I:** *Talking about yourself and others: subject pronouns and the present tense of the verb* **ser.**
- Tell students what to look for and/or how these concepts will add to the communicative goals of the course.
- Dismiss class using **adiós, hasta luego, nos vemos,** and **chao,** as students leave class.

Day 2:
Warm-up and Review

- Role-play dialogs in **Vocabulario: Saludos y despedidas** for three to five minutes. Students should pair up in male and female groups, if possible. After the second reading, students change partners and pair with another student. This time, encourage students to extend practice by using **preguntas formales** or **preguntas informales** and using **respuestas** and **despedidas,** accordingly.

Practice

- Select exercises from **¡A practicar! P-1 Meter la pata** and **P-2 ¿Qué dices?** and **En voz alta P-3 ¡A conocernos!** and **P-4 ¡Buenos días, professor(a)!** to confirm student comprehension.
- Begin class instruction with **Encuentro cultural: El lugar de encuentro: Las plazas.**
- Review the **Para pensar** and **Para discutir** sections to evaluate student comprehension of the reading.
- Practice **En contexto:** Ask students to quickly review the **En contexto** dialog (3 minutes).

Comprehension Check

- **¿Comprendiste?:** One pair of students volunteer to read the dialog, all others close their texts. Write **Cierto** and **Falso** on the board. After reading a statement, ask students to raise their hands if the statement is true. Count aloud the show of **ciertos** and repeat for **falsos.** Write the numbers on the board under each heading. Counting aloud in Spanish, count how many **chicos** said **cierto** and how many **chicas** said **falso.** Take another minute to clarify student questions or take the opportunity to add your own questions in Spanish.
- Point out the use of **nena** and **nene** in the **¿Nos entendemos?** section.
- Have students read **Encuentro cultural: ¿Ser informal o formal? *¿Tú o usted?***
- After going over the reading, provide a list of nouns or write on the board **un amigo, un doctor, una señora,** etc. Ask individual students how they would address the people as you go down the list. When a student responds, write **tú** or **usted** beside each noun. Ask the student why (**por qué**) he or she would use one or the other.
- Repeat the process with other students until you complete the list.
- Ask students to arrange their desks in two semi-circles facing each other.

Encourage students to use terms seen in **Palabras útiles** when appropriate as they are rearranging furniture for the semi-circles. Encourage students to practice informal and formal courtesies among themselves.

Estructura I: *Talking about yourself and others: subject pronouns and the present tense of the verb* ser

- Point out the uses of the verb **ser** and introduce the verb conjugation.
- Identify its uses in the model of the **Estructura** section.

Practice

- Go over **¡A practicar! P-5 ¿Sí or No?** Call on individual students to read the sentence aloud, providing the appropriate verb form. As students respond, ask the class: **¿Están de acuerdo? ¿Por qué sí o por qué no?**
- Pair students: one asks who someone is or who a group of people are and what they do, while the partner answers the question(s) posed.
- Select grammar exercises to do as a class from **¡A practicar! P-6 ¿Quiénes somos?** and **En voz alta P-7 ¿Quién entre nosotros?**
- Have students provide the correct form of the verb **ser**, for **P-6 ¿Quiénes somos?** and/or call on individual students to read the sentence aloud with the appropriate verb form.
- Do **P-7 ¿Quién entre nosotros?** in **En voz alta** in small groups or pairs. Encourage students to use adjectives they have learned to formulate questions and to ask each other to describe other classmates.

Así se dice: *Identifying quantities:* hay *and numbers 0–30*

- Begin presenting numbers 0–30 by showing students how Spanish-speakers use their fingers when using hands for counting.
- Begin the count with **cero,** and start using the thumb with one as you gesture to the students to join you on the counting. When you reach ten, open your palms facing the class with fingers spread out, and count in tens pulsing your hands back and forth. Have students start counting taking turns one by one, up and down the rows of students. Now, ask the females to take a count, then the males. Ask: **¿Cuántos chicos hay en la clase? ¿Cuántas chicas hay en la clase? ¿Cuántos son, X chicos más X chicas? ¿Cuántos estudiantes hay en la clase?**

Practice

- Do **¡A practicar! P-8 En la clase de español hay... , P-9 ¿Cuántos hay?, P-10 Problemas de matemáticas,** and **En voz alta P-11 ¿Hay o no hay?**
- Hint: Newspaper ads for grocery stores are large enough for students to see from the front of the classroom. They are colorful, are excellent for practicing the numbers, and can later be used for the unit on food.
- Review the **Vocabulario: Palabras interrogativas.** Begin by reviewing the words first.
- Point out the use of the upside-down punctuation marks and of the accent mark on questions words for stress. Model some questions for students to follow; for example: **¿Cuál es tú número de teléfono? ¿Cuál es tú dirección? ¿Cuál es tú número de seguro social?**
- Ask students to work in pairs and have them go over **¡A practicar! P-12 Preguntas** and **En voz alta P-13 Información personal.**

Comprehension Check

- Dictate short and simple questions with question words. Students are to provide (on the board or on paper) the correct use of questions marks and accents. If paper is used, students exchange papers and make corrections as needed. Collect papers for feedback and/or use for review the following day.

Wind-down and Preview

- While students are working on correcting the papers, go around the classroom and ask students questions. Begin with the greetings and use **pronombres, ser, números,** and **palabras interrogativas.** Praise students for doing so well by using **¡Gracias, muchas gracias! ¡Qué buenos estudiantes! ¡Qué inteligentes!**
- Tell students what they will learn in the next sections and what they will be able to do with the added skills.
- Have students study the **Cultura** annotation on telephone numbers; **Estructura II:** *Telling age: the present tense of the verb* **tener; Encuentro cultural: El mundo hispanoamericano, El alfabeto en español.**
- Dismiss class using **adiós, hasta luego, nos vemos,** and **chao,** as students leave class.

Day 3:
Warm-up and Review

- Greet students at the door, shake hands, ask each student one or two questions you may have used the day before. Encourage students to greet their classmates and to practice the questions they already know and feel comfortable using while waiting for class to begin.
- Before class, create a list of questions for a student handout with terms from **Saludos y despedidas, Preguntas formales e informales,** the verbs **ser** and **hay, los números, Palabras interrogativas,** and **Palabras útiles.**
- Begin the review by greeting students with questions from the list you created. Do not read directly from the list. Make the questions sound more like a mini-dialog, instead of an interview. The demonstration you present should serve as a model for students to mimic.
- Hand out the list and have students mingle with other students as they use the list to ask other students questions. The student asking the questions may be guided by the list, while the student listening should respond to the questions as best she/he understands.
- Students are to talk to two students and complete the list of questions in 5–7 minutes.
- Review **los números** using 3x5 index cards.
- Ask students to write on the index cards their name, address, and phone number.
- As students complete the information, pause in front of the students when you collect the cards. Briefly scan the card and verify that the information on the card is correct by asking the student: **¿Cómo se/te llama(s)? ¿Cúal es su/tu dirección? ¿Cuál es su/tu código postal? ¿Cuál es su/tu número de teléfono? ¿Cuál es su/tu número de seguro social?**
- Time permitting, you may choose to review **¡A practicar! P-12 Preguntas.**
- Begin class instruction with the **Cultura** annotation on telephone numbers. After reviewing the note with students and demonstrating how Spanish-speakers may answer the telephone, role-play an activity: have students make phone calls to one another. Encourage students to practice all the ways to use the phone. Expand the activity and have students add greetings and farewells.
- Present **Estructura II:** *Telling age: the present tense of the verb* **tener.**
- Ask volunteers to provide the verb forms while you write them on the board. If you wish, have students repeat the forms in chorus. Provide a list of subjects and have students give the appropriate verb form orally.

Comprehension Check

- Repeat the above activity in writing.

Practice

- Do **¡A practicar! P-15 Edades** and **En voz alta P-16 ¿Cuántos años tienes?**
- Ask students to ask at least three students how old they are. Use **¿Qué edad tienes? ¿Cuántos años tienes? ¿Cuántos años tiene tu/su mejor amigo(a)?** Tell students to respond to three questions about their age to classmates.
- Review the reading: **Encuentro cultural: El mundo hispanoamericano.**
- As time allows, utilize the additional **Para pensar** and **Para discutir** sections to give the students a panoramic view of **el mundo hispanoamericano.**
- Introduce **El alfabeto en español.**
- Have students repeat each letter as you name the Spanish letters. Then ask students: **¿Cómo se/te llama(s)?** When a student responds—for example, **Me llamo Joe,**— ask: **¿Cómo se deletrea?** or **¿Cómo se escribe?** Repeat the practice with especially long names, such as Christopher, and include those with not too common last names (refer to your class roll).
- Practice with several students using the same question, then have students ask other students their names and how to spell them. Follow up by asking students to spell the names of well-known people, while you write the names on the board.
- Brainstorm a list of familiar abbreviations (**siglas**): ABC, CBS, MSNBC, ESPN, FBI, CIA, PBS.

Comprehension Check

- Dictation: Using the letters of the Spanish alphabet, dictate a list of words and/or names. Students write what they hear. For corrections, provide the list of words on an overhead transparency. For example: Before putting up the transparency, dictate the list of words (**E–C–U–A–D–O–R**) on your list. When dictation is completed, go over one word at a time (cover the rest with a piece of paper). Say: **Ecuador–E–C–U–A–D–O–R–Ecuador.** Allow several students to pick up the spelling of each word and the pronunciation of the words for the rest of the list.

E–C–U–A–D–O–R	Ecuador
H–O–N–D–U–R–A–S	Honduras
V–E–N–E–Z–U–E–L–A	Venezuela
W–H–I–S–K–I	whiski
K–A–R–A–T–E	karate

Wind-down and Preview

- Go over **Capítulo 1 Chapter Opener** Communicative Goals and Cultural Information and tell students what they will be learning in that chapter.
- Point out the functions and tools in the next unit to let students know what will help them master the objective. You may want to pick up pencils, pens, books, and articles that are handy and found in a classroom and ask: **¿Qué es ésto _____? ¿Cuántos son? ¿Cuál es tu dirección? ¿Cómo se escribe el nombre de la calle?**
- Look for pictures from magazines or newspapers with pictures of people of various ages, including children and the elderly. Review **¿Cuántos años tiene?** or **¿Qué edad tiene él/ella?** The presentation of newspapers and magazines is a great way to wind down and good to use for a warm-up the following day. Students will most likely be familiar with articles and may be attracted to other words and pictures, which will help expand their interest to find out more.
- Have students study: **Vocabulario: En la clase, ¡A practicar! 1-1, 1-2,** and **1-3, En voz alta 1-4, 1-5, 1-6,** and **1-7, En contexto** (listen to audio), **Encuentro cultural: El español en los Estados Unidos, Estructura I:** *Talking about people, things, and concepts: definite and indefinite articles and how to make nouns plural,* **Vocabulario: Lenguas extranjeras, otras materias y lugares universitarios,** and **Encuentro cultural: La educación en Latinoamérica y España.**
- Dismiss class using **adiós, hasta luego, nos vemos,** and **chao,** as students leave class. You may wish to add **¡Hasta la próxima!**

Day 4:
Warm-up and Review

- Greet students at the door. Take the opportunity to use formal and informal greetings, handshakes, and perhaps a cheek-to-cheek greeting when appropriate. When students respond with positive and enthusiastic responses to your greetings, add **me alegro, fantástico, excelente.**
- In pairs or in small groups of three, instruct students to practice from the handout you created the day before for **saludos y preguntas.**
- Allow students to ask questions for clarification, before working with their peers. This is a good time to practice and model the word **hay.** You can ask **¿Hay preguntas? No, no hay preguntas** or **Sí, hay preguntas, hay dos (tres, etc.) preguntas. Joe, ¿tienes preguntas? Joe tiene una pregunta. Usted, ¿tiene una pregunta? ¿Cuántas preguntas hay? ¡Dios mío, hay muchas preguntas!** or **¡Qué bueno, no hay preguntas!**
- After the pair work, you may include some of the questions you used at the end of yesterday's class by asking students: **¿Qué es ésto ____? ¿Cuántos son? ¿Cuál es tu dirección? ¿Cómo se escribe el nombre de la calle?**
- Add to the Warm-up and Review: **¿De qué color(es) es (son) (el, la, los, las)____?** Encourage students to say **El libro es amarillo con azul.** However, one word is sufficient for now.
- Use your pictures from newspapers or fliers from an office supply store advertisement for additional vocabulary words.

Capítulo 1

- Introduce **Vocabulario: En la clase.** Include **Otras cosas, Otras Personas, Los colores,** and **Palabras útiles.**
- Practice by identifying items in the classroom related to the vocabulary given and have students repeat them aloud.
- Review the color brown in **¿Nos entendemos?** Point out that, like other adjectives, colors must agree in gender and number with the noun they describe.
- Since students are familiar with **hay** and **cuántos,** practice **En voz alta 1-4 ¿Cuántos hay?** As time and student level of comprehension and skills permit, include **1-5 Cosas y colores.** For students who are ready for a bit more of a challenge, practice can be expanded by adding personal questions such as: **¿Cuántos libros tiene(s) en la mochila? ¿Cuántos lápices tiene(s) en la mano? ¿De qué color es tu coche? ¿Tiene(s) un cuaderno rojo?**
- Show students a picture of a classroom and ask them to think of items they believe are missing, or ask them to shop from the newspaper for office supplies, that they believe are needed in a classroom. Start by asking a question: **¿Qué falta? ¿Qué es necesario? ¿Qué es (son) importante(s) para una clase?**
- Have students ask each other to describe an item with multiple colors, for example, **Es amarillo, verde y anaranjado.**

Comprehension Check

- Select activities from **¡A practicar!** **(1-1 ¿Cierto o Falso?, 1-2 ¿De qué color es... ?, 1-3 ¿Cuántos hay en la clase?)** and **En voz alta.** Include questions using interrogative words and color with the vocabulary just presented.

- **En contexto:** students listen to the audio or two students volunteer to read the dialog aloud, before breaking into small groups of 3–4 per group. After listening to / reading the dialog; one student reads statements in **¿Comprendiste?,** and the other students take turns answering whether statements are true or false. The student who reads the statements can provide assistance as needed.

- **Encuentro cultural: El español en los Estados Unidos:** review the new vocabulary by relating it to words they already have seen; i.e., **desde = de; algunos = unos;** also point out the cognates **mayoría, emigrar.**

- Have students work in small groups on the pre-reading activity **Para pensar.** Students may write their responses on paper (or the board) and compare their responses with those of another group, then present a brief report about the dialog to the class. The brief report can be in written form to turn in for feedback.
- Encourage students to contribute to the discussion followed by activity **Para discutir.**

- **Estructura I:** *Talking about people, things, and concepts: definite and indefinite articles and how to make nouns plural:* present a list of nouns on an overhead transparency and ask students to supply the appropriate definite /indefinite article, for example, **escritorio, pizarra, mochila, lápiz, estudiante, tiza, papel, borrador, mapa, libro, diccionario, clase, examen.** Then follow up by asking students to provide the plural forms and give the appropriate definite/indefinite articles for the items in the list.

- After reviewing rules of plural forms, have students write down the nouns and their definite/indefinite article as you give (aloud) a list of nouns. Some nouns you may wish to add/include are **reloj, mesas, ventana, mano, mujer, mapa, hombres, clases, muchacho(a, os, as).**

Practice

- Do as many **¡A practicar!** activities as time allows: **1-8 ¿El, la, los o las?, 1-9 ¿Qué es? ¿Qué son?, 1-10 ¿Hay una profesora en la clase?,** and **En voz alta 1-11 Cuestionario: ¿Cuántos tienes?**

- **Vocabulario: Lenguas extranjeras, otras materias y lugares universitarios:** to practice pronunciation and auditory comprehension, ask volunteers to read **Encuentro cultural: La educación en Latinoamérica y España.** As students are engaged in the activity, mark any pronunciation errors each student makes. After the paragraph is finished (do not interrupt students, while they are reading), model and write the word on the board and ask the entire class to repeat the word(s) in chorus.

- Continue the pronunciation practice to include: **Cursos y especializaciones, Más cursos y especializaciones, Lugares y edificios universitarios,** and **Palabras útiles.**

Comprehension Check

- As time allows and students needs require it, select some of the practice exercises to check student comprehension: **¡A practicar! 1-12 ¿Dónde... ?** or **1-13 ¿Qué lengua habla?** and **En voz alta 1-14 ¿Cierto o falso?** or **1-15 En la librería.**

Wind-down and Preview

- Point out or go over **¿Nos entendemos?** about **el castellano** and how Spanish speakers shorten words like **la facultad** to **la facu.**
- Before dismissing class, share with students some of the activities you do after class, using verbs they will see in the next day's lesson, for example, **Después de clase termino mi trabajo. Yo escucho música y hablo por teléfono. Mi amiga y yo caminamos por el parque y compramos agua en una tienda. Y tú, ¿estudias o trabajas después de clase? ¿Cuándo visitas a tus amigos? ¿Miras la tele después de la clase?**
- Have students prepare **Estructura II:** *Describing everyday activities: Present tense of regular -ar verbs,* **¡A practicar! 1-16, 1-17,** and **1-18, Así se dice:** *Expressing personal likes and dislikes:* **me gusta** + *infinitive,* **Así se dice:** *Telling time and talking about the days of the week:* **la hora y los días de la semana,** and **Encuentro cultural: El sistema de 24 horas.**
- Dismiss class using **adiós, hasta luego, nos vemos,** and **chao,** as students leave class. You may wish to add **¡Hasta la próxima!**

Day 5:

Warm-up and Review

- Greet students at the door with **saludos** in Spanish.
- Ask students to form pairs and work on the worksheet you created for Day 3. By this time, you may have the students add at least three questions using interrogative words, numbers, and the verb **tener.** Recycle questions using **ser, hay, vocabulario de la clase,** and the definite/indefinite articles. Include some questions about the **Encuentros culturales.** Use the questions you used for the wind-down, warm-up, and review, for example, **¿Qué estudias? ¿Dónde trabajas? ¿Cuándo visitas a los amigos? ¿Miras la tele después de clase?** Students work in pairs, using the handout as a guide to create a simple dialog between them. As you monitor the groups, encourage students to create and add their own questions. Allow 7–12 minutes for review.
- Present **Estructura II:** *Describing everyday activities: present tense of regular -ar verbs.* Begin instruction by presenting the verb forms in context, for example, point to your watch or the class clock on the wall (or other realia used) and state the time: **Son las 3:00 de la tarde. Estamos en la clase y estudiamos español. No hablamos inglés en la clase de español. La clase termina a las 4:00. Después de clase regreso a casa y hablo por teléfono con mi amigo(a, os, as).**
- Then ask students questions about what you have just told them about your activities: **¿Qué hora es? ¿Qué estudiamos? ¿Qué lengua hablamos en la clase? ¿A qué hora es la clase de español? ¿A qué hora termina la clase? ¿Cuándo regresa la profesora a casa?**

Practice

- Assign students to complete the paragraph given in **¡A practicar! 1-16.**
- Have students exchange or compare their responses, then ask volunteers to read the paragraph aloud. In addition, have two students write the verb forms on the board to verify the correct use of the verb.
- Continue with **¡A practicar! 1-17 La vida estudiantil.**
- Assign **1-18 La vida estudiantil estadounidense e hispana** for homework.
- Have students work in pairs and practice the exercises in **En voz alta: 1-19, 1-20,** and **1-21.** Allow 10–12 minutes.
- Given the list of verbs in **Estructura II,** ask students to compose questions to find out what their classmates do and do not do outside of class. Ask for questions using at least five different verbs for each student.
- Once information is gathered, ask students to volunteer to report to the class. Give students a time and length limit according to class schedule.
- If time allows, activity can be extended to have a comprehension check.

Comprehension Check

- While students are presenting their report, jot down who does what and be sure to take the names of the students doing the actions. Formulate questions based on the information students present. You may ask questions similar to the following list: **¿Quién estudia en el parque? ¿Quién trabaja por la noche? ¿Cuántas clases toma _____? ¿Dónde estudia _____? ¿A qué hora regresa ____ a casa? ¿Cómo se llama el amigo(a) de ____? ¿Cuándo mira ___ la tele? ¿Qué programa mira ____ en la tele? ¿Cuándo habla ____ por teléfono? ¿Qué materias estudia ____?**
- **Así se dice:** *Expressing personal likes and dislikes:* **me gusta** + *infinitive:* tell students about things you like and do not like, for example:

Me gusta la clase de español.
Me gusta comer en el parque.
Me gusta practicar deportes.
No me gusta hablar inglés en la clase.
No me gusta tomar café.
No me gusta tocar el piano en un lugar público.

- Now ask students to write at least four sentences—two about what they like to do and two about what they do not like to do. Allow them 5 minutes.
- Have two students volunteer to write their sentences on the board. Once students write their sentences on the board, have other students come up to the board and add to the list of likes and dislikes.

Wind-down

- Review the forms of **gustar** by asking students what famous people like to do, what their parents or friends like to do, etc.
- Have students study: **Así se dice:** *Telling time and talking about the days of the week:* **la hora y los días de la semana, Encuentro cultural: El sistema de 24 horas,** and the reading and writing activities in **Síntesis.**
- Bring a list of questions you may have in preparation for the Hour Exam.
- Dismiss class using **adiós, hasta luego, nos vemos, chao,** and **¡Hasta la próxima!,** as students leave class. You may wish to add **¡Buena suerte!**

In the case of a sixth day, any of the **Encuentro cultural** sections or **Síntesis** sections can be expanded to accommodate the additional time or you can include activities of your own creation.

Day 6:

- Present **Así se dice:** *Telling time and talking about the days of the week:* **la hora y los días de la semana** and **Encuentro cultural: El sistema de 24 horas.**
- Practice the reading and writing activities in the **Síntesis** section as a class.
- Give format of the Hour Exam.
- Respond to students' questions about the Exam.

If the majority of your students are false beginners[1], you may prefer to cover the opening chapters rather quickly and slow the pace when the material becomes more complicated, so that you can concentrate on appropriate activities. One possible way to divide the material in *Plazas* so as to provide your students and yourself with the time necessary to complete and practice the more involved structures and activities found in the later units is presented below:

	Term #1	Term #2	Term #3	Term #4
Semesters:	P/1–8(9)	9(10)–15		
Trimesters:	P/1–6	7–11	12–15	
Quarters:	P/1–4	5–8	9–12	13–15

MOTIVATION AND VARIETY: INSTRUCTIONAL GAMES

You can add variety and spice to your Spanish class by including word games in your lesson plans. They, too, meet the needs of your students in an entertaining way. You can invent your own, use those suggested below, or consult the authors listed under *References* at the end of this section. Start collecting fillers, that is, brief activities, which serve as transitions between activities and fill in those gaps that sometimes appear in spite of excellent planning. Locate books of games, read columns such as IDEAS in *Hispania* (the Journal of the AATSP), consult the *Plazas* Activity File, and, of course, your colleagues (and share your ideas with them!). You will find that starting a card file of ideas and gathering materials to use with them is a great help when you find yourself with a few minutes to spare or are looking for an innovative way to practice language skills. Here are a few suggestions with which to begin your collection:

---

[1] False beginners are students who have been exposed to Spanish either informally or studied it long enough ago for their skill to deteriorate.

- **Listas** Ask students to make lists of anything that comes to mind, from all the words that they can think of beginning with a particular letter or sound, to word families, where the students write down all the words they can think of that are associated with a particular topic, such as furniture in the house or a specific room, kinship terms, items associated with a date, etc. This is a marvelous and painless way to review vocabulary, orthography, and even pronunciation.
- **Los verbos** As the end of class approaches, ask students to close their books. Distribute index cards on which you have written an infinitive and inform them of the "tense or mood of the day." Give your students the opportunity to consult with one another (but not their texts). As each student approaches you, you supply the subject for which the student must provide the appropriate verb form in order to leave class. If the form is incorrect, the student must consult another available classmate, figure it out, and try again.
- **Detective** Choose a student to provide clues (one at a time), in Spanish, so that classmates can guess the identity of the "mystery" person, place, thing, or activity. This can also be done in teams so that once the item is identified, the successful team or student supplies the clues.
- **20 Preguntas** Students ask questions of the individual at the front of the room who has taken on another identity (person, place, thing, etc.). The person who correctly guesses, replaces the "celebrity."
- **Taboo en español** Based on the board game, students give clues so that the partner, or team members, can identify the word being described. Each clue needed decreases the point value. The first pair/team to reach a predetermined score wins the game. This is an excellent way to review vocabulary and practice oral/aural skills.
- **Chismes** One student (or the instructor) whispers a sentence or phrase in Spanish to a classmate, who repeats what she/he hears to another member of the class, and so on. The last person in the chain repeats what she/he heard. The initial statement and its final version are compared to see how (mis)communication takes place. This is an excellent (and amusing) way to practice auditory comprehension and/or pronunciation.
- **Cuentos chuecos** This activity requires a sheet of paper or index cards. Students are placed in groups and each group member writes either a sentence component or part of speech, according to the classification written on the index card (such as the subject, verb, direct object, preposition, noun, adjective, etc.). The different contributions are then read aloud in grammatical sequence to form complete sentences or discourse. This tends to result in some very amusing sentences/oral texts since each element is hidden from the other members of the group.
- **Arriésgate** *(Jeopardy en español)* This is a good activity for chapter review. You can set up a Jeopardy board rather inexpensively, and once constructed, it's simply a matter of changing topics to reflect the chapter contents. Since answers are required to be in question form, it provides an excellent opportunity for the practice and use of complete phrases and interrogative formation.

REFERENCES

Brow, H. Douglas. 1994. **Teaching By Principles.** Upper Saddle River, NJ: Prentice Hall.

Curtain, Helena and Carol Ann Bjornstad Pesola. 1994. **Languages and Children, Making the Match.** White Plains, NY: Longman.

Kellough, Richard D. and Patricia L, Roberts. 1998. **A Resource Guide for Elementary School Teaching.** 4th edition. Upper Saddle River, NJ: Prentice Hall.

Oller, Jr., John W. 1993. **Methods That Work.** New York: Heinle & Heinle.

Omaggio-Hadley, Alice. 1993. **Teaching Language in Context.** Boston: Heinle & Heinle Publishers, Inc.

Rivers, Wilga M. 1987. **Interactive Language Teaching.** Cambridge: Cambridge UP.

Stevick, Earl W. 1996. **Memory, Meaning & Method.** New York: Heinle & Heinle.

2-SEMESTER SYLLABUS: 4 DAYS A WEEK

WEEK	MONDAY	TUESDAY	WEDNESDAY	THURSDAY
1	Introductions Administrative requirements Hand out syllabus Show materials and explain how they will be used **Capítulo preliminar** **Vocabulario: Saludos y despedidas** **Una situación formal** **Una situación informal** **¿Nos entendemos?** (adiós, nos vemos, and chao)	**Capítulo preliminar** **Encuentro cultural: El lugar de encuentro: Las plazas** **Encuentro cultural: ¿Ser informal o formal? ¿Tú o usted?**	**Capítulo preliminar** **Estructura I:** *Talking about yourself and others: subject pronouns and the present tense of the verb* **ser** **Así se dice:** *Identifying quantities:* **hay** *and numbers 0–30*	**Capítulo preliminar** **Vocabulario: Palabras interrogativas** **Estructura II:** *Telling age: the present tense of the verb* **tener** **Encuentro cultural: El mundo hispanoamericano** **El alfabeto en español**
2	**Capítulo 1** **Vocabulario: En la clase, Los colores** **¿Nos entendemos? (el color café)** **Encuentro cultural: El español en los Estados Unidos**	**Capítulo 1** **Estructura I:** *Talking about people, things, and concepts: definite and indefinite articles and how to make nouns plural*	**Capítulo 1** **Vocabulario: Lenguas extranjeras, otras materias y lugares universitarios** **¿Nos entendemos? (el castellano)** **Encuentro cultural: La educación en Latinoamérica y España**	**Capítulo 1** **Estructura II:** *Describing everyday activities: present tense of regular* **-ar** *verbs* **Así se dice:** *Expressing personal likes and dislikes:* **me gusta + infinitive**
3	**Capítulo 1** **Así se dice:** *Telling time and talking about the days of the week:* **La hora y los días de la semana** **Encuentro cultural: El sistema de 24 horas**	Review Vocabulario **Síntesis: ¡A ver!, ¡A leer!, ¡A escribir!, or ¡A conversar!**	EXAM I	Oral Evaluation
4	**Capítulo 2** **Vocabulario: La familia** **¿Nos entendemos? (don/doña)** **Así se dice:** *Indicating ownership and possession: possession with* **de(l)** *and possessive adjectives* **Encuentro cultural: Los nombres y apellidos en español**	**Capítulo 2** **Estructura I:** *Describing people and things: common uses of the verb* **ser** **Así se dice:** *Describing people and things: agreement with descriptive adjectives* **¿Nos entendemos? (güero[a], canche, catire[a], mono[a], trigueño[a], moreno[a], pelirrojo[a])**	**Capítulo 2** **Encuentro cultural: La familia hispana** **Vocabulario: Las nacionalidades**	**Capítulo 2** **Estructura II:** *Describing daily activities at home or at school: present tense of regular* **-er** *and* **-ir** *verbs* **¿Nos entendemos? (deber / should)**
5	**Capítulo 2** **Así se dice:** *Expressing possesion and physical states: common uses of the verb* **tener** **Así se dice:** *Counting to 100:* **los números de 30 a 100**	**Capítulo 2** Review Vocabulario **Síntesis: ¡A ver!, ¡A leer!, ¡A escribir!, or ¡A conversar!**	EXAM II	Oral Evaluation

WEEK	MONDAY	TUESDAY	WEDNESDAY	THURSDAY
6	**Capítulo 3** **Vocabulario:** Los deportes y los pasatiempos **Encuentro cultural:** Los deportes en el mundo hispano	**Capítulo 3** **Estructura I:** *Expressing likes and dislikes:* **gustar** *+ infinitive and* **gustar** *+ nouns* **Vocabulario:** Los lugares	**Capítulo 3** **Estructura II:** *Expressing plans with* **ir:** **ir a** *+ destination and* **ir a** *+ infinitive* **Encuentro cultural:** El café en Colombia y en el mundo	**Capítulo 3** **Estructura III:** *Describing leisure-time activities: verbs with irregular yo forms* **¿Nos entendemos?** (idioms with **hacer** and other verbs that, like **hacer,** have irregular yo forms)
7	**Capítulo 3** **Así se dice:** *Expressing knowledge and familiarity:* **saber, conocer,** *and the personal* **a** **Así se dice:** *Talking about the months, seasons, and the weather*	**Capítulo 3** Review Vocabulario **Síntesis:** ¡A ver!, ¡A leer!, ¡A escribir!, or ¡A conversar!	**EXAM III**	**Oral Evaluation**
8	**Capítulo 4** **Vocabulario:** La casa **¿Nos entendemos?** (la heladera, la nevera, el refrigerador) **Encuentro cultural:** Gaudí y su obra	**Capítulo 4** **Estructura I:** *Describing household chores and other activities: present tense of stem-changing verbs:* **o** *to* **ue;** **e** *to* **ie;** **e** *to* **i** **Así se dice:** *Expressing physical conditions, desires, and obligations with* **tener**	**Capítulo 4** **Vocabulario:** Los quehaceres domésticos **Encuentro cultural:** Viviendas en Latinoamérica y España	**Capítulo 4** **Estructura II:** *Expressing preferences and giving advice: affirmative* **tú** *commands*
9	**Capítulo 4** **Estructura III:** *Talking about location, emotional and physical states, and actions in progress: the verb* **estar** **Así se dice:** *Counting from 100 and higher:* los números de 100 a 1.000.000	**Capítulo 4** Review Vocabulario **Síntesis:** ¡A ver!, ¡A leer!, ¡A escribir!, or ¡A conversar!	**EXAM IV**	**Oral Evaluation**
10	**Capítulo 5** **Vocabulario:** El cuerpo humano **¿Nos entendemos?** (useful expressions and **el cabello** and **el pelo**) **Encuentro cultural:** Bolivia y la salud	**Capítulo 5** **Estructura I:** *Talking about routine activities: reflexive pronouns and present tense of reflexive verbs*	**Capítulo 5** **Así se dice:** *Talking about things you have just finished doing:* **acabar de** *+ infinitive* **Vocabulario:** La salud	**Capítulo 5** **Estructura II:** *Describing people, things, and conditions:* **ser** *versus* **estar** **¿Nos entendemos?** (marital status)

WEEK	MONDAY	TUESDAY	WEDNESDAY	THURSDAY
11	Capítulo 5 Encuentro cultural: Tradición de hierbas: Yerba mate en Paraguay y las hojas de coca en los Andes Estructura III: *Pointing out people and things: demonstrative adjectives and pronouns*	Review Vocabulario Síntesis: ¡A ver!, ¡A leer!, ¡A escribir!, or ¡A conversar!	EXAM V (or review for Midterm Exam)	Oral Evaluation
12	Capítulo 6 Vocabulario: La comida ¿Nos entendemos? (un negrito, un marrón, un marroncito, un café con leche, etc.) Encuentro cultural: La comida típica venezolana	Capítulo 6 Estructura I: *Making comparisons: comparatives and superlatives* Vocabulario: El restaurante Encuentro cultural: Los postres venezolanos	Capítulo 6 Estructura II: *Describing past events: regular verbs and verbs with spelling changes in the preterite*	Capítulo 6 Estructura III: *Giving detailed description about past events: more verbs with stem changes in the preterite*
13	Capítulo 6 Review Vocabulario Síntesis: ¡A ver!, ¡A leer!, ¡A escribir!, or ¡A conversar!	EXAM VI	Oral Evaluation	Capítulo 7 Vocabulario: La ropa ¿Nos entendemos? (a cuadros, la pollera, la campera, etc.) Encuentro cultural: De compras en Buenos Aires
14	Capítulo 7 Así se dice: *Making emphatic statements: stressed possessive adjectives and pronouns* Estructura I: *Talking about singular and/or completed events in the past: verbs irregular in the preterite*	Capítulo 7 Vocabulario: De compras Encuentro cultural: El tango argentino Estructura II: *Simplifying expressions: direct object pronouns*	Capítulo 7 Estructura III: *Describing on-going and habitual actions in the past: the imperfect tense* Review the preterite and the imperfect	Capítulo 7 Review Vocabulario Síntesis: ¡A ver!, ¡A leer!, ¡A escribir!, or ¡A conversar!
15	EXAM VII (or review for Final Exam)	Oral Evaluation	Review Capítulos P–7 for Final Exam	FINAL EXAM

WEEK	MONDAY	TUESDAY	WEDNESDAY	THURSDAY
16	Second Semester Review: Capítulo preliminar and Capítulos 1–7	**Capítulo 8** **Vocabulario: Fiestas y celebraciones** **¿Nos entendemos? (¡Salud!)** **Encuentro cultural: Santo Tomás de Chichicastenango**	**Capítulo 8** **Así se dice:** *Inquire and provide information about people and events: interrogative words*	**Capítulo 8** **Estructura I:** *Narrating in the past: the preterite vs. the imperfect* **Vocabulario: La playa y el campo**
17	**Capítulo 8** **Encuentro cultural: El arzobispo Oscar Arnulfo Romero** **Estructura II:** *Stating indefinite ideas and quantities: affirmative and negative expressions*	**Capítulo 8** **Así se dice:** *Talking about periods of time since an event took place:* **hace** *and* **hace que** Review Vocabulario **Síntesis: ¡A ver!, ¡A leer!, ¡A escribir!, or ¡A conversar!**	EXAM VIII	Oral Evaluation
18	**Capítulo 9** **Vocabulario: Viajar en avión** **¿Nos entendemos?** (flight attendant and passenger) **Encuentro cultural: La República Dominicana: Santo Domingo, la primera ciudad de las Américas**	**Capítulo 9** **Estructura I:** *Simplifying expressions: indirect object pronouns* **Encuentro cultural: Cuba: Escuela Latinoamericana de Ciencias Médicas**	**Capítulo 9** **Estructura II:** *Simplifying expressions: double object pronouns*	**Capítulo 9** **Vocabulario: El hotel** **¿Nos entendemos? (un cuarto, una habitación)** **Así se dice:** *Giving directions: prepositions of location, adverbs, and relevant expressions*
19	**Capítulo 9** **Encuentro cultural: Puerto Rico: Estado Libre Asociado** **¿Nos entendemos? (puertorriqueños)** **Estructura III:** *Giving directions and expressing desires: formal and negative* **tú** *commands*	Review: Vocabulario **Síntesis: ¡A ver!, ¡A leer!, ¡A escribir!, or ¡A conversar!**	EXAM IX	Oral Evaluation
20	**Capítulo 10** **Vocabulario: Las relaciones sentimentales** **¿Nos entendemos? (amigo(a), novio(a), etc.)** **Encuentro cultural: Los novios en los países hispanoamericanos**	**Capítulo 10** **Estructura I:** *Describing recent actions, events, and conditions: the present perfect tense* **Así se dice:** *Describing reciprocal actions: reciprocal constructions with* **se, nos,** *and* **os**	**Capítulo 10** **Vocabulario: La recepción** **Encuentro cultural: Las bodas en el mundo hispano**	**Capítulo 10** **Así se dice:** *Qualifying actions: adverbial expressions of time and sequencing of events* **Estructura II:** *Using the Spanish equivalents of who, whom, that, and which: relative pronouns*

WEEK	MONDAY	TUESDAY	WEDNESDAY	THURSDAY
21	Review Vocabulario **Síntesis: ¡A ver!, ¡A leer!, ¡A escribir!, or ¡A conversar!**	EXAM X	Oral Evaluation	**Capítulo 11** **Vocabulario: Las profesiones y los oficios** **¿Nos entendemos? (policía, póliza, política)** **Encuentro cultural: El Canal de Panamá**
22	**Capítulo 11** **Estructura I:** *Making statements about motives, intentions, and periods of time:* **por vs. para** **Vocabulario: La oficina, el trabajo y la búsqueda de un puesto**	**Capítulo 11** **Estructura II:** *Expressing subjectivity and uncertainty: the subjunctive mood*	**Capítulo 11** **Encuentro cultural: Protocolo en los negocios en el mundo hispanohablante** **Vocabulario: Las finanzas personales**	**Capítulo 11** **Estructura III:** *Expressing desires and intentions: the present subjunctive with statements of volition*
23	Review Vocabulario **Síntesis: ¡A ver!, ¡A leer!, ¡A escribir!, or ¡A conversar!**	EXAM XI (or review for Midterm Exam)	Oral Evaluation	**Capítulo 12** **Vocabulario: La geografía rural y urbana** **¿Nos entendemos? (tico[a])** **Encuentro cultural: Costa Rica: Puros ingredientes naturales**
24	**Capítulo 12** **Estructura I:** *Expressing emotion and opinions: subjunctive following verbs of emotion, impersonal expressions, and ojalá*	**Capítulo 12** **Vocabulario: La conservación y la explotación** **Encuentro cultural: Costa Rica: Estación biológica La Selva**	**Capítulo 12** **Estructura II:** *Expressing doubts, uncertainty, and hypothesizing: the subjunctive with verbs, expressions of uncertainty, and with adjective clauses* **Vocabulario: Los animales y el refugio natural**	**Capítulo 12** Continue with present subjunctive with verbs, expressions of uncertainty, and with adjective clauses Review Vocabulario **Síntesis: ¡A ver!, ¡A leer!, ¡A escribir!, or ¡A conversar!**
25	EXAM XII	Oral Evaluation	**Capítulo 13** **Vocabulario: Programas y películas** **Encuentro cultural: La cinematografía en Latinoamérica**	**Capítulo 13** **Estructura I:** *Talking about anticipated actions: subjunctive with purpose and time clauses*

WEEK	MONDAY	TUESDAY	WEDNESDAY	THURSDAY
26	**Capítulo 13** Vocabulario: **Las artes Encuentro cultural: Oswaldo Guayasamín**	**Capítulo 13** **Estructura II:** *Talking about unplanned or accidental occurrences: no-fault se construction*	**Capítulo 13** **Así se dice:** *Describing completed actions and resulting conditions: use of the past participle as adjective*	Review Vocabulario **Síntesis:** ¡A ver!, ¡A leer!, ¡A escribir!, or ¡A conversar!
27	EXAM XIII	Oral Evaluation	**Capítulo 14** Vocabulario: **La política y el voto** Encuentro cultural: **El gobierno de Chile** **Estructura I:** *Talking about future events: the future tense*	**Capítulo 14** Continue with the future tense Vocabulario: **Las preocupaciones cívicas y los medios de comunicación** Encuentro cultural: **La libertad de la prensa**
28	**Estructura II:** *Expressing conjecture or probability: the conditional* **Estructura III:** *Making references to the present: the present perfect subjunctive*	Review Vocabulario **Síntesis:** ¡A ver!, ¡A leer!, ¡A escribir!, or ¡A conversar!	EXAM XIV	Oral Evaluation
29	**Capítulo 15** Vocabulario: **Los avances tecnológicos** Encuentro cultural: **Las telecomunicaciones en Uruguay**	**Capítulo 15** **Estructura I:** *Making statements in the past: past (imperfect) subjunctive* **Estructura II:** *Talking about hypothetical situations: if clauses*	**Capítulo 15** Vocabulario: **La computadora** Encuentro cultural: **Equipos: En la palma de la mano**	Review Vocabulario **Síntesis:** ¡A ver!, ¡A leer!, ¡A escribir!, or ¡A conversar!
30	EXAM XV (or review for Final Exam)	Oral Evaluation	Review Capítulos 8–15 for Final Exam	Final Exam

2-SEMESTER SYLLABUS: 5 DAYS A WEEK

WEEK	MONDAY	TUESDAY	WEDNESDAY	THURSDAY	FRIDAY
1	Introductions Administrative requirements Hand out syllabus Show materials and explain how they will be used **Capítulo preliminar** **Vocabulario: Saludos y despedidas** **Una situación formal** **Una situación informal** **¿Nos entendemos? (adiós, nos vemos, chao)**	**Capítulo preliminar** **Encuentro cultural: El lugar de encuentro: Las plazas** **Encuentro cultural: ¿Ser informal o formal? ¿Tú o usted?**	**Capítulo preliminar** **Estructura I:** *Talking about yourself and others: subject pronouns and the present tense of the verb ser*	**Capítulo preliminar** **Así se dice:** *Identifying quantities:* **hay** *and numbers 0–30* **Vocabulario: Palabras interrogativas**	**Capítulo preliminar** **Estructura II:** *Telling age: the present tense of the verb* **tener** **Encuentro cultural: El mundo hispanoamericano** **El alfabeto en español**
2	**Capítulo 1** **Vocabulario: En la clase,** **Los colores** **¿Nos entendemos?** **(el color café)** **Encuentro cultural: El español en los Estados Unidos**	**Capítulo 1** **Estructura I:** *Talking about people, things, and concepts: definite and indefinite articles and how to make nouns plural*	**Capítulo 1** **Vocabulario: Lenguas extranjeras, otras materias y lugares universitarios** **¿Nos entendemos?** **(el castellano)** **Encuentro cultural: La educación en Latinoamérica y España**	**Capítulo 1** **Estructura II:** *Describing everyday activities: present tense of regular* **-ar** *verbs*	**Capítulo 1** **Así se dice:** *Expressing personal likes and dislikes:* **me gusta** + *infinitive*
3	**Capítulo 1** **Así se dice:** *Telling time and talking about the days of the week:* **La hora y los días de la semana** **Encuentro cultural: El sistema de 24 horas**	Review **Vocabulario** **Síntesis: ¡A ver!, ¡A leer!, ¡A escribir!,** or **¡A conversar!**	EXAM I	Oral Evaluation	**Capítulo 2** **Vocabulario: La familia** **¿Nos entendemos? (don/doña)** **Así se dice:** *Indicating ownership and possession: possession with* **de(l)** *and possessive adjectives*

WEEK	MONDAY	TUESDAY	WEDNESDAY	THURSDAY	FRIDAY
4	**Capítulo 2** / **Encuentro cultural: Los nombres y apellidos en español** / **Estructura I:** *Describing people and things: common uses of the verb* **ser**	**Capítulo 2** / **Así se dice:** *Describing people and things: agreement with descriptive adjectives* / **¿Nos entendemos?** (güero(a), canche, catire(a) mono(a), trigueño(a), moreno(a), pelirrojo(a))	**Capítulo 2** / **Encuentro cultural: La familia hispana** / **Vocabulario: Las nacionalidades**	**Capítulo 2** / **Estructura II:** *Describing daily activities at home or at school: present tense of regular* **-er** *and* **-ir** *verbs* / **¿Nos entendemos?** (deber / should)	**Capítulo 2** / **Así se dice:** *Expressing possession and physical states: common uses of the verb* **tener** / **Así se dice:** *Counting to 100:* **los números de 30 a 100**
5	*Review Vocabulario* / **Síntesis: ¡A ver!, ¡A leer!, ¡A escribir!, or ¡A conversar!**	**EXAM II**	Oral Evaluation	**Capítulo 3** / **Vocabulario: Los deportes y los pasatiempos** / **Encuentro cultural: Los deportes en el mundo hispano**	**Capítulo 3** / **Estructura I:** *Expressing likes and dislikes:* **gustar** + *infinitive and* **gustar** + *nouns* / **Vocabulario: Los lugares**
6	**Capítulo 3** / **Estructura II:** *Expressing plans with* **ir: ir a** + *destination, and* **ir a** + *infinitive*	**Capítulo 3** / **Encuentro cultural: El café en Colombia y en el mundo**	**Capítulo 3** / **Estructura III:** *Describing leisure time activities: verbs with irregular yo forms* / **¿Nos entendemos?** (idioms with **hacer** and other verbs that, like **hacer**, have irregular yo forms)	**Capítulo 3** / **Así se dice:** *Expressing knowledge and familiarity:* **saber, conocer,** *and the* **personal a**	**Capítulo 3** / **Así se dice:** *Talking about the months, seasons, and the weather*
7	*Review Vocabulario* / **Síntesis: ¡A ver!, ¡A leer!, ¡A escribir!, or ¡A conversar!**	**EXAM III**	Oral Evaluation	**Capítulo 4** / **Vocabulario: La casa** / **¿Nos entendemos?** (la heladera, la nevera, el refrigerador) / **Encuentro cultural: Gaudí y su obra**	**Capítulo 4** / **Estructura I:** *Describing household chores and other activities: present tense of stem-changing verbs:* **o** *to* **ue; e** *to* **ie; e** *to* **i**
8	**Capítulo 4** / **Así se dice:** *Expressing physical conditions, desires, and obligations with* **tener**	**Capítulo 4** / **Vocabulario: Los quehaceres domésticos** / **Encuentro cultural: Viviendas en Latinoamérica y España**	**Capítulo 4** / **Estructura II:** *Expressing preferences and giving advice: affirmative* **tú** *commands*	**Capítulo 4** / **Estructura III:** *Talking about location, emotional and physical states, and actions in progress: the verb* **estar**	**Capítulo 4** / **Así se dice:** *Counting from 100 and higher:* **los números de 100 a 1.000.000**

WEEK	MONDAY	TUESDAY	WEDNESDAY	THURSDAY	FRIDAY
9	Review Vocabulario Síntesis: ¡A ver!, ¡A leer!, ¡A escribir!, or ¡A conversar!	EXAM IV	Oral Evaluation	**Capítulo 5** Vocabulario: El cuerpo humano ¿Nos entendemos? (*useful expressions and el cabello and el pelo*) Encuentro cultural: Bolivia y la salud	**Capítulo 5** **Estructura I:** *Talking about routine activities: reflexive pronouns and present tense of reflexive verbs*
10	**Capítulo 5** **Así se dice:** *Talking about things you have just finished doing:* **acabar de + infinitive** Vocabulario: La salud	**Capítulo 5** **Estructura II:** *Describing people, things, and conditions:* **ser versus estar** ¿Nos entendemos? (*marital status*)	**Capítulo 5** Encuentro cultural: Tradición de hierbas: Yerba mate en Paraguay y las hojas de coca en los Andes	**Capítulo 5** **Estructura III:** *Pointing out people and things: demonstrative adjectives and pronouns*	Review Vocabulario Síntesis: ¡A ver!, ¡A leer!, ¡A escribir!, or ¡A conversar!
11	**EXAM V** (or review for Midterm Exam)	Oral Evaluation	**Capítulo 6** Vocabulario: La comida ¿Nos entendemos? (un negrito, un marroncito, un marrón, un café con leche) Encuentro cultural: La comida típica venezolana	**Capítulo 6** **Estructura I:** *Making comparisons: comparatives and superlatives*	**Capítulo 6** Vocabulario: El restaurante Encuentro cultural: Los postres venezolanos
12	**Capítulo 6** **Estructura II:** *Describing past events: regular verbs and verbs with spelling changes in the preterite*	**Capítulo 6** **Estructura III:** *Giving detailed description about past events: more verbs with stem changes in the preterite*	Review Vocabulario Síntesis: ¡A ver!, ¡A leer!, ¡A escribir!, or ¡A conversar!	EXAM VI	Oral Evaluation
13	**Capítulo 7** Vocabulario: La ropa ¿Nos entendemos? (a cuadros, la pollera, la campera, etc.)	**Capítulo 7** Encuentro cultural: De compras en Buenos Aires **Así se dice:** *Making emphatic statements: stressed possessive adjectives and pronouns*	**Capítulo 7** **Estructura I:** *Talking about singular and/or completed events in the past: verbs irregular in the preterite*	**Capítulo 7** Vocabulario: De compras Encuentro cultural: El tango argentino	**Capítulo 7** **Estructura II:** *Simplifying expressions: direct object pronouns*

WEEK	MONDAY	TUESDAY	WEDNESDAY	THURSDAY	FRIDAY
14	**Capítulo 7** Estructura III: *Describing on-going and habitual actions in the past: the imperfect tense*	**Capítulo 7** Review the preterite and the imperfect	Review Vocabulario **Síntesis:** ¡A ver!, ¡A leer!, ¡A escribir!, or ¡A conversar!	EXAM VII	Oral Evaluation
15	Review Capítulos P–4 for Final Exam	Review Capítulos 5–7 for Final Exam	Final Exam	Oral Evaluation	Oral Evaluation
16	**Second Semester** **Review:** Capítulos P–7	**Capítulo 8** Vocabulario: Fiestas y celebraciones ¿Nos entendemos? (¡Salud!) Encuentro cultural: Santo Tomás de Chichicastenango	**Capítulo 8** Así se dice: *Inquire and provide information about people and events: interrogative words*	**Capítulo 8** Estructura I: *Narrating in the past: the preterite vs. the imperfect*	**Capítulo 8** Vocabulario: La playa y el campo Encuentro cultural: El arzobispo Oscar Arnulfo Romero
17	**Capítulo 8** Estructura II: *Stating indefinite ideas and quantities: affirmative and negative expressions*	**Capítulo 8** Así se dice: *Talking about periods of time since an event took place:* **Hace** *and* **hace que**	Review Vocabulario **Síntesis:** ¡A ver!, ¡A leer!, ¡A escribir!, or ¡A conversar!	EXAM VIII	Oral Evaluation
18	**Capítulo 9** Vocabulario: Viajar en avión ¿Nos entendemos? (flight attendant and passenger) Encuentro cultural: La República Dominicana: Santo Domingo, la primera ciudad de las Américas	**Capítulo 9** Estructura I: *Simplifying expressions: indirect object pronouns*	**Capítulo 9** Encuentro cultural: Cuba: Escuela Latinoamericana de Ciencias Médicas	**Capítulo 9** Estructura II: *Simplifying expressions: double object pronouns*	**Capítulo 9** Vocabulario: El hotel ¿Nos entendemos? (un cuarto, una habitación) **Así se dice:** *Giving directions: prepositions of location, adverbs, and relevant expressions*
19	**Capítulo 9** Encuentro cultural: Puerto Rico: Estado Libre Asociado ¿Nos entendemos? (puertorriqueños)	**Capítulo 9** Estructura III: *Giving directions and expressing desires: formal and negative* **tú** *commands*	*Review* Vocabulario **Síntesis:** ¡A ver!, ¡A leer!, ¡A escribir!, or ¡A conversar!	EXAM IX	Oral Evaluation

WEEK	MONDAY	TUESDAY	WEDNESDAY	THURSDAY	FRIDAY
20	Capítulo 10 Vocabulario: Las relaciones sentimentales ¿Nos entendemos? (amigo(a), novio(a), etc.) Encuentro cultural: Los novios en los países hispanoamericanos	Capítulo 10 Estructura I: *Describing recent actions, events, and conditions: the present perfect tense*	Capítulo 10 Así se dice: *Describing reciprocal actions: reciprocal constructions with se, nos, and os* Vocabulario: La recepción	Capítulo 10 Encuentro cultural: Las bodas en el mundo hispano Así se dice: *Qualifying actions: adverbial expressions of time and sequencing of events*	Capítulo 10 Estructura II: *Using the Spanish equivalents of who, whom, that, and which: relative pronouns*
21	Review Vocabulario Síntesis: ¡A ver!, ¡A leer!, ¡A escribir!, or ¡A conversar!	EXAM X	Oral Evaluation	Capítulo 11 Vocabulario: Las profesiones y los oficios ¿Nos entendemos? (policía, póliza, política) Encuentro cultural: El Canal de Panamá	Capítulo 11 Estructura I: *Making statements about motives, intentions, and periods of time:* por vs. para
22	Capítulo 11 Vocabulario: La oficina, el trabajo y la búsqueda de un puesto	Capítulo 11 Estructura II: *Expressing subjectivity and uncertainty: the subjunctive mood*	Capítulo 11 Vocabulario: Las finanzas personales Encuentro cultural: Protocolo en los negocios en el mundo hispanohablante	Capítulo 11 Estructura III: *Expressing desires and intentions: the present subjunctive with statements of volition*	Review Vocabulario Síntesis: ¡A ver!, ¡A leer!, ¡A escribir!, or ¡A conversar!
23	EXAM XI (or review for Midterm Exam)	Oral Evaluation	Capítulo 12 Vocabulario: La geografía rural y urbana ¿Nos entendemos? (tico(a), etc.) Encuentro cultural: Costa Rica: Puros ingredientes naturales	Capítulo 12 Estructura I: *Expressing emotion and opinions: subjunctive following verbs of emotion, impersonal expressions, and* ojalá	Capítulo 12 Vocabulario: La conservación y la explotación Encuentro cultural: Costa Rica: Estación biológica La selva
24	Capítulo 12 Estructura II: *Expressing doubts, uncertainty and hypothesizing: the subjunctive with verbs, expressions of uncertainty, and with adjective clauses*	Capítulo 12 Continue with subjunctive with verbs of uncertainty and doubt Vocabulario: Los animales y el refugio natural	Review Vocabulario Síntesis: ¡A ver!, ¡A leer!, ¡A escribir!, or ¡A conversar!	EXAM XII	Oral Evaluation

WEEK	MONDAY	TUESDAY	WEDNESDAY	THURSDAY	FRIDAY
25	**Capítulo 13** **Vocabulario: Programas y películas** Encuentro cultural: La cinematografía en Latinoamérica	**Capítulo 13** **Estructura I:** *Talking about anticipated actions: subjunctive with purpose and time clauses*	**Capítulo 13** **Vocabulario: Las artes** Encuentro cultural: Oswaldo Guayasamín	**Capítulo 13** **Estructura II:** *Talking about unplanned or accidental occurrences: no-fault* **se** *construction*	**Capítulo 13** **Así se dice:** Describing completed actions and resulting conditions: use of the past participle as adjective
26	Review Vocabulario Síntesis: ¡A ver!, ¡A leer!, ¡A escribir!, or ¡A conversar!	EXAM XIII	Oral Evaluation	**Capítulo 14** **Vocabulario: La política y el voto** Encuentro cultural: El gobierno de Chile	**Capítulo 14** **Estructura I:** *Talking about future events: the future tense*
27	**Capítulo 14** **Vocabulario: Las preocupaciones cívicas y los medios de comunicación** Encuentro cultural: La libertad de la prensa **Estructura II:** *Expressing conjecture or probability: the conditional*	**Capítulo 14** Continue with the conditional **Estructura III:** *Making references to the present: the present perfect subjunctive*	**Capítulo 14** Review **Vocabulario** Síntesis: ¡A ver!, ¡A leer!, ¡A escribir!, or ¡A conversar!	EXAM XIV	Oral Evaluation
28	**Capítulo 15** **Vocabulario: Los avances tecnológicos** Encuentro cultural: Las telecomunicaciones en Uruguay	**Capítulo 15** **Estructura I:** *Making statements in the past: past (imperfect) subjunctive*	**Capítulo 15** **Vocabulario: La computadora** Encuentro cultural: En la palma de la mano	**Capítulo 15** **Estructura II:** *Talking about hypothetical situations: if clauses*	Review **Vocabulario** Síntesis: ¡A ver!, ¡A leer!, ¡A escribir!, or ¡A conversar!
29	EXAM XV	Oral Evaluation	Review Capítulos 8–10 for Final Exam	Review Capítulos 11–15 for Final Exam	FINAL EXAM
30	Practice for Oral Evaluation	Oral Evaluation	Oral Evaluation	Individual consultations, as needed	End of semester

3-SEMESTER SYLLABUS: 4 DAYS A WEEK

WEEK	MONDAY	TUESDAY	WEDNESDAY	THURSDAY
1	Introductions Administrative requirements Hand out syllabus Show materials and explain how they will be used **Capítulo preliminar** **Vocabulario: Saludos y despedidas** **Una situación formal** **Una situación informal** **¿Nos entendemos?** (adiós, nos vemos, chao)	**Capítulo preliminar** **Encuentro cultural: El lugar de encuentro: Las plazas** **Encuentro cultural: ¿Ser informal o formal? ¿Tú o usted?**	**Capítulo preliminar** **Estructura I:** *Talking about yourself and others: subject pronouns and the present tense of the verb* **ser**	**Capítulo preliminar** **Así se dice:** *Identifying quantities:* **hay** *and numbers 0–30* **Vocabulario: Palabras interrogativas**
2	**Capítulo preliminar** **Estructura II:** *Telling age: the present tense of the verb* **tener**	**Capítulo preliminar** **Encuentro cultural: El mundo hispanoamericano** **El alfabeto en español**	**Capítulo 1** **Vocabulario: En la clase, Los colores** **¿Nos entendemos? (el color café)** **Encuentro cultural: El español en los Estados Unidos**	**Capítulo 1** **Estructura I:** *Talking about people, things, and concepts: definite and indefinite articles and how to make nouns plural*
3	**Capítulo 1** **Vocabulario: Lenguas extranjeras, otras materias y lugares universitarios** **¿Nos entendemos? (el castellano)** **Encuentro cultural: La educación en Latinoamérica y España**	**Capítulo 1** **Estructura II:** *Describing everyday activities: present tense of regular* **-ar** *verbs* **Así se dice:** *Expressing personal likes and dislikes:* **me gusta + infinitive**	**Capítulo 1** **Así se dice:** *Telling time and talking about the days of the week:* **la hora y los días de la semana** **Encuentro cultural: El sistema de 24 horas**	Review Vocabulario **Síntesis: ¡A ver!** and/or **¡A conversar!**
4	**Síntesis: ¡A leer!** and/or **¡A escribir!**	EXAM I	Oral Evaluation	**Capítulo 2** **Vocabulario: La familia** **¿Nos entendemos? (don/doña)** **Así se dice:** *Indicating ownership and possession: possession with* **de(l)** *and possessive adjectives*

WEEK	MONDAY	TUESDAY	WEDNESDAY	THURSDAY
5	**Capítulo 2** Encuentro cultural: Los nombres y apellidos en español Estructura I: *Describing people and things: common uses of the verb* **ser**	**Capítulo 2** **Así se dice:** *Describing people and things: agreement with descriptive adjectives* ¿**Nos entendemos?** (güero(a), canche, catire(a) mono(a), trigueño(a), moreno(a), pelirrojo(a)) Encuentro cultural: La familia hispana	**Capítulo 2** **Vocabulario: Las nacionalidades** **Estructura II:** *Describing daily activities at home or at school: present tense of* **-er** *and* **-ir** *verbs* ¿**Nos entendemos?** (deber / should)	**Capítulo 2** **Así se dice:** *Expressing possession and physical states: common uses of the verb* **tener** **Así se dice:** *Counting to 100:* los números de 30 a 100
6	Review Vocabulario Síntesis: ¡A ver! and/or ¡A conversar!	Síntesis: ¡A leer! and/or ¡A escribir!	**EXAM II**	**Oral Evaluation**
7	**Capítulo 3** **Vocabulario: Los deportes y los pasatiempos** Encuentro cultural: Los deportes en el mundo hispano	**Capítulo 3** **Estructura I:** *Expressing likes and dislikes:* **gustar** + *infinitive and* **gustar** + *nouns* **Vocabulario: Los lugares**	**Capítulo 3** **Estructura II:** *Expressing plans with* **ir:** **ir a** + *destination, and* **ir a** + *infinitive* Encuentro cultural: El café en Colombia y en el mundo	**Capítulo 3** **Estructura III:** *Describing leisure time activities: verbs with irregular* **yo** *forms* ¿**Nos entendemos?** *(idioms with* **hacer** *and other verbs that, like* **hacer,** *have irregular* **yo** *forms)*
8	**Capítulo 3** **Así se dice:** *Expressing knowledge and familiarity:* **saber, conocer,** *and the* **personal a**	**Capítulo 3** **Así se dice:** *Talking about the months, seasons, and the weather*	Review Vocabulario Síntesis: ¡A ver! and/or ¡A conversar!	Síntesis: ¡A leer! and/or ¡A escribir!
9	**EXAM III** (or review for Midterm Exam)	**Oral Evaluation**		
10	**Capítulo 4** **Así se dice:** *Expressing physical conditions, desires, and obligations with* **tener**	**Capítulo 4** **Vocabulario: Los quehaceres domésticos** Encuentro cultural: Viviendas en Latinoamérica y España	**Capítulo 4** **Vocabulario: La casa** ¿**Nos entendemos?** (la heladera, la nevera, el refrigerador) Encuentro cultural: Gaudí y su obra	**Capítulo 4** **Estructura I:** *Describing household chores and other activities: present tense of stem-changing verbs:* **o** *to* **ue;** **e** *to* **ie;** **e** *to* **i**
			Capítulo 4 **Estructura II:** *Expressing preferences and giving advice: affirmative* **tú** *commands*	**Capítulo 4** **Estructura III:** *Talking about location, emotional, and physical states, and actions in progress: the verb* **estar** **Así se dice:** *Counting from 100 and higher:* los números de 100 a 1.000.000

WEEK	MONDAY	TUESDAY	WEDNESDAY	THURSDAY
11	Review Vocabulario Síntesis: ¡A ver! and/or ¡A conversar!	Síntesis: ¡A leer! and/or ¡A escribir!	EXAM IV	Oral Evaluation
12	Capítulo 5 Vocabulario: El cuerpo humano ¿Nos entendemos? (useful expressions and el cabello and el pelo) Encuentro cultural: Bolivia y la salud	Capítulo 5 Estructura I: *Talking about routine activities: reflexive pronouns and present tense of reflexive verbs*	Capítulo 5 Así se dice: *Talking about things you have just finished doing:* acabar de + infinitive Vocabulario: La salud	Capítulo 5 Estructura II: *Describing people, things, and conditions:* ser vs. estar ¿Nos entendemos? (marital status)
13	Capítulo 5 Encuentro cultural: Tradición de hierbas: Yerba mate en Paraguay y las hojas de coca en los Andes	Capítulo 5 Estructura III: *Pointing out people and things: demonstrative adjectives and pronouns*	Review Vocabulario Síntesis: ¡A ver! and/or ¡A conversar!	Síntesis: ¡A leer! and/or ¡A escribir!
14	EXAM V	Oral Evaluation	Review Capítulos P–3 for Final Exam	Review Capítulos 4 y 5 for Final Exam
15	FINAL EXAM	Practice for Oral Evaluation	Oral Evaluation	Oral Evaluation
16	Second semester Administrative requirements Hand out syllabus	Review: Capítulo preliminar y Capítulos 1 and 2	Review: Capítulos 3 and 4	Review: Capítulo 5
17	Capítulo 6 Vocabulario: La comida ¿Nos entendemos? (un negrito, un marrón, un marroncito, un café con leche, etc.)	Capítulo 6 Encuentro cultural: La comida típica venezolana	Capítulo 6 Estructura I: *Making comparisons: comparatives and superlatives*	Capítulo 6 Vocabulario: El restaurante Encuentro cultural: Los postres venezolanos
18	Capítulo 6 Estructura II: *Describing past events: regular verbs and verbs with spelling changes in the preterite*	Capítulo 6 Estructura III: *Giving detailed description about past events: more verbs with stem changes in the preterite*	Review Vocabulario Síntesis: ¡A ver! and/or ¡A conversar!	Síntesis: ¡A leer! and/or ¡A escribir!

WEEK	MONDAY	TUESDAY	WEDNESDAY	THURSDAY
19	EXAM VI	Oral Evaluation	**Capítulo 7** **Vocabulario: La ropa** **¿Nos entendemos?** (a cuadros, la pollera, la campera, etc.) **Encuentro cultural: De compras en Buenos Aires**	**Capítulo 7** **Así se dice:** *Making emphatic statements: stressed possessive adjectives and pronouns*
20	**Capítulo 7** **Estructura I:** *Talking about singular and/or completed events in the past: verbs irregular in the preterite*	**Capítulo 7** **Vocabulario: De compras** **Encuentro cultural: El tango argentino**	**Capítulo 7** **Estructura II:** *Simplifying expressions: direct object pronouns*	**Capítulo 7** **Estructura III:** *Describing on-going and habitual actions in the past: the imperfect tense*
21	Review Vocabulario **Síntesis: ¡A ver!** and/or **¡A conversar!**	**Síntesis: ¡A leer!** and/or **¡A escribir!**	EXAM VII	Oral Evaluation
22	**Capítulo 8** **Vocabulario: Fiestas y celebraciones** **¿Nos entendemos?** (¡Salud!) **Encuentro cultural: Santo Tomás de Chichicastenango**	**Capítulo 8** **Así se dice:** *Inquire and provide information about people and events: interrogative words*	**Capítulo 8** **Estructura I:** *Narrating in the past: the preterite vs. the imperfect*	**Capítulo 8** **Vocabulario: La playa y el campo** **Estructura II:** *Stating indefinite ideas and quantities: affirmative and negative expressions*
23	**Capítulo 8** **Así se dice:** *Talking about periods of time since an event took place:* **hace and hace que**	**Capítulo 8** **Encuentro cultural: El arzobispo Oscar Arnulfo Romero**	Review Vocabulario **Síntesis: ¡A ver!** and/or **¡A conversar!**	**Síntesis: ¡A leer!** and/or **¡A escribir!**
24	**EXAM VIII** (or review for **Midterm Exam**)	Oral Evaluation	**Capítulo 9** **Vocabulario: Viajar en avión** **¿Nos entendemos?** (flight attendant and passenger) **Encuentro cultural: La República Dominicana: Santo Domingo, la primera ciudad de las Américas**	**Capítulo 9** **Estructura I:** *Simplifying expressions: indirect object pronouns*

WEEK	MONDAY	TUESDAY	WEDNESDAY	THURSDAY
25	**Capítulo 9** Encuentro cultural: Cuba: Escuela Latinoamericana de Ciencias Médicas	**Capítulo 9** **Estructura II:** *Simplifying expressions: double object pronouns* **Vocabulario: El hotel** **¿Nos entendemos? (un cuarto, una habitación)**	**Capítulo 9** **Así se dice:** *Giving directions: prepositions of location, adverbs, and relevant expressions* **Encuentro cultural: Puerto Rico: Estado Libre Asociado** **¿Nos entendemos? (puertorriqueños)**	**Capítulo 9** **Estructura III:** *Giving directions and expressing desires: formal and negative tú commands*
26	Review Vocabulario Síntesis: ¡A ver! and/or ¡A conversar!	Síntesis: ¡A leer! and/or ¡A escribir!	EXAM IX	Oral Evaluation
27	**Capítulo 10** **Vocabulario: Las relaciones sentimentales** **¿Nos entendemos? (amigo(a), novio(a), etc.)** **Encuentro cultural: Los novios en los países hispanoamericanos**	**Capítulo 10** **Estructura I:** *Describing recent actions, events, and conditions: the present perfect tense*	**Capítulo 10** **Así se dice:** *Describing reciprocal actions: reciprocal constructions with se, nos, and os*	**Capítulo 10** **Vocabulario: La recepción** **Encuentro cultural: Las bodas en el mundo hispano**
28	**Capítulo 10** **Así se dice:** *Qualifying actions: adverbial expressions of time and sequencing of events*	**Capítulo 10** **Estructura II:** *Using the Spanish equivalents of who, whom, that, and which: relative pronouns*	Review Vocabulario Síntesis: ¡A ver! and/or ¡A conversar!	Síntesis: ¡A leer! and/or ¡A escribir!
29	**EXAM X**	Oral Evaluation	Review Capítulos 6–8 for Final Exam	Review Capítulos 9 and 10 for Final Exam
30	**FINAL EXAM**	Practice for Oral Evaluation	Oral Evaluation	Oral Evaluation
31	**Third Semester** Administrative requirements Hand out syllabus	Review: Capítulos 6–8	Review: Capítulos 9 and 10	Lab and Workbook assignments for review
32	**Capítulo 11** **Vocabulario: Las profesiones y los oficios** **¿Nos entendemos? (policía, póliza, política)** **Encuentro cultural: El Canal de Panamá**	**Capítulo 11** **Estructura I:** *Making statements about motives, intentions, and periods of time:* **por** *vs.* **para**	**Capítulo 11** **Vocabulario: La oficina, el trabajo y la búsqueda de un puesto**	**Capítulo 11** **Estructura II:** *Expressing subjectivity and uncertainty: the subjunctive mood*

WEEK	MONDAY	TUESDAY	WEDNESDAY	THURSDAY
33	**Capítulo 11** Encuentro cultural: Protocolo en los negocios en el mundo hispanohablante **Vocabulario: Las finanzas personales**	**Capítulo 11** **Estructura III:** *Expressing desires and intentions: the present subjunctive with statements of volition*	**Capítulo 11** Review use of subjunctive presented in Estructuras II y III	Review Vocabulario Síntesis: ¡A ver! and/or ¡A conversar!
34	Síntesis: ¡A leer! and/or ¡A escribir!	Exam XI	Oral Evaluations	**Capítulo 12** **Vocabulario: La geografía rural y urbana** ¿Nos entendemos? (tico[a]) Encuentro cultural: Costa Rica: Puros ingredientes naturales
35	**Capítulo 12** **Estructura I:** *Expressing emotion and opinions: subjunctive following verbs of emotion, impersonal expressions, and ojalá*	**Capítulo 12** **Vocabulario: La conservación y la explotación** Encuentro cultural: Costa Rica: Estación biológica La Selva	**Capítulo 12** **Estructura II:** *Expressing doubts, uncertainty, and hypothesizing: the subjunctive with verbs, expressions of uncertainty, and with adjective clauses*	**Capítulo 12** Review use of subjunctive presented in Estructuras I y II **Vocabulario: Los animales y el refugio natural**
36	Review Vocabulario Síntesis: ¡A ver! and/or ¡A conversar!	Síntesis: ¡A leer! and/or ¡A escribir!	EXAM XII	Oral Evaluations
37	**Capítulo 13** **Vocabulario: Programas y películas** Encuentro cultural: La cinematografía en Latinoamérica	**Capítulo 13** **Estructura I:** *Talking about anticipated actions: subjunctive with purpose and time clauses*	**Capítulo 13** **Vocabulario: Las artes** Encuentro cultural: Oswaldo Guayasamín	**Capítulo 13** **Estructura II:** *Talking about unplanned or accidental occurrences: no-fault se construction*
38	**Capítulo 13** Continue with forming the no-fault se construction and verbs used in the constructions	**Capítulo 13** **Así se dice:** *Describing completed actions and resulting conditions: use of the past participle as adjective*	Review Vocabulario Síntesis: ¡A ver! and/or ¡A conversar!	Síntesis: ¡A leer! and/or ¡A escribir!
39	**Exam XIII** (or review for Midterm Exam)	Oral Evaluations	**Capítulo 14** **Vocabulario: La política y el voto** Encuentro cultural: El gobierno de Chile	**Capítulo 14** **Estructura I:** *Talking about future events: the future tense*

WEEK	MONDAY	TUESDAY	WEDNESDAY	THURSDAY
40	**Capítulo 14** **Vocabulario: Las preocupaciones cívicas y los medios de comunicación** **Encuentro cultural: La libertad de la prensa**	**Capítulo 14** **Estructura II:** *Expressing conjecture or probability: the conditional*	**Capítulo 14** **Estructura III:** *Making references to the present perfect subjunctive*	Review **Vocabulario** **Síntesis: ¡A ver!** and/or **¡A conversar!**
41	**Síntesis: ¡A leer!** and/or **¡A escribir!**	**EXAM XIV**	**Oral Evaluation**	**Capítulo 15** **Vocabulario: Los avances tecnológicos** **Encuentro cultural: Las telecomunicaciones en Uruguay**
42	**Capítulo 15** **Estructura I:** *Making statements in the past: past (imperfect) subjunctive*	**Capítulo 15** **Vocabulario: La computadora** **Encuentro cultural: Equipos: En la palma de la mano**	**Capítulo 15** **Estructura II:** *Talking about hypothetical situations: if clauses*	**Capítulo 15** Practice using the past subjunctive forms Practice using *if* clauses
43	Review **Vocabulario** **Síntesis: ¡A ver!** and/or **¡A conversar!**	**Síntesis: ¡A leer!** and/or **¡A escribir!**	**EXAM XV**	**Oral Evaluation**
44	Review **Capítulos 11–13** for Final Exam	Review **Capítulos 14 and 15** for Final Exam	**FINAL EXAM**	Practice for **Oral Evaluation**
45	**Oral Evaluation**	**Oral Evaluation**	Individual consultations, if necessary	Students complete unfinished and/or make-up assignments Students turn in final reports or projects

3-SEMESTER SYLLABUS: 5 DAYS A WEEK

WEEK	MONDAY	TUESDAY	WEDNESDAY	THURSDAY	FRIDAY
1	Introductions Administrative requirements Hand out syllabus Show materials and explain how they will be used **Vocabulario: Saludos y despedidas** Una situación formal Una situación informal ¿Nos entendemos? (adiós, nos vemos, chao)	**Capítulo preliminar** **Encuentro cultural: El lugar de encuentro: Las plazas** **Encuentro cultural: ¿Ser informal o formal?** ¿Tú o usted?	**Capítulo preliminar** **Estructura I:** *Talking about yourself and others: subject pronouns and the present tense of the verb* **ser**	**Capítulo preliminar** **Así se dice:** *Identifying quantities:* hay *and numbers 0–30* **Vocabulario: Palabras interrogativas**	**Capítulo preliminar** **Estructura II:** *Telling age: the present tense of the verb* **tener**
2	**Capítulo 1** **Encuentro cultural: El mundo hispanoamericano** El alfabeto en español	**Capítulo 1** **Vocabulario: En la clase, Los colores** ¿Nos entendemos? (el color café) **Encuentro cultural: El español en los Estados Unidos**	**Capítulo 1** **Estructura I:** *Talking about people, things, and concepts: definite and indefinite articles and how to make nouns plural*	**Capítulo 1** **Vocabulario: Lenguas extranjeras, otras materias y lugares universitarios** ¿Nos entendemos? (el castellano) **Encuentro cultural: La educación en Latinoamérica y España**	**Capítulo 1** **Estructura II:** *Describing everyday activities: present tense of regular* **-ar** *verbs*
3	**Capítulo 1** **Así se dice:** *Expressing personal likes and dislikes:* **me gusta** + *infinitive*	**Capítulo 1** **Así se dice:** *Telling time and talking about the days of the week:* la hora y los días de la semana	**Capítulo 1** **Encuentro cultural: El sistema de 24 horas**	Review Vocabulario **Síntesis: ¡A ver!** and/or **¡A conversar!**	**Síntesis: ¡A leer!** and/or **¡A escribir!**
4	**EXAM I**	**Oral Evaluation**	**Capítulo 2** **Vocabulario: La familia** ¿Nos entendemos? (don/doña)	**Capítulo 2** **Así se dice:** *Indicating ownership and possession: possession with* **de(l)** *and possessive adjectives*	**Capítulo 2** **Encuentro cultural: Los nombres y apellidos en español**

WEEK	MONDAY	TUESDAY	WEDNESDAY	THURSDAY	FRIDAY
5	**Capítulo 2** / **Estructura I:** *Describing people and things: common uses of the verbs* **ser**	**Capítulo 2** / **Así se dice:** *Describing people and things: agreement with descriptive adjectives* / **¿Nos entendemos?** (güero(a), canche, catire(a) mono(a), trigueño(a), moreno(a), pelirrojo[a])	**Capítulo 2** / **Encuentro cultural:** La familia hispana / **Vocabulario:** Las nacionalidades	**Capítulo 2** / **Estructura II:** *Describing daily activities at home or at school: present tense of* **-er** *and* **-ir** *verbs* / **¿Nos entendemos?** (deber / should)	**Capítulo 2** / **Así se dice:** *Expressing possession and physical states: common uses of the verb* **tener**
6	**Capítulo 2** / **Así se dice:** *Counting to 100:* los números de 30 a 100	Review **Vocabulario** / **Síntesis:** ¡A ver! and/or ¡A conversar!	**Síntesis:** ¡A leer! and/or ¡A escribir!	**EXAM II**	**Oral Evaluation**
7	**Capítulo 3** / **Vocabulario:** Los deportes y los pasatiempos / **Encuentro cultural:** Los deportes en el mundo hispano	**Capítulo 3** / **Estructura I:** *Expressing likes and dislikes:* **gustar** + *infinitive and* **gustar** + *nouns*	**Capítulo 3** / **Vocabulario:** Los lugares	**Capítulo 3** / **Estructura II:** *Expressing plans with* **ir:** **ir a** + *destination, and* **ir a** + *infinitive*	**Capítulo 3** / **Encuentro cultural:** El café en Colombia y en el mundo
8	**Capítulo 3** / **Estructura III:** *Describing leisure time activities: verbs with irregular yo forms* / **¿Nos entendemos?** (idioms with **hacer** and other verbs that, like **hacer**, have irregular yo forms)	**Capítulo 3** / **Así se dice:** *Exressing knowledge and familiarity:* **saber, conocer,** *and the personal* **a**	**Capítulo 3** / **Así se dice:** *Talking about the months, seasons, and the weather*	Review **Vocabulario** / **Síntesis:** ¡A ver! and/or ¡A conversar!	**Síntesis:** ¡A leer! and/or ¡A escribir!
9	**EXAM III** (or review for Midterm Exam)	**Oral Evaluation**	**Capítulo 4** / **Vocabulario:** La casa / **¿Nos entendemos?** (la heladera, la nevera, el refrigerador)	**Capítulo 4** / **Encuentro cultural:** Gaudí y su obra	**Capítulo 4** / **Estructura I:** *Describing household chores and other activities: present tense of stem-changing verbs:* o to ue; e to ie; e to i
10	**Capítulo 4** / Continue with stem-changing verbs / **Así se dice:** *Expressing physical conditions, desires, and obligations with* **tener**	**Capítulo 4** / Continue with **tener** expressions / **Vocabulario:** Los quehaceres domésticos	**Capítulo 4** / **Encuentro cultural:** Viviendas en Latinoamérica y España	**Capítulo 4** / **Estructura II:** *Expressing preferences and giving advice: affirmative* **tú** *commands*	**Capítulo 4** / **Estructura III:** *Talking about location, emotional and physical states, and actions in progress: the verb* **estar**

WEEK	MONDAY	TUESDAY	WEDNESDAY	THURSDAY	FRIDAY
11	**Capítulo 4** / **Así se dice:** *Counting from 100 and higher:* **de 100 a 1.000.000**	Review Vocabulario / Síntesis: **¡A ver!** and/or **¡A conversar!**	Síntesis: **¡A leer!** and/or **¡A escribir!**	**EXAM IV**	Oral Evaluation
12	**Capítulo 5** / Vocabulario: **El cuerpo humano** / **¿Nos entendemos?** (useful expressions and *el cabello* and *el pelo*)	**Capítulo 5** / Encuentro cultural: **Bolivia y la salud**	**Capítulo 5** / **Estructura I:** *Talking about routine activities: reflexive pronouns and present tense of reflexive verbs*	**Capítulo 5** / **Así se dice:** *Talking about things you have just finished doing:* **acabar de + infinitivo**	**Capítulo 5** / Vocabulario: **La salud**
13	**Capítulo 5** / **Estructura II:** *Describing people, things, and conditions:* **ser vs. estar** / **¿Nos entendemos?** (marital status)	Continue with **ser vs. estar**	**Capítulo 5** / Encuentro cultural: **Tradición de hierbas: Yerba mate en Paraguay y las hojas de coca en los Andes**	**Capítulo 5** / **Estructura III:** *Pointing out people and things: demonstrative adjectives and pronouns*	Review Vocabulario / Síntesis: **¡A ver!** and/or **¡A conversar!**
14	Síntesis: **¡A leer!** and/or **¡A escribir!**	**EXAM V**	Oral Evaluation	Review **Capítulos P–2** for **Final Exam**	Review **Capítulos 3–5** for **Final Exam**
15	**FINAL EXAM**	Practice for **Oral Evaluation**	Oral Evaluation	Oral Evaluation	Individual consultations, if necessary / **End of Semester**
16	**Second semester** / Administrative requirements / Hand out syllabus	Review: **Capítulo preliminar** and **Capítulo 1**	Review: **Capítulos 2 and 3**	Review: **Capítulos 4 and 5**	Lab and Workbook assignments for review
17	**Capítulo 6** / Vocabulario: **La comida** / **¿Nos entendemos?** (un negrito, un marrón, un marroncito, un café con leche, etc.)	**Capítulo 6** / Encuentro cultural: **La comida típica venezolana**	**Capítulo 6** / **Estructura I:** *Making comparisons: comparatives and superlatives*	**Capítulo 6** / Vocabulario: **El restaurante**	**Capítulo 6** / Encuentro cultural: **Los postres venezolanos**

WEEK	MONDAY	TUESDAY	WEDNESDAY	THURSDAY	FRIDAY
18	**Capítulo 6** **Estructura II:** *Describing past events: regular verbs and verbs with spelling changes in the preterite*	**Capítulo 6** **Estructura III:** *Giving detailed description about past events: more verbs with stem changes in the preterite*	**Capítulo 6** *Review spelling changes and stem changes in the preterite*	Review Vocabulario **Síntesis: ¡A ver!** and/or **¡A conversar!**	**Síntesis: ¡A leer!** and/or **¡A escribir!**
19	**EXAM VI**	Oral Evaluation			**Capítulo 7** **Así se dice:** *Making emphatic statements: stressed possessive adjectives and pronouns*
20	**Capítulo 7** **Estructura I:** *Talking about singular and/or completed events in the past: verbs irregular in the preterite*	**Capítulo 7** **Encuentro cultural: El tango argentino**	**Capítulo 7** **Vocabulario: La ropa** **¿Nos entendemos?** (a cuadros, la pollera, la campera, etc.) **Capítulo 7** **Vocabulario: De compras**	**Capítulo 7** **Encuentro cultural: De compras en Buenos Aires** **Capítulo 7** **Estructura II:** *Simplifying expressions: direct object pronouns*	**Capítulo 7** **Estructura III:** *Describing on-going and habitual actions in the past: the imperfect tense*
21	Review Vocabulario **Síntesis: ¡A ver!** and/or **¡A conversar!**	**Síntesis: ¡A leer!** and/or **¡A escribir!**	**EXAM VII**	Oral Evaluation	**Capítulo 8** **Vocabulario: Fiestas y celebraciones** **¿Nos entendemos?** (¡Salud!)
22	**Capítulo 8** **Encuentro cultural: Santo Tomás de Chichicastenango**	**Capítulo 8** **Así se dice:** *Inquire and provide information about people and events: interrogative words*	**Capítulo 8** **Estructura I:** *Narrating in the past: the preterite vs. the imperfect*	**Capítulo 8** *Continue with the preterite vs. the imperfect*	**Capítulo 8** **Vocabulario: La playa y el campo**
23	**Capítulo 8** **Estructura II:** *Stating indefinite ideas and quantities: affirmative and negative expressions*	**Capítulo 8** **Así se dice:** *Talking about periods of time since an event took place:* **hace** *and* **hace que**	**Capítulo 8** **Encuentro cultural: El arzobispo Oscar Arnulfo Romero**	Review Vocabulario **Síntesis: ¡A ver!** and/or **¡A conversar!**	**Síntesis: ¡A leer!** and/or **¡A escribir!**

WEEK	MONDAY	TUESDAY	WEDNESDAY	THURSDAY	FRIDAY
24	EXAM VIII (or review for Midterm Exam)	Oral Evaluation	Capítulo 9 Vocabulario: Viajar en avión ¿Nos entendemos? (flight attendant and passenger)	Capítulo 9 Encuentro cultural: La República Dominicana: Santo Domingo, la primera ciudad de las Américas	Capítulo 9 Estructura I: *Simplifying expressions: indirect object pronouns*
25	Capítulo 9 Encuentro cultural: Cuba: Escuela Latinoamericana de Ciencias Médicas	Capítulo 9 Estructura II: *Simplifying expressions: double object pronouns* Review indirect and double object pronouns	Capítulo 9 Vocabulario: El hotel ¿Nos entendemos? (un cuarto, una habitación)	Capítulo 9 Así se dice: *Giving directions: prepositions of location, adverbs, and relevant expressions*	Capítulo 9 Encuentro cultural: Puerto Rico: Estado Libre Asociado ¿Nos entendemos? (puertorriqueños)
26	Capítulo 9 Estructura III: *Giving directions and expressing desires; formal and negative* **tú** *commands*	Review Vocabulario Síntesis: ¡A ver! and/or ¡A conversar!	Síntesis: ¡A leer! and/or ¡A escribir!	EXAM IX	Oral Evaluation
27	Capítulo 10 Vocabulario: Las relaciones sentimentales ¿Nos entendemos? (amigo(a), novio(a), etc.)	Capítulo 10 Encuentro cultural: Los novios en los países hispanoamericanos	Capítulo 10 Estructura I: *Describing recent actions, events, and conditions: the present perfect tense*	Capítulo 10 Así se dice: *Describing reciprocal actions: reciprocal constructions with* **se, nos,** *and* **os**	Capítulo 10 Vocabulario: La recepción
28	Capítulo 10 Encuentro cultural: Las bodas en el mundo hispano	Capítulo 10 Así se dice: *Qualifying actions: adverbial expressions of time and sequencing of events*	Capítulo 10 Estructura II: *Using the Spanish equivalents of who, whom, that, and which: relative pronouns*	Review Vocabulario Síntesis: ¡A ver! and/or ¡A conversar!	Síntesis: ¡A leer! and/or ¡A escribir!
29	EXAM X	Oral Evaluation	Review Capítulos 6 and 7 for Final Exam	Review Capítulos 8 and 9 for Final Exam	Review Capítulo 10 for Final Exam

WEEK	MONDAY	TUESDAY	WEDNESDAY	THURSDAY	FRIDAY
30	FINAL EXAM	Practice for Oral Evaluation	Oral Evaluation	Oral Evaluation	Individual consultations, if necessary End of Semester
31	Third semester Administrative requirements Hand out syllabus	Review: Capítulos 6 and 7	Review: Capítulos 8 and 9	Review: Capítulo 10	Lab and Workbook assignments for review.
32	Capítulo 11 Vocabulario: Las profesiones y los oficios ¿Nos entendemos? (policía, póliza, política)	Capítulo 11 Encuentro cultural: El Canal de Panamá	Capítulo 11 Estructura I: *Making statements about motives, intentions, and periods of time:* por vs. para	Capítulo 11 Vocabulario: La oficina, el trabajo y la búsqueda de un puesto	Capítulo 11 Estructura II: *Expressing subjectivity and uncertainty: the subjunctive mood*
33	Capítulo 11 Encuentro cultural: Protocolo en los negocios en el mundo hispanohablante	Capítulo 11 Vocabulario: Las finanzas	Capítulo 11 Estructura III: *Expressing desires and intentions: the present subjunctive with statements of volition*	Capítulo 11 Review use of subjunctive presented in Estructuras II y III	Review Vocabulario Síntesis: ¡A ver! and/or ¡A conversar!
34	Síntesis: ¡A leer! and/or ¡A escribir!	EXAM XI	Oral Evaluation	Capítulo 12 Vocabulario: La geografía rural y urbana ¿Nos entendemos? (tico[a])	Capítulo 12 Encuentro cultural: Costa Rica: Puros ingredientes naturales
35	Capítulo 12 Estructura I: *Expressing emotion and opinions: subjunctive following verbs of emotion, impersonal expressions, and ojalá*	Capítulo 12 Vocabulario: La conservación y la explotación	Capítulo 12 Encuentro cultural: Costa Rica: Estación biológica La Selva	Capítulo 12 Estructura II: *Expressing doubts, uncertainty, and hypothesizing: the subjunctive with verbs, expressions of uncertainty, and with adjective clauses*	Capítulo 12 Vocabulario: Los animales y el refugio natural
36	Capítulo 12 Review use of subjunctive presented in Estructuras I y II	Review Vocabulario Síntesis: ¡A ver! and/or ¡A conversar!	Síntesis: ¡A leer! and/or ¡A escribir!	EXAM XII	Oral Evaluation

WEEK	MONDAY	TUESDAY	WEDNESDAY	THURSDAY	FRIDAY
37	**Capítulo 13** Vocabulario: Programas y películas	**Capítulo 13** Encuentro cultural: La cinematografía en Latinoamérica	**Capítulo 13** **Estructura I:** *Talking about anticipated actions: subjunctive with purpose and time clauses*	**Capítulo 13** Continue with conjunctions of purpose and time	**Capítulo 13** Vocabulario: Las artes
38	**Capítulo 13** Encuentro cultural: Oswaldo Guayasamin	**Capítulo 13** **Estructura II:** *Talking about unplanned or accidental occurrences: no-fault* **se** *construction*	**Capítulo 13** Continue with forming the no-fault **se** construction and verbs used in the constructions	**Capítulo 13** **Así se dice:** *Describing completed actions and resulting conditions: use of the past participle as adjective*	Review Vocabulary **Síntesis: ¡A ver!** and/or **¡A conversar!**
39	**Síntesis: ¡A leer!** and/or **¡A escribir!**	**EXAM XIII** (or review for **Midterm Exam**)	Oral Evaluation		**Capítulo 14** Encuentro cultural: El gobierno de Chile
40	**Capítulo 14** **Estructura I:** *Talking about future events: the future tense*	**Capítulo 14** Vocabulario: Las preocupaciones cívicas y los medios de comunicación	**Capítulo 14** Encuentro cultural: La libertad de la prensa	**Capítulo 14** **Estructura II:** *Expressing conjecture or probability: the conditional*	**Capítulo 14** **Estructura III:** *Making references to the present: the present perfect subjunctive*
41	Review Vocabulary **Síntesis: ¡A ver!** and/or **¡A conversar!**	**Síntesis: ¡A leer!** and/or **¡A escribir!**	**EXAM XIV**	Oral Evaluation	**Capítulo 15** Vocabulario: Los avances tecnológicos
42	**Capítulo 15** Encuentro cultural: Las telecomunicaciones en Uruguay	**Capítulo 15** Review indicative vs. subjunctive	**Capítulo 15** **Estructura I:** *Making statements in the past: past (imperfect) subjunctive*	**Capítulo 15** Encuentro cultural: Equipos: En la palma de la mano	**Capítulo 15** **Estructura II:** *Talking about hypothetical situations: if clauses*
43	**Capítulo 15** Practice using the past subjunctive forms Practice using if clauses	Review Vocabulary **Síntesis: ¡A ver!** and/or **¡A conversar!**	**Síntesis: ¡A leer!** and/or **¡A escribir!**	**EXAM XV**	Oral Evaluation
44	Review **Capítulos 11 y 12** for Final Exam	Review **Capítulos 13 y 14** for Final Exam	Review **Capítulo 15** for **Final Exam**	**FINAL EXAM**	Practice for Oral Evaluation
45	Oral Evaluation	Oral Evaluation	Individual consultations, if necessary	Students complete unfinished and/or make-up assignments	Students turn in final reports or projects

P ¡Mucho gusto!

CHAPTER OPENER (page 2)

Introduce the chapter by describing the picture using simple Spanish, redundancies, gestures, and indicating items in the picture so that students are able to follow along. Use cognates whenever possible to enhance comprehension and show students that they already know some Spanish. Emphasize the communication aspects of language study so students understand that language is a useful tool instead of a set of grammar structures and rules that must be memorized.

Explain that they don't have to understand everything they hear, but just listen attentively and pick up what they can. Use the photo as a point of departure. You can begin with: **Son dos personas, un hombre y una mujer. Ellos son estudiantes. Son hispanos. Se saludan (se besan). Están en la plaza. Él tiene...** etc. Don't be afraid to repeat words, phrases, or sentences to help students understand. Develop the theme expressed in the picture. Act out some of the phrases that you use with your students so that they can more fully understand.

VOCABULARIO Saludos y despedidas (pages 4–5)

Begin this section on the very first class meeting by introducing yourself in Spanish: **Buenos días (Buenas tardes), clase. Soy el (la) profesor(a)... (Me llamo... y soy el (la) profesor[a] de español.)** and write your name on the board. Repeat, **Me llamo...** emphasizing your name. Then, turning to a student, ask her/him: **¿Y usted? ¿Cómo se llama?** Don't force your students to respond in complete sentences, simply stating their names will suffice. Remember, we want to use Spanish for true communication, so this is precisely how language functions in the real world! After several other students give their names, ask them to identify others: **Y, ¿cómo se llama él/ella? Y él/ella, ¿cómo se llama?** If they don't know each other, they can then use the question you've been using to find out. The purpose is to show students that they understand although they may not know every element in the sentence, and at the same time they begin learning their classmates' names.

Next, state, **Yo estoy bien (mal).** and use gestures to indicate how you are feeling. Continue by asking, **¿Cómo está usted? ¿Bien? ¿Muy bien? ¿Así, así? ¿Mal?** Use facial expressions and gestures to signal meanings, or draw representative faces on the board and label them if you like. Continue, asking others, **Y usted, ¿cómo está?**

Now mix the questions and encourage students to ask each other and respond when asked. **Buenos días, ¿cómo se llama usted? ¿Cómo está usted? ¡Qué bueno!** This amount of Spanish will suffice for the moment. Now you can present **Una situación formal** on page 4.

Be sure to point out that the adjective **encantada** changes according to the person speaking. This can be done through modeling so that the examples are contextualized and communicative in nature, rather than presented as lexical items or grammar rules. Also point out that questions in Spanish, unlike English, begin with an "upside-down" question mark, which is not optional but required.

After several pairs of students role-play, go on to **Una situación informal** and repeat the same process, pointing out differences between formal and informal situations and when each is used. For example: **¡Hola! ¿Qué tal? (¿Cómo estás?)** versus **Buenos días. ¿Cómo está usted?** and **¿Cómo te llamas?** rather than **¿Cómo se llama usted?** Don't forget comprehension checks so as not to lose anyone early on.

Finally, present the formal and informal questions as groupings or expressions rather than isolated words, as intonation and parsing is different from sentential elements. They tend to be pronounced as if they were one word, rather than a group. The method employed for previous vocabulary works well.

¡OJO! Unlike English, Spanish does not require every sentence to have an overt subject. Neither does it require the use of subject pronouns. This trait, in conjunction with others, classifies Spanish (along with Italian and others) as a *pro-drop* language. The uniformity of the verb paradigms and the verb-final morphology makes it possible to identify the sentential subject. Therefore, although we teach students the personal subject pronouns, it is advisable to discourage their use when referring to readily recognizable subjects such as **yo, tú, nosotros(as), vosotros(as)** as well as the third-person forms when context eliminates any ambiguity. This can be accomplished by calling students' attention to the dialog and contrasting **¿Cómo está** *usted*? with **Soy el profesor Benjamín Rico Torres.** (Ø is the symbol used by linguists to indicate that an element present in the underlying or deep structure is absent from the surface structure.)

¡OJO! It is equally important to point out that subject pronouns are also unnecessary with reflexive verbs such as **me llamo.** Spanish requires redundancy with third-person singular and plural forms in order to clear up any ambiguity, which is not resolved by content. For example: **Quiero presentarte(le) a dos amigos.** *Él* **se llama Miguel y** *ella* **se llama Marta.**

¿NOS ENTENDEMOS? (pages 4–5)

Show the social meanings of **Adiós, Hasta luego, Nos vemos,** and **Chao (Ciao)** when ending an encounter.

¡A PRACTICAR! (page 6)

In addition to activities **P-1** and **P-2,** write a number of questions and answers on the board. With closed books, ask students to write down or tell you how they would respond. Be sure that they pay attention to indications of formality or familiarity when answering. Another activity is to put students in pairs with a set of pages, one containing questions, the other responses. One member of the pair asks a question, and the other must respond appropriately. Above each set of questions/responses, a setting can be specified in order to practice different structures.

EN VOZ ALTA (page 6)

Model the dialogs from activities **P-3** and **P-4** with a student or have a pair of students model them for the rest of the class. Then, ask them to create their own dialog based on the expressions and other vocabulary they have learned. Have them change partners several times so that they can learn about each other, thereby using Spanish for real communication. Be sure to circulate to help students with questions or to supply needed vocabulary. Train students to ask questions in Spanish from the very beginning, by giving the necessary format: **¿Cómo se dice** (word or expression) **en español?** If they need clarification, **¿Qué es (significa)... ?** This is also a good opportunity to teach them the courtesy associated with the Spanish language and culture, and the use of **Por favor, (Muchas) gracias, Perdón, Disculpe**, etc., when requesting information or responding to an inquiry.

ENCUENTRO CULTURAL (page 7)

After reading the excerpt and answering the questions that follow, either in class or as homework, have volunteers ask each other questions in Spanish similar to those just discussed in English.

EN CONTEXTO (page 8)

This section can be introduced by means of the Student Text Audio CD or can be read aloud by members of the class while the others read along. Write down mispronounced words so that they can be practiced once the dialog is completed. Do not interrupt the reading, this will destroy the fluidity of the interaction unnecessarily and may embarrass the student. Instead, use choral repetition so that the entire class has the opportunity to repeat and practice the correct pronunciation of the words or phrases you have noted. Be sure to remind your students that it is not necessary to understand every word they read. They should try to get the gist of the conversation and guess the meanings of the rest. Don't forget your comprehension checks along the way to avoid completely losing anyone or use **¿Comprendiste?** for that purpose. For additional practice, either written or oral, have students correct those statements that are false.

¡OJO! It is imperative that phonetic problems be noted and minimized or corrected as soon as possible to avoid fossilization and to help students' interlanguage (See Selinker 1972) to approximate the target language as much and as quickly as possible.

ENCUENTRO CULTURAL (page 9)

After reading the text, use **Para discutir** or make up your own list of individuals. Put students in pairs or small groups. Have them take turns pretending to be different people so that their classmates can ask them questions or make comments using the appropriate pronoun and verb forms.

¡OJO! The sociolinguistic aspects inherent in the use of **tú** and **usted** may have unforeseen and serious consequences due to ignorance. According to Brown & Gilman, the choice of pronoun is determined by factors of power and solidarity, distance and intimacy. A speaker demonstrates power and distancing by employing **tú** with an interlocutor of lesser power and/or status, thereby creating distance between them. The person being addressed responds with **usted,** corroborating the lack of power and/or status and their lack of solidarity. When both speakers want to express membership in the same "in-group," both employ the same pronoun of address, regardless which one is chosen. **Usted** is also used as a sign of respect, be it for age or education, and is used with older individuals, religious persons, and professionals. As a show of intimacy, most Hispanics employ **tú** when addressing their deity. Small children are often addressed as **usted** in order to teach them the appropriate way to address adults and persons they don't know. Once the rules of protocol are established, the parents and other adults will begin using **tú** to indicate their lesser status and age.

ESTRUCTURA I Talking about yourself and others: subject pronouns and the present tense of the verb *ser* (page 10)

To present the subject pronouns and present tense forms of the verb **ser** together, draw pictures / stick figures of persons on the board and label them with your name and the names of members of the class. Placement is also important, so make sure you place the figures alone (for the singular forms) and in groups (for the plural forms). If you are artistically challenged, you can purchase paper doll figures or cut out figures from magazines or newspapers and attach them to the chalkboard. Or, you can use members of the class to demonstrate. Begin by pointing to yourself and saying, **Yo soy** (your name). **Soy profesor(a) de español.** Address a member of the class, **Tú eres** (student's name). **Eres estudiante de español.** You can intersperse the questions **¿Quién/Qué soy yo? ¿Quién/Qué eres tú?** and ask the student(s) to respond. Then go on to use the **usted** form, followed by **él/ella.** Then place students in pairs or groups and place yourself in one group so that you can demonstrate **nosotros(as), vosotros(as), ustedes, ellos/ellas.**

Note that when the pronouns and verb forms are placed in the traditional order, students are often confused. The **usted** form can be placed beneath the **tú** form to show that both are second person pronouns, one formal, one informal (concepts to which they have already been introduced), and the same with the plurals. Thus, you can use an overhead to change the placement:

1p	yo soy	nosotros(as) somos
2pi*	tú eres	ustedes son (vosotros(as) sois)
2pf**	usted es	ustedes son
3p	él/ella es	ellos/ellas son

*2pi = segunda persona informal
**2pf = segunda persona formal

Remind your students that they have already seen many of the verb forms and pronouns in the dialogs they have heard and read. **¡OJO!** Unlike English, Spanish subject pronouns have specific functions and narrow applications so that they do not appear in every sentence. In addition, they can refer only to people, and cannot have animals, objects, or concepts as their antecedents.

Therefore, when a noun referring to one of the latter categories is to be replaced by a pronoun, the slot reserved for the pronoun must be left unoccupied (blank) at the surface because, among other reasons, Spanish lacks the pronoun "it," which English uses for this purpose. Thus, **¿Qué es un perro?** can only elicit the response **(Ø) Es un animal.**, leaving the subject position empty, while **¿Qué es Juan José?** can be answered by **Él es profesor de español.** or **(Ø) Es profesor de español.** The fact that the subject of the second set of sentences is a [+ human] subject allows for the option of placing the pronoun **él** in the slot reserved for the subject.

¡A PRACTICAR! (page 11)

Do **P-5** orally in class and have students do **P-6** at home and then go over it orally in class. Call on individual students to read the sentence aloud, providing the appropriate verb form. Once you have made sure that everyone understands, place students in pairs. One asks who someone is or who a group of people are and what she/he does or they do, while the partner answers the question(s) posed and asks the next one. This can be done orally or in written form.

¿Quién soy yo? As an alternative to **P-6,** you can use pictures of well-known people or describe them so that the students can identify them. This can be done as a class or you can divide the class into teams and make it a contest.

EN VOZ ALTA (page 11)

¿Cómo es... ? In addition to the suggestions in the *IAE,* you can give students a list of adjectives (cognates) to use in describing individuals they know or are familiar with (**mi mamá, mi papá, mi novio(a),** etc.; **Raúl Juliá, Juan Leguizamo, Gloria Estéfan, Jon Secada, Ricky Martin, Antonio Banderas,** etc.**).**

ASÍ SE DICE Identifying quantities: *hay* and numbers 0–30 (page 12)

Assign the numbers as homework and review them by using items to represent the different numbers from 0 to 10, making sure that students understand **un(a)** can mean both *one* and *an* and agree in gender and number with the noun that they precede (*un* **profesor,** *una* **profesora),** and that the masculine **uno** is used when counting. Continue with the numbers 11 to 20, pointing out the two options for writing 16 to 19. Then move on to 21 to 30, making sure to again present the options for the numbers. Also mention that with the exception of one and any number ending with one (1, 21, 31, etc.), numbers do not agree with the noun: *una* **profesora** but *diez* **profesoras,** *veintitrés* **profesoras,** and so on.

Use index cards on which you have written the numbers and display them for choral repetition by the students. Begin in numerical order until they show you they know them, then mix them up or have them count by two's, three's, five's from 0 to 30. You can continue this activity by calling on individuals. You may prefer to bring in the page of a large calendar to practice the numbers. If you can hang it up on the board, do so, since it leaves you free to move around and point to the individual numbers first in order and then out of sequence.

Now write **1 + 4 = 5,** saying it out loud as you point to the elements: **uno y (más) cuatro son cinco** or **6 – 2 = 4.** Continue the activity, either writing additional problems on the board, showing flashcards with problems written on them, or simply stating them orally while the students say or write the solutions. Keep them simple at first and increase the difficulty as students become more confident.

¡OJO! Impersonal **haber** has only one form per tense—third-person singular—and is known as an expletive or "place holder." While it may be followed by numerals and indefinite articles, **hay** cannot be followed by definite articles. It also differs from the locative *there* (as opposed to *here*) in sentences such as *There is my father* (*Allí* está mi padre).

¡A PRACTICAR! (page 13)

Using **P-8** as a point of departure, ask: **¿Cuántos estudiantes hay en la clase? ¿Cuántas profesoras hay en la clase? ¿Hay tres profesoras en la clase? ¿Cuántos chicos hay en la clase? ¿Hay XX chicas en la clase?** Place students in groups or pairs to review their answers to activities **P-9** and **P-10,** which they did for homework.

EN VOZ ALTA (page 13)

In addition to activity **P-11** you can bring a poster or large picture of a scene containing numerous items. If you don't have one, use an overhead transparency. Ask students questions regarding the number of each of the various items in the scene. To continue the exercise, put students into groups and hand each group a different picture for them to describe, using **hay,** the different forms of the verb **ser,** and numbers.

VOCABULARIO Palabras interrogativas (page 14)

Assign this vocabulary for homework. Begin by reviewing words they have already used; they are your jumping-off point to introduce the new ones. Remind your students that Spanish questions begin with "upside-down" question marks as well as end with closing question marks (¿?). Stress the need for accent marks and make sure students understand that they can only appear above vowels and that they have a function, which changes the meaning of the word by its presence or absence. If they are made aware of the importance of certain details from the outset, many errors and much confusion can be avoided or minimized.

Use visuals to form questions using the different interrogative words. These can be done as a handout so that each student has a copy, or by using a transparency or poster. Point to a particular illustration and ask questions, changing the interrogative word. For example, a picture with three individuals in a group and another facing them. Two of the individuals in the group have names above their heads while the remaining one has ¿? instead of a name. One individual (who has a name) is pointing to this unidentified individual, and asks **¿Quién es/eres?** [you choose!] and you can also include other interrogatives such as **¿Dónde? ¿Cuántos? ¿Quién(es)?** The question **¿Cuál?** can be illustrated by showing an individual being given a choice of items or being asked to identify which item belongs to her/him: **¿Cuál es tu perro? ¿Cuáles son los actores buenos/malos?**

For additional practice, provide students with a worksheet on which there is a dialog with blanks, which the student must complete in a logical manner while maintaining the flow of the conversation. For example:

Carlos and Isabel attend the same university. It is the beginning of their first semester and they bump into each other outside the Modern Languages Building. Isabel has dropped her books and Carlos helps her. The following conversation takes place.

CARLOS: Hola. Buenos días. Soy Carlos Morales. ¿Cómo te llamas?

ISABEL: _____

CARLOS: Mucho gusto.

ISABEL: _____

CARLOS: Muy bien, gracias. ¿Y tú?

ISABEL: _____

CARLOS: Soy de Lima, Perú. ¿Y tu familia?

ISABEL: _____

CARLOS: Hay cinco personas en mi familia. Es pequeña *(small)*.

ISABEL: Mi familia es grande.

CARLOS: _____

ISABEL: Estudio español, inglés, psicología y ciencias políticas.

CARLOS: _____

ISABEL: Hay 25 estudiantes en la clase de inglés y 18 en la clase de psicología.

CARLOS: Yo también *(also)* estudio inglés. ¿Quién es tu profesor?

ISABEL: _____

CARLOS: ¿Ah sí? Él es mi profesor también.

ISABEL: Mi número de teléfono es 486-0203. Es tarde. *(It's late.)* Adiós.

CARLOS: _____

EN VOZ ALTA (page 15)

In addition to activities **P-13** and **P-14** you can pair students and ask one to be the reporter and the other to be a famous personality. Have them pick the personality out of a hat where you have placed names. Have the two prepare a written list of questions they will use for the interview. Then, the reporter will ask the questions, which the interviewee will answer. A second personality can be chosen and the roles reversed. After 10 minutes or so, choose a pair and have them perform the "live" interview for the audience, who will be asked to identify the celebrity. Another possibility for this type of activity is for you to assume the persona of someone with whom all of the students are familiar, and you have a press interview. Each student takes notes and then goes home to write up her/his report. You can collect these the following day and grade them. This will allow students to see that they have learned quite a bit in a short period of time and are capable of integrating the four skills as they have had to speak, listen, write, and read (if they are going to turn in a good piece of work). This section is also a good opportunity for a round of Jeopardy, the quiz show that provides the answers and has the contestants provide the questions. You read the answers to the students and the first one to raise her/his hand gets to provide the question. You can add the proviso that once a student has answered a question, she/he must wait two or three turns before trying again. This allows everyone to participate but does not put any-one on the spot. You can include vocabulary that has been presented and cognates to round out the possibilities.

You	The Student(s)
Me llamo Sara Aguirre.	¿Cómo te llamas?¿Cómo se llama?
Estoy muy bien, gracias.	¿Cómo está(s)?
Mi dirección es 3899 de la Avenida de la Reforma.	¿Cuál es tu dirección?
Mi clase favorita es español.	¿Cuál es tu clase favorita?
El profesor se llama Francisco Pérez.	¿Cómo se llama el profesor?
Él es de Guatemala.	¿De dónde es él?
El profesor es muy inteligente.	¿Cómo es el profesor?
Este (This) semestre tengo cinco clases.	¿Cuántas clases tiene(s) este semestre?
Mi profesora de inglés es la Sra. Smith.	¿Quién es tu profesora de inglés?
La clase es por la tarde.	¿Cuándo es la clase?
Hay quince chicos en la clase.	¿Cuántos chicos hay en la clase?
Estudio español porque es interesante.	¿Por qué estudia(s) español?

ESTRUCTURA II Telling age: the present tense of the verb *tener* (page 16)

Assign students to look over the verb forms for homework. Build the verb paradigm with your students by asking volunteers to provide the verb forms while you write them on the board and have the students repeat the forms in chorus. Now provide a variety of subjects and have students produce the appropriate verb form, first orally and then in writing. Then reverse the process (a good review of subject pronouns).

Now practice some uses of the verb. Begin by stating your age and asking one of your students hers/his: **Tengo 50 años. Y tú** (student's name), **¿cuántos años tienes? ¿Cuántos años tiene tu mamá/papá/mejor amigo(a),** etc. ? Show a number of pictures of individuals of various ages. Ask students, **¿Cuántos años tiene... ?** and select someone to answer.

¡OJO! In many countries, **¿Qué edad tiene(s)?** is as common as **¿Cuántos años tienes?** for inquiring about someone's age. In some places, the former is considered much more polite and in better taste as well as more educated. You might wish to point this out when discussing social differ-ences between the U.S. and Spanish-speaking countries.

Move on to practice the possessive function of the verb. Use pictures and ask individuals **¿Cuán-tos libros tiene el chico?** or **¿Qué tiene la chica en la mano?** (Even though they don't yet know the word for hand, you can gesture.)

ENCUENTRO CULTURAL (pages 17–19)

Since these sections are in English they can be read at home in preparation for class discussion. Simplify the information so that you can use Spanish as much as possible. Some suggested ques-tions are given on the next page to get you started. You can do this exercise aloud or in writing.

Preguntas en español:

1. ¿Cómo se dice *car* en español?
2. En Cuba, ¿cómo se dice **autobús**? ¿Y en México?
3. ¿En qué países de Latinoamérica no es el español la lengua principal?
4. ¿Cómo se llaman unas *(some)* naciones de Sudamérica?
5. ¿Cuántas personas hay en Chile?
6. ¿Cuál es la capital de la Argentina? ¿Y de Perú? ¿Bolivia? ¿Ecuador?
7. ¿Cuántos hispanos hay en los Estados Unidos?
8. ¿Dónde hay muchos hispanos en los Estados Unidos?
9. ¿Qué significa EE.UU.?
10. ¿Cuál es la capital de México?
11. ¿Qué hay en la península de Yucatán?
12. ¿Dónde están las islas de Cuba, Puerto Rico y la República Dominicana?
13. ¿Cuál es la capital de Cuba?
14. ¿Cuál es la capital de Portugal?

EL ALFABETO EN ESPAÑOL (page 20)

Point out to students that several letters in Spanish have more than one sound and that the pronunciation of some letters differs from the way they are pronounced in English.

- **Las vocales** All vowels in Spanish are pronounced the same way, regardless of their location in the word. Have them repeat the five vowel sounds according to tongue placement: **a** (central, low), **e** (posterior, mid), **i** (anterior, high), **o** (posterior, mid), and **u** (posterior, high).

The long vowel sounds of English correspond to diphthongs in Spanish. A diphthong is a combination of two vowel sounds, which have a combined length of a single vowel and are part of the same syllable. For example:

English *a* of *cape* or *save*	[ei] or [ey]	**reina; buey**
English *i* of *I*, *sigh*, or *lie*	[ai] or [ay]	**traigo; hay**
English *o* of *rope* or *soap*	[ou]	**estadounidense**
English *u* of *use* or *clue*	[iu]	**ciudad**

- **Las consonantes** The consonants that differ in pronunciation from English are:
  b, p word initial, they are aspirated in English; that is, there is a puff of air that escapes when the word begins with either of these plosives. In Spanish they are not aspirated in any position.
  d in intervocalic position is pronounced much the same way as the *th* of *this*. It is almost silent when it is in word final position, so that words like **ciudad** are pronounced **ciudá.**
  h this letter is silent; it is never pronounced.
  j pronounced like the *h* of *house*
  ll pronounced like the *y* of *you* or *yankee*
  ñ pronounced like the *ni / ny* of *onion* or *canyon*
  q pronounced like *k* rather than *kw*
  v pronounced like *b*; Spanish shows no difference between **b** and **v**
  z pronounced like English *s*; Spanish has no equivalent to the sound of English *z*

  Multiple pronunciations:
  c → **s** when followed by **e** or **i**; → **k** when followed by **a, o,** or **u**
  g → **h** when followed by **e** or **i**; → **g** when followed by **a, o,** or **u**
  r → **rr** when in word-initial position; otherwise it is a flap such as the *tt* in *butter* or the *dd* in *ladder*
  x → **s** in words such as **Xochimilco** pronounced **[sochimilko]**; → **h** in words such as **Xavier** also spelled **Javier;** and → **ks** in words such as **extra** or **experto**
  y → **y** when it is considered a consonant and is in the syllable onset in words such as **yo** or **rayo;** → **i** when part of a word-final diphthong in words such as **soy, mamey**

Give the names of each Spanish letter. Have students repeat the names of each letter. Ask students their names and then ask them how they are spelled. For example: **¿Cómo te llamas?** Student responds by giving her/his first name: **Elizabeth.** You then ask, **¿Cómo se escribe?** *(How is it written?)* or **¿Cómo se deletrea?** *(How is it spelled?)* The student then spells her/his name using the names of the letters.

Acronyms are an excellent way to practice the letters of the alphabet and learn about culture and language at the same time. Below is a list of acronyms used in the Spanish-speaking world and their Spanish acronyms and names. You can reproduce them for students, write them on the board, or make an overhead transparency of them.

Las siglas

AIDS	SIDA	Síndrome de Inmunodeficiencia Adquirida
Associated Free State	ELA	Estado Libre Asociado (Puerto Rico)
European Common Market	MCE	Mercado Común Europeo
Incorporated Business/Enterprise	SA	Sociedad Anónima
Mexico City, Federal District	DF	Distrito Federal (Capital de México)
Organization of American States	OEA	Organización de Estados Americanos
	ONA	Organización de Naciones Americanas
Post Script (PS)	PD	Posdata
Revolutionary Armed Forces	FAR	Fuerzas Armadas Revolucionarias (Guatemala)
United Nations	ONU	Organización de Naciones Unidas
United States	EE.UU.	Estados Unidos
World War II	SGM	Segunda Guerra Mundial

You can eliminate some and add others according to your needs. You can use these in various ways, by either providing the acronym and asking for its meaning or what type of activity it is associated with or vice versa. Ask students to add others by looking for them in books, on the Web, in Spanish newspapers, in Spanish magazines, or other resources.

En una clase de español: Los Estados Unidos

VOCABULARIO En la clase (page 24)

Begin by pointing to items in the classroom, identifying them orally in Spanish and having the students repeat them aloud. This can be followed by a Pictionary activity in which students guess what the instructor is drawing on the chalkboard. Include **Otras cosas** and **Otras personas** in the activity as well.

Then ask students to orally answer **¿De qué color es?** This can be combined with the classroom vocabulary once placement and agreement of adjectives have been reviewed by asking students questions such as **¿Tienes un cuaderno rojo?** and modeling the answer expected, for example, **Tengo un cuaderno azul.** or **No tengo un cuaderno rojo. Tengo un cuaderno azul.**

¡A PRACTICAR! (page 25)

Begin the section by doing activities **1-1** and **1-3**. Continue by asking students to identify objects you hold up or point to either in a picture or in class. They are to write down the name of the item, preferably using an article or a short sentence such as **Es un libro.** Some items you can include are: **escritorio, profesora, estudiante, mochila, pluma, lápiz, borrador, tiza, pizarra, cuaderno, papel.** Follow this by writing out the sentences on the board or on an overhead transparency and have the students write out, either individually or in pairs, whether the statements are **cierto o falso** and correct those that are **falso.** Some examples you can use include: **Hay 20 estudiantes en la clase. No hay profesores en la clase.** (student's name) **tiene tres libros en la mochila.** (student's name) **tiene un bolígrafo en la mano. Hay una pizarra en la clase. Hay muchos papeles en el escritorio.** etc.

After completing activity **1-2**, put the following list (or a similar one) on the board and ask students, **¿De qué color es generalmente? (1) el dinero (2) un lápiz (3) la pluma de la profesora (4) la pizarra (5) la tiza (6) el uniforme del policía (7) una bola de fútbol.**

EN VOZ ALTA (page 26)

After completing activity **1-4,** place students in small groups and give each group a picture or drawing of a typical classroom scene. Ask students to write a list of what items and how many of each item are found in the scene. The lists can then be collected or you can have groups exchange them and go over them. Another version of this activity is **¿Qué falta? (¿Qué no hay?)** in which students identify the items missing from typical classroom scenes. When the item(s) are identified, students can answer, **¿Es (Son) importante(s)/necesario(s)?**

As an expansion to activity **1-5,** have students ask each other to describe an item by describing its color(s) until her/his partner is able to identify it. Add colors and supplementary vocabulary such as **de cuadros, de rayas,** if necessary. For example: **Es amarillo, verde y anaranjado. (Tu cuaderno.) Son blancos. (Los papeles en la mesa.) Es negra y rosada. (La mochila de Fernando.),** and so on.

EN CONTEXTO (page 27)

After completing ¿**Comprendiste?**, follow up by asking students to write, in English, three statements about the students in the dialog that have not been mentioned. Then ask them to write three questions in Spanish (good review of interrogative words) about the dialog to ask a classmate. Finally, as a class activity, have each individual choose a classmate to answer the most interesting of the three questions written, or as a paired activity, have each ask the partner chosen to answer all three of the questions and then reverse the process. This way everyone has the opportunity to both ask and answer questions. If there are any errors committed, ask them to correct each other by consulting the passage.

ENCUENTRO CULTURAL (page 28)

Review the new vocabulary by relating them to words they already have seen; i.e, **desde = de; algunos = unos;** also point out the cognates: **mayoría, emigrar.** Add the following questions to **Para discutir.**

5. When did many Cubans arrive in Miami?
6. Where do most Mexicans reside in the U.S.?

The above questions, together with those from **Para discutir** can be asked in Spanish, requiring only a single word or short phrasal answer. For example:

1. ¿Qué grupos hispanohablantes viven en los Estados Unidos?
2. ¿Qué fiestas hispanas se celebran en los Estados Unidos?
3. ¿Dónde se reúne la mayoría de los hispanohablantes para hablar?
4. ¿Dónde se reúnen tú y tus amigos para hablar? ¿Por qué?
5. ¿Cuándo llegó el grupo cubano?
6. ¿Dónde vive la mayoría de los mexicanoamericanos?

¡OJO! Point out that in Spanish, the nationality of people is not capitalized as in English; **cubanos** *(Cubans),* **mexicanos** *(Mexicans),* **puertorriqueños** *(Puerto Ricans).* Be sure to also mention that Mexican-Americans are referred to as both **mexicanoamericanos** and **méxico-americanos,** and as **chicanos,** in some areas of the Southwest U.S.

Ask students to identify the nationality of a number of well-known celebrities of Latin American origin: **Rigoberta Menchú** (Nobel Peace Prize winner from Guatemala, now living in exile in Mexico); **Gloria Estéfan** (Cuban-American singer); **Ricky Martin** (Puerto Rican singer/actor); **Frida Kahlo** (Mexican painter who lived in Chicago for many years); **Sergio García** (Spanish golfer); **Tito Puente** (Puerto Rican salsa musician); **Emilio Estévez** (Mexican-American actor); to name a few. Add or substitute names of your favorites.

ESTRUCTURA I Talking about people, things, and concepts: definite and indefinite articles and how to make nouns plural (page 29)

Assign the section to be read for homework. Then build an explanation by drawing data from your students. For example, write the word **amigo** on the board. Ask students to supply the two articles that modify (are used with) the noun. If they have read the material or studied some Spanish before, they will respond **el/un.** Follow with **amiga** in order to elicit the feminine forms, **la/una.** Then produce their plurals, **amigos/amigas,** and ask for the appropriate plural articles **(los/unos, las/unas).**

Deduce the rule for regular nouns: Nouns ending in **-o** are masculine, add **-s** to pluralize; nouns ending in **-a** are feminine, add **-s** to make plural; nouns ending in **-e** can be either masculine or feminine (**la clase, el hombre**), add **-s** to make plural. Now proceed to nouns ending in consonants, and follow the same procedure: pluralizing nouns ending in consonants:

1. Nouns ending in **-r** or **-l** are masculine, add **-es** to pluralize: **el profesor, los profesores; un papel, unos papeles.**
2. Nouns ending in **-ión** or **-d** are feminine, also add **-es** to pluralize: **una lección, unas lecciones; la universidad, las universidades.**

Some nouns, however, don't follow the gender rules (**el día, la mano, el mapa, la flor**) and must be memorized. Remembering is made easier by learning them with an article.

Point to items found in your classroom and ask students to supply the appropriate definite (indefinite) article: (1) **escritorio** (2) **pizarra** (3) **mochila** (4) **lápiz** (5) **estudiante** (6) **profesor** (7) **tiza** (8) **cuaderno** (9) **mujer** (10) **pluma** (11) **papel** (12) **borrador** (13) **mapa** (14) **libro** (15) **bolígrafo** (16) **diccionario** (17) **clase** (18) **examen.** Follow up by asking students to provide the plural forms and appropriate definite/indefinite articles for the items in the list.

Then review these additional rules of pluralization:

1. Singular nouns whose final syllable carries a written accent mark form their plurals by dropping the accent mark before adding **-es: la lección, las lecciones; el francés, los franceses; el refrán, los refranes** (refrain[s]); **el pizarrón, los pizarrones.**
2. Singular nouns ending in **-z** change the **-z** to **-c** before adding **-es: el lápiz, los lápices; el pez, los peces; la vez, las veces.**

Point out to students that compound words tend to pluralize the noun following the preposition: **el (los) compañero(s) de clase.**

Have students write down the nouns and their definite article as you say aloud:

reloj	ventana	borradores
mesas	mano	mapas
bolígrafo	mujer	hombres
clases	mochila	libro

¡A PRACTICAR! (page 30)

Begin by using the activities in the book and continue by pointing to the items as you say: **¿Qué hay en** _____ **(la pared, el escritorio de** [name of student]**, la mochila de** [name of student]**)?** Then show a photograph or an overhead to the class and ask them to write the answer to **¿Qué hay en la foto?**

VOCABULARIO Lenguas extranjeras, otras materias y lugares universitarios (pages 31–32)

Begin by pointing at a map of the world or an enlargement (or overhead) of the map in the book. Say each country's name out loud as you point to it and have students repeat them in chorus: **el alemán → Alemania; el inglés → Inglaterra; el estadounidense → los Estados Unidos,** etc.

Continue with questions related to the map. **¿Dónde hablan alemán? ¿inglés?**, etc. followed by **¿Qué hablan en China? ¿Japón? ¿Francia? ¿Ecuador? ¿Puerto Rico?** This last place can be used as a point of departure for a quick discussion of bilingualism, or cultural mixing. Perhaps a student or students have traveled to Puerto Rico, or speak another language or languages. This is a good opportunity to break down stereotypes. Even if the discussion turns to English since their vocabulary is limited, it is a worthwhile endeavor!

¡OJO! Be sure to stress that one of the orthographic differences between English and Spanish is that the names of countries are capitalized while the names of languages are not. It is also important that the students be shown that the adjectives of nationality share their masculine form with the language but have feminine (in most cases) and plural forms as well. For example: En *Hungría* hablan *húngaro*. **Gertrudis es *húngara* y sus padres son *húngaros*. Su amigo Pierre no es *húngaro*, es *francés* y habla *francés*.**

Ask students to tell what courses they are taking this semester. Have them locate the names in **Cursos y especializaciones, Más cursos y especializaciones,** or under **Palabras útiles.** If one is not included, have them ask you in Spanish how to say it. It is important to personalize this activity so that they can discuss what they study, what they want to study, what they want to specialize in, etc. This will lead to greater oral and written production, not to mention class participation!

Finally, ask students what they do at the different locations or where certain activities take place. For example: **Andrés, ¿dónde estudias para tu examen? (Estudio en la biblioteca; En la biblioteca.) ¿Qué hacen los estudiantes en el centro estudiantil? (Comen, Descansan, Comemos, Hablamos,** etc.). Remember, you are practicing vocabulary, one word or a phrase is acceptable. In a conversation, people don't always answer in complete sentences.

¿NOS ENTENDEMOS? (page 32)

Additional common abbreviated words include: **la uni** for **la universidad, (la) seño** for **(la) señora, el bus** for **el autobús, la tele** for **la televisión.** Many of these expressions or words started out as adolescent or street slang as a sign of in-group solidarity.

¡A PRACTICAR! (page 33)

Do activity **1-12** in class and assign **1-13** for homework. As a follow-up to **1-13**, have students identify the language the following celebrities and other famous people speak/spoke. Perhaps they can even identify the country to which they belong(ed). This can be done orally or in writing.

Shakespeare	la princesa Diana	Miguel Ángel
John F. Kennedy	el rey Juan Carlos	Hercule Poirot
Francisco Franco	Fidel Castro	Mozart
Evita Perón	Mao Tse Tung	el emperador Hirohito

EN VOZ ALTA (page 33)

After completing the activities you want to do in the book, continue by pairing students and asking them to pretend one is a reporter for the school newspaper while the other has been chosen **Estudiante del día** and is being interviewed. It is the reporter's job to find out as much interesting information about this "celebrity" as possible so that she/he can report it. They can then exchange roles. Some suggestions are: **¿Cómo te llamas? ¿Cuántos años tienes? ¿De dónde eres? ¿Qué clases tienes? ¿Quién es tu profesor(a) de... ? ¿Qué libro usas en la clase de... ? ¿Cómo se llama el libro de... ? ¿Cuántas personas hay en tu clase de... ?**

For homework, have students write up the article for the newspaper. These articles can then be read aloud in class or used for peer editing activities during the next class meeting. This activity recycles material from previous lessons and adds to their target language production while integrating various skills (listening comprehension, speaking, writing, and then reading).

ENCUENTRO CULTURAL (page 34)

After **Para pensar**, ask volunteers to read aloud. This serves two functions, pronunciation and auditory comprehension practice. Mark the pronunciation errors each student makes but do not interrupt her/him until the paragraph is finished. Then say the words yourself and ask the entire class to repeat the word. This will avoid embarrassing the student and everyone will have an opportunity to work on the correct way sounds are said.

Afterwards, add this third question to **Para discutir:** What other differences did you notice about the school systems of Spanish-speaking countries and those of the U.S. or the lifestyles of American versus Spanish-speaking students? This question can also be asked in Spanish, although in simpler terms: **¿Qué diferencias hay entre el sistema de las escuelas en los Estados Unidos y en España/América Latina? ¿Qué diferencias hay entre los estudiantes en Estados Unidos y España y Latinoamérica?**

¡OJO! Use various ways of referring to the same things in your classroom so students can become accustomed to the variations that exist in Spanish across the world. They need to be aware that there are dialects of Spanish and that one is not better or worse than another. There are seven dialects of Spanish in Spain alone! The most similar to the Spanish of the Americas is that spoken in Andalucía (southern Spain). The main differences between dialects tend to be phonetic and lexical, with most of the latter related to food, plants, animals, kinship terms, place names (toponyms), and words borrowed from or blended with terms from the many indigenous languages with which Spanish came in contact.

ESTRUCTURA II Describing everyday activities: present tense of regular *-ar* verbs (page 35)

Assign this section for homework to study the verb endings and the meanings of the verbs on the list. Present the material by stating something like this: **Son las 3:00 de la tarde** (point to your watch or draw one on the board). **Estoy en la clase y siempre** *hablo* **español. No** *hablamos* **inglés en la clase de español. La clase** *termina* **a las 4:00. Luego** *regreso* **a casa y** *descanso* **por una hora.** Continue by asking students questions regarding what you have just told them and writing the verb forms on the board as they say them. For example: **¿Qué hablo en la clase?** Write down **(yo) hablo.** Your students should provide **Usted habla español.** Write down **(usted) habla.** This way the verb forms are presented in context and the verb paradigm is built cooperatively. The same procedure can be used to show the different uses of the present tense: **Generalmente** *hablamos* **español en clase. En este momento** *tú y yo hablamos* **de los verbos en español. Mañana** *ustedes hablan* **de sus clases en español.** By using these or similar examples you can show the various functions of the present tense in Spanish.

¡A PRACTICAR! (page 36)

Activities **1-16, 1-17,** and **1-18** can be done orally by having students take turns reading the sentences and filling in the blanks with the appropriate verb form. Follow those activities by displaying pictures that show a variety of activities and either calling out the subject to be used with each one or by writing the subject on the picture or the board. Students can then either write a sentence or simply supply the verb form. Rather than displaying the picture, you can make a worksheet to be distributed to the students to be done in class or as homework.

EN VOZ ALTA (page 37)

Using **1-20** and **1-21** as points of departure, place some students in pairs and others in groups of three or four (to practice the **tú, él/ella,** and **Uds.** and **ellas/ellos** forms, respectively) to find out about what their classmates do and don't do outside class. For this reason ask them to choose people with whom they are not well acquainted in order to make this a real communicative activity. Once they have gathered sufficient information (give them an appropriate time limit), ask for volunteers to report to the class. Those in pairs will use **tú** for data-gathering and **él/ella** or the student's name for reporting, while those in groups will use the plural in addition to the singular forms. This must be explained to them at the start of the activity in order to ensure that the appropriate forms are used.

ASÍ SE DICE Expressing personal likes and dislikes:
me gusta + infinitive (page 38)

Add **te** and **le** as options in the structure **me gusta** + infinitive so as to enable students to discuss the likes and dislikes of others and to be able to ask others what they (dis)like. These are easy to integrate simply by stating a sentence beginning with **Me** and then changing the person involved. **Me gusta escuchar música clásica. Juan, ¿te gusta escuchar música clásica? (No me gusta. Me gusta escuchar la música latina.) Y señor Ortega, ¿le gusta escuchar música clásica? (Sí, me gusta.)** Practice the model by showing drawings depicting actions and asking questions. **¿Te gusta o no?** These or others can be used in the **¡A practicar!** section.

ASÍ SE DICE Telling time and talking about the days of the week:
la hora y los días de la semana (page 39)

Assign this section for homework so that it can be practiced during the next class meeting. Review time expressions by drawing clock faces on the board and asking **¿Qué hora es?** Add the phrase **en punto** when showing the exact hour: **Son las nueve en punto.**

¡OJO! With the advent and popularity of digital timepieces, it is now accepted practice to also use **y** beyond the thirty minutes. As an alternative, *It's 7:45.* can now be expressed both as **Son las ocho menos cuarto** and **Son las siete (y) cuarenta y cinco.** This applies to any number between 31 and 59 minutes past the hour.

¡A PRACTICAR! (page 40)

In addition to the activities in the book, draw a series of clock faces on the board. Write **a.m.** and **p.m.** so that you can indicate whether the time indicated is in the morning, afternoon, or evening. Then ask **¿Qué hora es?** This can be done as a written exercise by making a worksheet with clock faces and either a sun or a moon to indicate the time of day. Along with the clock faces, you can include an infinitive on the worksheet and ask at what time the indicated activity takes place. Thus a clock face indicating 7:30 p.m. and the verb **hablar por teléfono** asks for **¿A qué hora hablas por teléfono?** requesting the answer **Hablo por teléfono a las siete y media de la tarde/noche.** The exercises in the book can be assigned for homework and later collected or they can be done in class.

EN VOZ ALTA (page 40)

Provide students with questions for them to practice with a partner. They can take turns asking and answering. Some suggestions:

> STUDENT 1: **Yo estudio español a las cuatro de la tarde, y tú, ¿a qué hora estudias?**

> STUDENT 2: **Estudio español a las diez de la mañana. (A las diez de la mañana.)**

Other options: **regresar a la residencia, hablar con mi novio(a), mirar la tele, escuchar la radio, escuchar música, terminar de estudiar, llegar a la clase, tomar café, cenar.**

Contextualize activities **1-26** and **1-27** by telling students: You are conducting a survey regarding the hours at which university students perform numerous activities. Ask several classmates the following questions in order to gather the needed information. **¿Cuándo tienes clase de... ? ¿Cuándo llegas a la universidad por la mañana? ¿A qué hora terminan tus clases? ¿A qué hora regresas a casa?** Then report to the class what activities they do and do not have in common and how the schedules differ.

ENCUENTRO CULTURAL (page 41)

Assign the reading for homework. In order to review the material, ask questions such as: **¿Qué tipo de eventos siempre empieza a tiempo? ¿Qué cosas empiezan tarde? ¿Qué frase usa la gente para llegar a tiempo a una reunión social?** Then, personalize the material in **Para discutir** by asking the following questions or similar ones. **¿Te gusta tener fiestas? Generalmente, ¿llegan los invitados a tiempo o tarde a las fiestas? ¿A qué eventos llegas temprano?** Finally, after working with the schedule provided, ask students to think about their own schedules during the week and on weekends. After sketching out the times and activities, have them write a composition detailing those activities for homework.

SÍNTESIS

As an alternative to the **¡A escribir!** activity, you may close the chapter with an activity that employs all the language skills that your students have been developing. The following series of activities calls all the information from the chapter into play. It involves various stages, some of which are done in class and some outside.

1. Ask students to interview a classmate to find out about her/his likes, dislikes, weekend schedules, and activities.
2. Students will then write a short essay about the individual interviewed based on the information she/he provided.
3. Next, students will again get together with the classmate so that she/he can verify the accuracy of the information included in the essay and for peer editing.
4. A final draft of the essay will then be turned in to you to be graded.

This final activity will give students opportunities to practice what they have learned and give them a sense of accomplishment and progress.

En una reunión familiar: México

VOCABULARIO La familia (page 50)

Assign the vocabulary of the chapter for homework so that the time in class can be used for practicing the material rather than presenting it! Using the picture of Juan Carlos García Martínez's family, begin by introducing him (Juan Carlos) to the class, saying **Aquí está Juan Carlos García Martínez. Es un joven de veinte años. Ésta es su familia. La señora es la madre de la familia; el hombre es el padre de la familia**, and so on.

Begin the in-class presentation by drawing and then describing the members of your family and their relationship to you and to each other while the students follow along. Using your family tree and transparencies E-1 and E-2, ask the students to describe the similarities and differences between them and their own family trees (which they prepared at home). Then, by pointing to individual members of either family, ask for identification saying **¿Quién es esta persona?** or **¿Es él/ella un/a pariente/a** (relative) **de Juan Carlos?**

¡OJO! In some countries of Latin America, rather than using **el nombre** to designate a first name, people use **el nombre de pila** for the given name, **el apellido** to designate the family or last name, and **el nombre** to indicate the entire name (first and last).

Add other common pets such as **el perro/el cachorro** and **el gato/el gatito,** perhaps even adding such odd but common, pets: **la culebra, la tortuga, el pato/el patito, los pollitos, la gallina, el gallo,** etc., to the presentation on **Las mascotas.**

¡A PRACTICAR! (page 51)

To begin this section, go back to the family tree you drew on the board. Begin with easy relationships, such as making statements regarding the nuclear family, moving to the extended family, then including in-laws and step-relatives, if applicable. When the statements are false, ask students to correct the statements, either by changing the name of the individual or indicating the correct relationship. You may specify which way or allow students to determine how they wish to rectify the situation.

EN VOZ ALTA (page 51)

As an addition to activity **2-3,** ask students to pair up and, using their family trees, ask their partners to identify the members of their family as they point to them. **¿Quién es este hombre/esta mujer?** Another version is to describe the relationship and ask for the name that appears beneath it. **¿Cómo se llama el hermano de tu madre? ¿Quién es el padre de** (name of person)?

As a change of pace, choose famous people who also are related to celebrities or commonly known individuals. This can be done in groups, pairs, or as a class activity in which you provide the clues for the class to identify:

1. La esposa de Brad Pitt. (Jennifer Aniston)
2. El esposo de Melanie Griffith. (Antonio Banderas)
3. El nombre de pila de la hija de Madonna. (Lourdes)
4. Uno de los hijos de Julio Iglesias. (Enrique Iglesias)
5. El abuelo de Mariel Hemingway. (Ernest Hemingway)
6. La esposa de Will Smith. (Jada Pickett)
7. La esposa del rey Juan Carlos de España. (la reina Sofia)
8. La hermana de Ashley Judd. (Wynona)

You can vary activity **2-4** by asking students to prepare a short description of their favorite family member that they will read to the class. Classmates will be asked to identify the individual from the information given. You can give the students a list of information that must be included, such as: **Su edad (¿Cuántos años tiene?), el color del pelo, su trabajo (Es doctor, profesora,** etc.). This can later be converted into a written activity to practice that skill.

EN CONTEXTO (page 52)

Have students listen to the Student Text Audio CD, following along in the text. Then ask them to look at the questions in activity **¿Comprendiste?** and listen again to the Student Text Audio CD to check for the applicable answers, but with the book closed. Write the questions on the board or stop the CD at various points.

¿NOS ENTENDEMOS? (page 52)

Inasmuch as diminutives are discussed, also include the terms of endearment common to Central America and Mexico, **m'hijito(a),** which are as common as those indicated in the text. **Nene** and **nena** are employed in Central America to refer to one's children, regardless of their age, while Mexicans and Mexican-Americans along the Texas-Mexico border and in New Mexico commonly refer to their children when young and teenagers as **chavalo(a).** You can include these terms either as part of the previous sections, or integrate the information during the appropriate **Encuentro cultural.**

ASÍ SE DICE Indicating ownership and possession: possession with *de(l)* and possessive adjectives (page 53)

Tell your students that, unlike English contractions, Spanish has only two, both of which are obligatory when the syntactic environment is presented. This occurs only when the prepositions **a** and **de** are followed by the masculine singular definite article: **de + el = del** and **a + el = al.**

ENCUENTRO CULTURAL (page 56)

It has been in vogue since the late 1980's in Central America, the Spanish Caribbean, and Mexico to give children foreign, especially American, names. It is also worthy of note that although many older Hispanic women still use **de** between their maiden name and that of their husband, as in **Margarita González *de* Marañón,** younger women, especially those who have traveled to the U.S. or live here, no longer observe this tradition, opting instead for the American custom of simply hyphenating them: **Margarita González-Marañón.**

ESTRUCTURA I Describing people and things: common uses of the verb *ser* (page 57)

Note that unlike English, Spanish does not use *a/an* (**un[a]**) before a "Bare NP," that is, a bare noun phrase, one that contains a noun that is not modified. Yet, when the noun is modified by a descriptive adjective, **un(a)** is employed. For example: **Pedro es médico. Pedro es un médico excelente.** Also, please note that **ser** is also used to indicate religious affiliation the same way it is used to designate profession or vocation. For example: **María es católica. María es una católica devota.**

¡A PRACTICAR! (page 58)

Assign activities **2-9** and **2-10** for homework or skip them and use the following contextualized activity in the form of a letter that might be sent to a relative as a substitute for or an addition to exercise **2-9.** It can be copied and distributed or placed on an overhead.

Fill in the blanks with the appropriate form of **ser** according to the context.

Querido tío Raúl:

Hoy _____ el 2 de mayo _____ lunes por la tarde. (Yo) _____ estudiante en una escuela secundaria

de Houston. Tengo una novia mexicana. Ella _____ muy inteligente y habla francés, inglés y español.

También _____ muy bonita. Pero (yo) _____ extrovertido y ella _____ un poco introvertida. _____

un pequeño problema. _____ las tres de la tarde y tengo clase de matemáticas. Tengo un examen

en cinco minutos. ¡_____ una situación terrible! El padre de Elena, mi novia, _____ mi profesor.

Un abrazo de tu sobrino,

_____

ASÍ SE DICE Describing people and things: agreement with descriptive adjectives (pages 59–60)

Assign all the sections regarding adjectives for homework and review them in class using overheads, illustrations in the text, or examples of the adjectives describing your students or items in the class.

¡OJO! The adjectives **hermosa** and **linda** can be added as synonyms for **bonita** in order to give students options. Besides, in some Latin American countries, these options are more commonly used (in Central America, for example). An explanation of **guapo** should be added, as this adjective is generally applied only to men in most countries. However, it is common for Spaniards to use the feminine **guapa**. This practice is uncommon in Spanish-speaking America.

¡OJO! The adjective **haragán (haragana)** is more common in some regions as either an alternative or as a replacement for **perezoso(a).**

¡OJO! Many adjectives that form opposites in English by adding prefixes such as **in-, im-, ir** tend to do so in Spanish as well: **(in)tolerante, (im)paciente, (ir)responsable.**

VOCABULARIO Las nacionalidades (page 63)

The nickname for a native of Guatemala is **chapín** and for a Nicaraguan is **nica.**

¡A PRACTICAR! (page 64)

Here is an additional activity to practice languages, nationalities, and origins. Have the students fill in the blanks with the correct form of the appropriate adjective.

Llena el blanco con el idioma, la nacionalidad o el origen apropiado.

1. París es la capital _____ y Berlín _____.
2. El Misisipí es un río _____ pero el Seine es _____.
3. Frida Kahlo fue *(was)* pintora mexicana; su idioma es _____.
4. El fútbol es un deporte _____.
5. Un Rottweiller es un perro _____ pero un chihuahua es _____.
6. Sofía Loren es una actriz _____ y habla italiano.
7. Pero Brigitte Bardot es francesa y habla _____.
8. Jon Secada y Ricky Martin son latinoamericanos; cantan en _____.
9. Andrei Putin es el presidente de Rusia, habla _____.
10. Beijing y Taipei son ciudades _____.

EN VOZ ALTA (page 64)

Review **-ar** verbs by having students answer the following questions orally rather than doing activity **2-19** or by using it in addition thereto.

1. ¿Hablas ruso? ¿Qué idiomas hablas? ¿Te gusta practicar el español?
2. ¿Qué clases tomas este semestre? ¿Tienes amigos en tus clases? ¿Qué clases toman ellos?
3. ¿Dónde estudias? ¿Con quién estudias español? ¿Hablan español tus amigos?
4. ¿A qué hora llegas a la universidad? ¿A qué hora regresas a tu casa?
5. ¿Miras la tele o escuchas música por la noche? ¿Qué programas te gusta mirar?

Generalmente, ¿qué clase de música te gusta?

ESTRUCTURA II Describing daily activities at home or at school: present tense of *-er* and *-ir* verbs (page 65)

Assign forms as homework. Review in class only to clarify any questions. Teach verbs with the prepositions that generally follow them. This diminishes errors in usage. Examples in the list provided include **asisitir a** and **creer en.** Point out that **deber** + infinitive means *must* or *ought* but it can also mean *to owe* when followed by a noun as in **Juan (le) debe cien dólares a Pablo.**

¡A PRACTICAR! (page 66)

After activity **2-21** add the following activity, which can be done orally or in writing.

Identify the activity associated with the following items. Give students the opportunity to give as many verbs as possible.

1. los libros; el periódico; la revista *Time* (leer)
2. el café; té; Coca Cola (beber)
3. una carta; una postal; un telegrama (leer, recibir, escribir)
4. el apartamento; tu casa; la residencia (vivir)
5. la cafetería; el restaurante (comer)
6. Santa Claus; Dios (creer en)

7. la puerta; el libro de texto (abrir)
8. el teatro; un concierto (asistir a)
9. la lección; los verbos; el vocabulario (aprender, comprender)
10. el español en clase; bailar el tango (aprender)

ASÍ SE DICE Expressing possession and physical states: common uses of the verb *tener* (page 67)

Present the section by pantomiming while making statements describing the state of being (resultant condition). Act out the idioms in the order they appear in the text and ask students to follow along or guess, and then provide them with the additional expressions if you choose to include them. Then pass out the following worksheet of fill-in-the-blanks for them to do in pairs.

1. Si no como por 24 horas, _____. (tengo hambre)
2. Son las tres de la mañana. Enrique _____. (tiene sueño)
3. La clase de español es a las dos. Son las dos menos cinco y Marta está en casa. Ahora ella _____. (tiene prisa)
4. Carlos es el presidente de su compañía y su hermana, Sara, es una excelente doctora; tienen mucho dinero. Los dos hermanos _____. (tienen éxito)
5. Los exploradores están en el desierto sin agua. _____. (Tienen sed)
6. Tú dices «diez y diez son veinte»; tú _____. (tienes razón)

ASÍ SE DICE Counting to 100: *los números de 30 a 100* (page 69)

Assign the numbers as homework. Review by writing them on the board and pointing to them first in order, then randomly, and have the students identify them in chorus. This is an opportunity to practice pronunciation as well as the numbers. A quick (and easy) practice exercise is **Patrones,** which you can do orally or at the board in teams.

Identifica el próximo número en la serie:

1. 10 20 30 (40)
2. 72 60 48 (36)
3. 100 90 80 (70)
4. 99 90 81 (72)
5. 5 10 15 (20)
6. 66 72 78 (84)
7. 60 55 50 (45)
8. 42 40 38 (36)
9. 30 33 36 (39)
10. 54 56 58 (60)
11. 48 44 40 (36)
12. 88 77 66 (55)
13. 15 30 45 (60)
14. 30 50 70 (90)
15. 11 22 33 (44)
16. 84 81 78 (75)

¡A PRACTICAR! (page 69)

Here's a quick ¿**Cierto o falso?** activity to practice numbers. Ask students to correct those statements that are **falso.** This can either be used as a substitute for or in addition to exercise **2-28.**

1. Hay 45 personas en la clase de español.
2. Hay 100 centavos en un dólar.
3. Mayo tiene 31 días.
4. Hay 50 semanas en un año.
5. Mi abuelo tiene 31 años.
6. Hay 99 años en un siglo.
7. Hay 11 personas en un equipo de fútbol americano.
8. Una hora tiene 70 minutos.
9. Hay 72 horas en tres días.
10. Junio, julio y agosto tienen 90 días.

SÍNTESIS

¡OJO! Remind students that numbers are considered adjectives of quantity so they must precede the noun to which they refer. In response to the question **¿Cuántos animales tienes en casa?,** an individual might answer **Tengo cinco gatos y tres perros en casa.** When expressing possession, point out to students that the owner follows while the item owned precedes the preposition **de.** Thus, in the statement **Café es el gato de Sara, gato** is the item owned by **Sara.**

You can bring together a variety of skills in the following activity. Place students in groups of three or four and have them ask each other questions so that everyone finds out about the others' families. Then, separate them and have each individual write a description of one of the members of her/his group. This second step can be given as a homework assignment. The group can then re-form to "peer edit" the composition. As a final step, several students can be chosen to read aloud the composition to see if the rest of the class (nongroup members) can identify the individual. The compositions can then be turned in for correction and grading. You can provide your students with questions to guide the composition, or suggestions on what information might be included. This is a good way to bring together the information from this chapter and also an excellent mechanism to recycle previously learned material.

3 El tiempo libre: Colombia

CHAPTER OPENER (pages 76–77)

Ask students to identify what the people are doing in the photo. See if they can identify relationship, colors, and other items that will help to recycle the previous vocabulary. To jump-start the chapter, ask the following questions to review old vocabulary, **gustar,** and **tener** idioms.

These can be done orally since it is a review.

1. ¿Qué tienes en la mochila?
2. ¿Cuánto dinero tienes (en la bolsa) hoy?
3. ¿Te gusta la clase de español? ¿Es fácil o difícil?
4. ¿Te gusta (vivir en) la residencia? ¿Cómo es tu compañero(a) de cuarto?
5. ¿Qué libros te gustan? ¿Cuándo lees?
6. ¿Cuándo tienes hambre o sed? ¿Qué bebes cuando tienes sed?
7. ¿Tienes razón frecuentemente?
8. ¿Quién tiene razón con más frecuencia, tú o la profesora?

VOCABULARIO Los deportes y los pasatiempos (page 78)

After assigning the vocabulary for home study, use the items labeled in the illustrations to review the pronunciation of the vocabulary.

¡OJO! It is important to point out to students the differences in the following verbs, all of which are translated as *to play:* **jugar** *(to play games, board games);* **practicar** *(to play sports);* and **tocar** *(to play musical instruments).* Also explain the difference between **un juego** *(card or board game)* and **un partido** *(game of sports).* Point out the word **el equipo,** which they can use to talk about favorite teams.

¡A PRACTICAR! (page 79)

After students have completed the activities **3-1** and **3-2,** have them do some additional vocabulary work by completing the following matching game. Instruct them either in English or Spanish to match the locations in **Columna A** with the sports in **Columna B.** The columns can be placed on an overhead, on the board, or made into a handout for each student.

Columna A	Columna B
el Estadio de Forest Hills	esquiar en agua
Madison Square Garden	la natación
Shea Stadium	montar a caballo
una playa en California	el golf
Pebble Beach	esquiar
Churchill Downs, KY	levantar pesas y hacer ejercicio
una piscina olímpica	el vólibol
Vail, CO	el béisbol
Cypress Gardens, FL	el básquetbol
el Gimnasio de GOLD	el tenis

EN VOZ ALTA (page 79)

To give your students more oral practice, do the following activity upon completion of activities **3-3** and **3-4.** Ask students to pick a slip of paper out of a hat/box on which you have written the name of a celebrity. Students must tell the class what the individual does for fun on weekends. They should indicate either the sport they are known for, a pastime they are known to enjoy, or a place associated with a pastime. They can give one or more hints so that their classmates can guess who has been chosen. You can provide hints on the pieces of paper on which the names appear or allow them to "start from scratch."

Michele Kwan	patina en hielo; exhibición de patinaje; la tele
Tiger Woods	practica el golf; anuncia en la tele
Brett Favre	el fútbol americano; el golf
Shaquile O'Neal	el baloncesto; las películas (actuar)
Jewel	tocar la guitarra; cantar
Blink 182	la música; los conciertos
Salvador Dalí	la pintura; el museo; el arte surrealista

EN CONTEXTO (page 80)

Have your students practice the dialog in small groups so that they can get used to the intonation and rhythm of Spanish. Have them listen carefully the first time, then practice once or twice, listen again, and then practice once more. Finally, you can choose one or more groups to present before the class. You can also have them create their own situations employing the vocabulary and structures they have been practicing. This should be followed by completion of **¿Comprendiste?** so that you can determine whether or not they have understood.

ENCUENTRO CULTURAL (page 81)

After students read the passage and answer the questions in activity **Para discutir,** ask them to answer the questions below. These can be done either orally or in writing, depending on which of the skills needs more practice at this point in the acquisition process.

1. Compara los aficionados al fútbol en Latinoamérica con los aficionados al básquetbol o al fútbol americano en los Estados Unidos. ¿Qué tienen en común? ¿En qué se diferencian? ¿Actúan igual?
2. ¿Quién es el futbolista estadounidense que ayuda o trabaja con niños necesitados? ¿Qué hace?
3. ¿Cuál es el deporte más popular en los Estados Unidos? ¿Por qué crees eso?

ESTRUCTURA I Expressing likes and dislikes: *gustar* + infinitive and *gustar* + nouns (page 82)

Review the information supplied to the students regarding **gustar** used both with infinitives and with nouns. Be sure to point out that the order appears to be "backwards" from what they come to consider the word order of Spanish.

¡OJO! **Gustar** and verbs that employ the same constructions are considered ergative verbs. This means that the Noun Phrase (NP) that appears to be the superficial direct object of the verb is really the subject. If **gustar** is translated as *to be pleasing to* or *to please,* comprehension and usage become less difficult. Thus, **Me gustan los deportes.** is interpreted as *Sports are pleasing to (please) me* (rather than *I like sports*). In order to clarify or emphasize, you can explain that the prepositional phrase corresponding to the individual(s) being pleased is preposed, as in *A Juan* **le gustan** los deportes. (clarification) and *A nosotros* **nos gusta el fútbol.** (emphasis).

Next, practice the structure(s) with your students orally using a quick question-and-answer session:

1. A mí me gustan los deportes acuáticos. Y a ti, ¿qué deporte te gusta?
2. ¿Qué deporte le gusta a tu papá? Y a tus abuelos, ¿les gusta el boxeo?
3. A (student's name) le gustan los Rockets de Houston. ¿Qué equipo (de básquetbol) te gusta a ti?
4. A mi madre no le gustan los deportes, pero tiene varios pasatiempos. A ella le gusta ir al cine y ver muchas películas. ¿Te gusta ir al cine también? ¿Con quién te gusta ir? Generalmente, ¿cuándo van ustedes?
5. ¿A tus parientes les gusta sacar fotos durante las fiestas? ¿A quién le gusta ser el fotógrafo? ¿Saca buenas fotos?

You can continue adding questions that will provide personal information for the students regarding their classmates and you.

¡A PRACTICAR! (page 83)

After completing activities **3-5** and **3-6,** include the following written activity so that students can practice answering in complete sentences.

1. A tú papá, ¿qué le gusta mirar en la televisión? Y a tu mamá, ¿le gustan los mismos programas?
2. ¿Cuántos hermanos tienes? ¿Te gustan? ¿Cuál es tu hermano favorito? ¿Qué deportes les gustan a ustedes? ¿Van a muchos partidos? ¿Cuál de los jugadores te gusta más? ¿Por qué?
3. A tus abuelos, ¿les gusta ir a la playa? ¿Nadan mucho o les gusta sólo tomar el sol?
4. ¿Quién es tu mejor amigo? ¿Cómo les gusta pasar el tiempo? ¿Qué les gusta hacer los sábados por la noche? ¿Qué les gusta hacer durante las vacaciones?
5. ¿Qué películas les gustan a los niños pequeños? Y a ti, ¿te gustan las películas románticas o las de acción?

EN VOZ ALTA (page 83)

Have students complete the oral practices in the text (activities **3-7, 3-8,** and **3-9**). Pair students and have them ask each other what the following people like.

¿Qué les gusta a las siguientes personas famosas?

1. Shakira
2. Ricky Martin
3. Jennifer López
4. Manny Rodríguez
5. Isabel Allende
6. Enrique Iglesias
7. Laura Esquivel
8. al rey Juan Carlos
9. Fidel Castro
10. Antonio Banderas

VOCABULARIO: Los lugares (page 84)

Introduce some of these places by asking students **¿Cuál es tu lugar favorito para descansar? ¿Qué lugar deseas visitar después del banco? ¿Qué hay en el banco? ¿En el cine? ¿En el centro comercial?** etc.

Point out to your students that the place where a particular item is sold often carries the suffix **-ería** added on to some version of the name of the item.

fruta	frutería	joya	joyería
libro	librería	papel	papelería

¡OJO! Another word for **la peluquería** is **el salón de belleza**. In some countries, **la peluquería** is reserved for a barber shop and **el salón de belleza** is used for a beauty salon.

¡A PRACTICAR! (page 85)

Assign activities **3-10** and **3-11** for students to complete as homework and go over their answers in class to clear up any problems. Then, if they need more practice, have them do the following activity, **¿Adónde vamos a ir?** Match the items needed found in Column A with the appropriate location in Column B.

Necesitamos...	Vamos a...
1. Bananas y peras	la iglesia
2. Mandar cartas	la papelería
3. Ver una película	la piscina
4. Tomar una taza de café	el restaurante
5. Nadar	la gasolinera
6. Mirar los pájaros	el mercado
7. Comprar recuerdos (*souvenirs*)	la frutería
8. Depositar un cheque	el centro comercial
9. Comprar muchas cosas diferentes	el cine
10. Rezar	el correo
11. Llenar el carro	la plaza
12. Comprar un lápiz	el banco

¿NOS ENTENDEMOS? (page 85)

In Central America the word for warehouse is **la bodega,** while in many other places it refers to a small corner grocery and even a liquor store.

ESTRUCTURA II Expressing plans with *ir: ir a* + destination, and *ir a* + infinitive (page 86)

Remind students that contractions in Spanish are obligatory, not optional. Any time **a + el** appears, **al** must be used.

¡A PRACTICAR! (page 87)

¡OJO! Tell your students that in Spanish, each clause contains only one conjugated verb. All other verbs must appear in the form of an infinitive or a present participle in the case of some verbs/ constructions such as the progressive tenses (**Estamos hablando.**) or following **continuar/seguir** (**Pedro continúa hablando sin parar. Mis hermanos siguen comiendo y ya están llenos.**).

The following activity can be substituted for or used in addition to activities **3-14** and **3-15.**

MODELO: E1: Me gusta caminar.
E2: Pues, vamos al parque.
E1: A mi mamá le gusta comer.
E2: Pues, debe ir al restaurante La Cucaracha Contenta.

1. Me gustan las películas. Pues,...
2. A Pedro le gustan los libros de misterio. Pues,...
3. Necesito un libro de texto. Pues,...
4. A mi primo le gusta el drama. Pues,...
5. Nos gusta hacer ejercicio. Pues, ¿por qué...
6. A mi abuela le gusta la lucha libre *(wrestling).* Pues,...
7. A mi novia le gusta esquiar en agua. Pues,...
8. A todos mis amigos les gusta bailar. Pues,...

If you feel students need more practice, you can include the activity below after completing activity **3-16.**

Las vacaciones son en junio. ¿Qué vas a hacer? Completa la oración, usando el sujeto y la actividad.

1. Tú   viajar a Europa
2. Marcos   esquiar en Acapulco
3. Mi hermano y yo   nadar en el sur de España
4. Mis primos   hacer ejercicio en el gimnasio
5. Yo   ir al cine los sábados
6. Papá y tío Berto   practicar béisbol
7. Mi tía Sofía   escribir cartas
8. La profesora   descansar bajo un árbol

EN VOZ ALTA (page 88)

After completing activities **3-17** and **3-18,** have students get together with a friend in the class to plan their dream vacation. They have just won an all-expense-paid trip for two (or four) to the location of their choice for two weeks. What will they do with all that time and spending money? Here's a good way to find out while practicing **ir a** + *infinitive* and all the previous verbs they have learned. They can, of course, include sports and pastimes, since they will have all desires met! After planning, a number of students can tell their classmates about their plans and take questions and suggestions to improve their "once-in-a-lifetime" opportunity.

ENCUENTRO CULTURAL (page 89)

Add the following questions to activity **Para dicutir** to stimulate discussion.

1. ¿Qué otros países son famosos por producir café excelente?
2. ¿Es el café algo especial en tu vida? ¿Por qué?

ESTRUCTURA III Describing leisure-time activities: verbs with irregular *yo* forms (page 90)

Assign the section for homework so that students will be familiar with the verbs and their forms and meanings when they arrive in class. Spend the time your students are in class practicing the language rather than simply discussing it.

¡OJO! Point out to your students that the **vosotros** form of **dar,** like that of **ver,** does not carry a written accent mark on the root vowel, e.g., **veis** and **dais** since they are monosyllabic verb forms.

¡A PRACTICAR! (page 91)

After activities **3-19** and **3-20** have been completed for homework, review your students' listening comprehension and spelling abilities by writing the infinitives of the **yo** forms that you say aloud.

1. salgo
2. tengo
3. doy
4. traigo
5. voy
6. hago
7. sé
8. veo
9. pongo
10. soy
11. conozco

EN VOZ ALTA (page 91)

After students complete activity **3-22,** continue your review by giving students varied subjects and an infinitive and asking them to orally provide the appropriate verb form. If you want to make this a bit more complex, ask students to provide their answers in complete sentences.

1. Estela   hacer
2. los estudiantes   poner
3. vosotros   dar
4. tú y tus primos   saber
5. un niño   traer
6. yo   conocer
7. Juan y Carlos   ver
8. nosotros   salir
9. tú   saber
10. el tío   ver

ASÍ SE DICE Expressing knowledge and familiarity: *saber, conocer,* and the personal *a* (page 92)

Assign these explanations as homework and go over them briefly. **Saber no es para personas. Es para acciones (o actividades) e información. Conocer es para la identidad de personas, cosas o lugares. Aquí hay unos ejemplos:**

Conocer: Conozco a (personas) los primos de José. También conozco (lugar) el barrio donde viven.

Saber: Y sé (información) dónde viven y que saben jugar (actividad) béisbol muy bien.

¡A PRACTICAR! (page 93)

After reviewing the uses of the verbs and completing activities **3-23** and **3-24,** students can continue with the following exercise: **¿Qué sabes y a quién conoces?**

1. ¿Conoces al presidente de los Estados Unidos?
2. ¿Conoces a una persona famosa?
3. ¿Conoce tu mamá a tu novio(a)?
4. ¿Conocen tus compañeros a tus abuelos?
5. ¿Qué deporte sabes jugar bien?
6. En tu opinión, ¿quién sabe jugar béisbol bien?
7. ¿Sabe Tiger Woods jugar fútbol? ¿Qué sabe jugar él?
8. ¿Sabes todos nuevos los verbos?

EN VOZ ALTA (page 93)

Have students choose a partner and work on activities **3-25** and **3-26.** If you feel additional oral work is needed, have students take turns asking and answering the questions provided above.

ASÍ SE DICE Talking about the months, seasons, and the weather (page 94)

Have students study the names of the months and the seasons of the year outside of class. For ease in memorization, they may organize the months according to the season to which they belong. Thus, in the Northern Hemisphere, they will be arranged as:

el invierno
diciembre   enero   febrero

el verano
junio   julio   agosto

la primavera
marzo   abril   mayo

el otoño
septiembre   octubre   noviembre

¡OJO! Point out to your students that the months and seasons of the year are not written with a capital letter in Spanish as they are in English. They are considered common nouns in Spanish.

¡OJO! Make sure that you explain to students that **muy** *(very)* is used with **está nublado** while **mucho** *(a lot)* is used with **llueve, nieva,** and expressions with **hace.** In addition, **hace mal tiempo** is used to indicate that the weather is bad.

¡A PRACTICAR! (page 95)

Activity **3-27** should be assigned for homework and gone over quickly to make sure there is no confusion.

Ask students to complete activity **3-28,** which you can then follow up with the questions provided below.

¿Qué tiempo hace...
1. en Alaska en diciembre?
2. en la playa en agosto?
3. en octubre en Maine?
4. en los picos de los Andes en mayo?
5. en la selva amazónica en el verano?
6. cuando no hace sol?
7. en Boston en marzo?
8. en Kansas en la primavera?

EN VOZ ALTA (page 95)

Ask students to work with someone they have not worked with before and complete activity **3-29.**

SÍNTESIS

As an alternative to the writing task, have students write up their notes for an article on "Sports Around the World" as telegraph messages to the newspaper editor for whom they work.

As an activity that winds up all the sections of **Capítulo 3,** have students work with one or two classmates. The contextual situation is as follows: They are copy editors at a major advertising agency doing work for World-Wide Travel. They are working on a multi-media advertising campaign. The students are to choose the location being advertised, the activities and other amenities offered, and the weather at different times of the year that make it the ideal location for any occasion. After discussing the "ad campaign," the "advertising executives" must then write up the material they have designed so that the "clients" (their classmates) can review them. Taking the advice and comments of their "clients," the ad men and women must then edit their copy and present it to the head of the company, **you,** for final approval (and a grade!).

Remember to provide a clear rubric that explains exactly how and on what you will be grading the students.

4 En la casa: España

CHAPTER OPENER (page 106)

To begin the chapter, ask students to take a good look at the photo of the plaza and to make a list of its characteristics. Could there be apartments overlooking the plaza? This is a good way of recycling previous vocabulary as well as introducing the new lexicon. The lists made by different students can then be shared and discussed by the whole class.

VOCABULARIO La casa (page 108)

Assign the vocabulary items to be studied at home so that they can be used during class. After discussing the lists that the students make up, go inside the house to begin discussing rooms and their furnishings. Add the following vocabulary to round out the **Palabras útiles** list: **el (la) dueño(a), el (la) inquilino(a), el alquiler, alquilar.**

¿NOS ENTENDEMOS? (page 108)

Add the following terms to the list of variations: **la tina = la bañera; el lavabo (en el baño) = el fregadero (en la cocina); el piso = el suelo.** Be sure to explain that in Spain the term **el piso = el apartamento.**

¡A PRACTICAR! (page 109)

Assign activities **4-1, 4-2, 4-3,** and **4-4** for homework, and as an additional activity to practice furniture and parts of the house, have students identify which of the items does not belong to the group.

1. el espejo	el cuadro	el sillón	la ventana
2. el lavabo	el estante	la bañera	el inodoro
3. el comedor	la sala	el garaje	el dormitorio
4. la cama	la cómoda	el sofá	la mesita de noche
5. la silla	el sillón	el armario	la alfombra
6. la terraza	el jardín	la ducha	el patio
7. la puerta	la ventana	la pared	la alfombra

EN VOZ ALTA (page 110)

After students complete activities **4-5, 4-6,** and **4-7,** place them in teams (of 2, 3, or 4 students) to play Pictionary. This is an entertaining way to polish pronunciation while repeating the vocabulary items.

EN CONTEXTO (page 111)

Have students listen to the Student Text Audio CD and see how many items they can identify from the vocabulary list. Then play it a second time to see if they have been able to identify additional items.

¡OJO! In Central America the word used for *grass* is **la grama** rather than **el césped;** in other parts of Latin America, the term used is **la hierba (la yerba).**

¿NOS ENTENDEMOS? (page 111)

Many young people in Central America and the Caribbean use the term **un montón** rather than **un mogollón.**

ENCUENTRO CULTURAL (page 112)

Have students read the text and then answer the questions in **Para discutir** as well as the following additional questions.

1. ¿En qué parte/región de España se encuentran?
2. ¿Cuáles son algunos aspectos especiales de la arquitectura de Gaudí?
3. ¿Conoces al arquitecto estadounidense Frank Lloyd Wright? ¿Crees que estos dos hombres tienen algo en común? Explica tu opinión.
4. ¿A cuál de los dos arquitectos prefieres? ¿Por qué?

ESTRUCTURA I Describing household chores and other activities: present tense of stem-changing verbs (*e → ie; e → i; o → ue*) (page 113)

Introduce the topic by pointing out to your students that it is always the stressed (tonic) syllable of the verb stem that changes. When the stress falls on the personal ending, there is no vowel change. **Nosotros** and **vosotros** show no stem change because the verb endings carry the stress, regardless of the type of vowel change exhibited: **perder → pierdo, perdemos, perdéis; contar → cuento, contamos, contáis; pedir → pido, pedimos, pedís.**

¡A PRACTICAR! (page 114)

After you review exercises **4-8, 4-9,** and **4-10** (which students have completed as homework), add the following questions, which you can ask orally and have the students answer orally or in writing.

1. ¿A qué hora comienzas el día durante la semana?
2. ¿Qué prefieres comer para el desayuno? ¿Dónde lo preparas?
3. ¿Vives en una casa, un apartamento o en una residencia? ¿Dónde prefieres vivir? ¿Qué quieres tener en tu dormitorio que no tienes ahora?
4. ¿A qué hora vienes a la universidad? ¿Cierras la puerta con llave cuando sales?
5. ¿Cuándo vuelves a casa (a tu cuarto)?
6. ¿Quiénes vienen a tu casa de visita los fines de semana? ¿Qué les sirves para comer y beber a tus visitas?
7. Cuando tus amigos están en tu casa/cuarto, ¿qué hacen?
8. ¿Puedes estudiar con tus amigos en tu cuarto o prefieres estudiar solo(a)?
9. Por lo general, ¿cuántas horas duermes durante la semana? Y durante los fines de semana, ¿duermes más?
10. ¿Piensas conseguir un buen trabajo después de terminar la universidad?

EN VOZ ALTA (page 115)

Students should be placed in pairs or groups of three or four individuals in order to complete activities **4-11** and **4-12.** Pair your students if they are not already paired to continue with activity **4-13.** Since your students are already in pairs, have each report the results of the interview to the rest of the class. A poll can be taken to see how many individuals share the same ideas, preferences, etc.

ASÍ SE DICE Expressing physical conditions, desires, and obligations with *tener* (page 116)

Recycle the previously studied **tener** idioms by having students answer the following questions.

1. ¿Qué hace tu madre cuando tiene sed?
2. ¿Por qué duermes mucho los fines de semana?
3. ¿Qué come tu papá cuando tiene hambre?
4. ¿Qué haces tú cuando tienes frío?
5. ¿Qué llevas cuando tienes calor?
6. ¿Por qué estás corriendo? (¿Qué haces cuándo tienes prisa?)

¡A PRACTICAR! (page 117)

Having had students complete activities **4-14** and **4-15** at home, you can now go over the answers as a class. As students have already been exposed to other **tener** idioms, these two activities should suffice.

EN VOZ ALTA (page 117)

Once students and their partners complete activities **4-16, 4-17,** and **4-18,** give them an additional opportunity to practice the new **tener** idioms by giving their reactions to each of the situations presented. They should take turns asking and answering.

1. Tu novio(a) está besando a tu mejor amigo(a).
2. Hay una serpiente en tu cama.
3. Hay mucho tráfico pero estás escuchando un buen CD.
4. Es un día muy bonito. Hace calor y sol y vas a la playa.
5. Mi banda favorita está en el club ¡Olé! esta noche. Quiero escuchar música con mis amigos y bailar.
6. Tengo una «A» en la clase de español. Tú tienes una «C» en la clase y no estás contento(a).
7. Soy tutor(a) de niños con problemas. Paso mucho tiempo explicando todo.
8. A Isabel no le gustan los lugares altos ni los ascensores. Hoy necesita subir al piso 30.

VOCABULARIO Los quehaceres domésticos (page 118)

Begin by asking students what chores they are accustomed to doing. You can also ask which ones they like and which ones they dislike performing. You can add the following vocabulary to help students communicate more fully: **secar (los platos, la ropa); sacudir (los muebles, el polvo).**

¡A PRACTICAR! (pages 118–119)

Assign activity **4-19** to be done for homework and go over it in class in order to determine that everyone understands the appropriate answers.

EN VOZ ALTA (page 119)

Do **¡A practicar!** activity **4-20** and **En voz alta** activities **4-21** and **4-22** in class, so that students have plenty of opportunity for oral practice. The activity below is offered in addition to or as an alternative to the previous three, depending on how much practice you feel your students require.

¿Qué haces cuando...

1. los platos están sucios?
2. la alfombra tiene polvo?
3. no hay ropa limpia?
4. las plantas necesitan agua?
5. el césped está muy alto?
6. tu camisa está arrugada?
7. hay muchas cosas en el garaje?
8. hay basura en el piso?
9. los muebles tienen polvo?
10. la cama está desordenada?

ENCUENTRO CULTURAL (page 120)

Have students read the short narrative and answer the questions that follow **(Para discutir)** to which we have added a few more. They are provided to provoke discussion and allow students to share information with each other.

1. ¿Qué diferencia hay entre la enumeración de los pisos en los edificios de algunos países de Latinoamérica y la de los Estados Unidos?
2. ¿Por qué no hay viviendas típicas en Latinoamérica? ¿Hay casas típicas en los Estados Unidos? Explica tu respuesta.
3. ¿En qué tipo de casa prefieres vivir tú? ¿Por qué?

ESTRUCTURA II Expressing preferences and giving advice: affirmative *tú* commands (page 121)

As an introduction to the formation of affirmative informal commands, remind students that there are two ways of addressing an individual: either as **tú** or as **usted.** The informal (or familiar) form of address is **tú,** and there are times that they must directly ask or tell someone to do something. Thus, students must be able to employ the appropriate **tú** command verb forms.

¡A PRACTICAR! (page 122)

Have students complete **4-23** and **4-24** as homework assignments and then go over them orally in class while you write the appropriate form on the board, so that there is no doubt in any student's mind regarding the spelling. Complete the following activity with your class.

Consejos a un amigo Give your friend advice appropriate to the situation identified below.

1. Quiero ponerme estos vaqueros pero están sucios. _____
2. Hoy es jueves y los basureros vienen a recoger la basura los viernes. _____
3. Las plantas necesitan agua. _____
4. Hay mucho polvo en el suelo. _____
5. Tengo sueño. _____
6. Son las dos de la tarde y tengo hambre. _____
7. Tengo un examen mañana por la tarde. _____
8. Necesito comprar comida para preparar la cena. _____
9. Mi cama está desordenada. _____
10. Quiero ir al cine contigo. _____

EN VOZ ALTA (page 122)

Ask students to complete activity **4-25** with a classmate. Once they have finished, have them change partners and share with the new partner the advice that they compiled in the previous activity.

ESTRUCTURA III Talking about location, emotional and physical states, and actions in progress: the verb *estar* (pages 123–124)

Remind students of the uses of **ser** and that you will now focus on the second Spanish verb meaning *to be*. Review the forms associated with the verb so that they don't have to focus on form and can pay attention to function. Point out to your students that **estar + en** can also be translated as being "at" a location in expressions such as: **Juan José está en casa.** *(Juan José is at home.)* and **Cristina está en la universidad de San Marcos.** *(Cristina is at the University of San Marcos.)*

Also explain to students that in Spanish, the present progressive indicates that the individual is in the act of doing something. Unlike English, where we tend to employ this verb tense to describe ongoing actions, Spanish uses the simple present for this. For example: **Estos días no miro mucha televisión.** *(These days I'm not watching [I don't watch] much television.)* **Hoy estoy mirando varios programas para mi curso de cine.** *(Today I am watching various programs for my film course.)*

¡OJO! In Spanish the present progressive is not used with verbs of motion. For example: **Vamos al cine.** *(We're going to the movies.)*

¡A PRACTICAR! (pages 124–126)

Assign activities **4-26, 4-27,** and **4-28** for homework so that all three of them can be gone over as a class in order to clarify any errors or misconceptions. You may then do **4-29** orally as a class. Ask students to continue working on the present progressive by completing the sentences below.

¿Qué está pasando?

1. Pedro está cansado, por eso _____. (está durmiendo)

2. Marta y María tienen hambre, por eso _____. (están cocinando, comiendo)

3. Tú tienes examen mañana, por eso _____. (estás estudiando)

4. Mi falda está arrugada, por eso _____. (estoy planchando)

5. Terminamos de comer, por eso _____. (estamos quitando la mesa)

6. El basurero está lleno, por eso Pamela _____. (está botando/tirando la basura).

7. Quiero saber cómo termina la novela, por eso _____. (estoy leyendo)

8. Hay polvo en la mesa y la lámpara. Carlota y Vilma _____. (están sacudiendo)

Once finished with this activity, if students need extra practice with **estar** for location or emotional and physical states, have them pair up and complete the activity below.

Match the answers in **Columna B** that most appropriately complete the phrases in **Columna A.**

Columna A	Columna B
1. Tienes un examen difícil.	A. Hoy él está emocionado.
2. Hay ropa en el piso de tu cuarto.	B. Estás nervioso.
3. Sus hermanos pierden su dinero.	C. Ella está muy ocupada.
4. Juanita se gana la lotería.	D. Mamá está muy contenta porque los hijos ayudan.
5. Los chicos pasan la aspiradora y barren el piso.	E. Estás preocupada.
6. Tu hijo tiene fiebre.	F. La alcoba está desordenada.
7. Mamá tiene mucho que hacer.	G. Están furiosos.
8. Paquito va a Europa mañana.	H. Ella está muy contenta.

EN VOZ ALTA (page 126)

For additional oral practice after completing activities **4-30, 4-31,** and **4-32,** have students play Family Feud. Have students answer the following questions in writing. Then select one or two of them to tally the four or five most popular answers. Then form several "families" (teams), as on the TV show, where they attempt to match the most popular answer and receive the number of points equal to the number of people who match your answer. The first team to reach a set number of points wins!

1. ¿Cuándo están contentos tus padres?
2. ¿Por qué está aburrido(a) tu novio(a)?
3. ¿Quiénes están ocupados al fin del semestre?
4. ¿Cuándo estás emocionado(a)?
5. ¿Por qué están ustedes nerviosos?
6. ¿Cuándo está ordenada tu habitación?
7. ¿Quiénes están contentos en el verano?
8. ¿Cuándo están enfermas muchas personas?
9. ¿Cuándo es necesario estar sano?
10. ¿Cuándo estás aburrido(a)?

ASÍ SE DICE Counting from 100 and higher:
Los números de 100 a 1.000.000 (page 127)

¡OJO! The expression **millón** is always followed by **de** and does not change gender to agree with the noun that follows the preposition: **un millón de dólares; un millón de monedas** *(coins)*.

Also remind students that **millón** loses its written accent when used in the plural—**millones**—but maintains the same structure: **diez millones de madres; ciento diez millones de dólares.**

¡A PRACTICAR! (page 128)

As an additional expansion after completing activity **4-33**, ask students to supply the dates for the following "historical" events in their lives:

1. La fecha de tu cumpleaños
2. El año de tu graduación de la secundaria
3. El año de tu graduación de la universidad
4. La fecha de la boda *(wedding)* de tus padres
5. La fecha del cumpleaños de tu novio(a)

EN VOZ ALTA (page 129)

Activities **4-35** and **4-36** should provide adequate practice of **los números.**

SÍNTESIS

This section provides students with a final opportunity to bring together all of their newly acquired skills in a single project. This activity may serve as an additional assignment or a replacement assignment.

You are a world-famous architect who has just been hired by (a celebrity to be played by a classmate). You have been chosen to design and build a house, which will express the celebrity's personality while addressing her/his needs and status. Before you can set about your task, you must get to know her/him so that your creation will have a unique flavor. Each pair of students will turn in a "project" and report to the banking officer (you) for financing.

1. Interview the celebrity to ascertain specific information to help you design the structure.
2. With the information from the interview, design the house. Draw the plans for the house and make sure you label rooms, furnishings, landscaping, etc.
3. Get together with the celebrity once again to explain what you've done and to get approval to continue. Any additional details or information necessary to complete the project should be written down for inclusion in revisions.
4. Discuss any changes she/he wants made and discuss the reasons for them.
5. Make any changes and adjustments to your plans.
6. Write up a report to go with the plans, which will then be submitted to the bank (the instructor) for financing.

5 La salud: Bolivia y Paraguay

CHAPTER OPENER (page 138)

Ask students to look at the photo of the plaza and comment on the various aspects represented. Ask them to flip back to the plaza depicted on page 106 of **Capítulo 4** to compare and contrast the two (one in Spain and one in South America).

VOCABULARIO El cuerpo humano (page 140)

The vocabulary for the human body and its parts is self-explanatory, so simply assign the vocabulary items for home study in order to be able to practice them during the class period. You can also add the following vocabulary to help students talk about their body: **la cintura, el pecho, el (dedo) pulgar,** and **los labios.** Initial review of the vocabulary can be done either by pointing to your own body and asking for identification (**¿Qué es esto(a),** etc.?) or by pointing to a student's body part (but be careful!) and asking the same sort of question. An alternative question you might use is **¿Dónde tienes el/la/los/las... ?** or **Enséñame el/la/los/las...**

¿NOS ENTENDEMOS? (page 140)

Another expression in this category is the Spanish expression **ser codo** (while cupping one's right hand to hold the left elbow) which indicates the person referred to is *cheap, tight, stingy.*

¡A PRACTICAR! (page 141)

Have students complete activities **5-1, 5-2,** and **5-3** at home as part of the same assignment with the vocabulary. Then you can add the following activity and ask students to identify the part of the body described.

¿Qué parte del cuerpo es?

1. Hay cinco en la mano. (los dedos)
2. Es necesario para pensar. (el cerebro)
3. Usamos esta parte para oír música. (el oído, la oreja)
4. Me duele cuando como mucho. (el estómago)
5. Necesitas estas partes para correr. (los pies, las piernas)
6. Son necesarios para mirar la tele. (los ojos)
7. Tengo 32 y sirven para masticar. (los dientes)
8. Cuando tengo resfriado me duele mucho. (la garganta, la nariz, la cabeza)
9. Tengo dos y sirven para llevar mis libros y abrazar *(to hug)* a mi mamá. (los brazos)

EN VOZ ALTA (page 141)

The following activities can be done either before or after activity **5–4.** You can use the activity suggested above under **Vocabulario** as an introduction to **Simón dice (tócate la nariz,** etc.). Two other activities that are good ways to practice vocabulary words are Hangman and Pictionary. An activity that is more complicated is **¡Ay, doctor, me duele!,** followed by the part of the body that hurts. This also helps to practice **doler,** which conjugates like **gustar,** and can be quickly reviewed by giving a few examples before beginning the game.

EN CONTEXTO (page 142)

Ask students if they ever pretended to be ill in order to play hooky from school. If so, ask them what happened. Keep in mind that you will have to either provide the preterite forms of verbs or ask them to relate the incident as if they were still pretending to be ill to avoid classes. Then play the CD and ask them if they recognize Carolina's illness. Have them look at the questions prior to listening and then replay the dialog so that they can check their answers to **¿Comprendiste?**

ENCUENTRO CULTURAL (page 143)

After reading the passage, ask if anyone has been to Bolivia. If so, ask for a description of how she/he felt while there. If not, ask if anyone has visited a place (Denver, in the U.S., comes to mind) of high altitude. Again, ask for the same information. If there is no one who has experienced the symptoms firsthand, go on to discuss the information from the text. Here are some additional questions you can add to **Para discutir:**

1. ¿Cómo se llama la región donde está la capital de Bolivia?
2. ¿Por qué es tan severo el mareo?

ESTRUCTURA I Talking about routine activities: reflexive pronouns and present tense of reflexive verbs (pages 144–145)

Reflexive verbs are those whose actions fall back onto the subject. This means that the subject and the direct object are one; therefore, the pronoun employed must reflect the same grammatical person as the verb-final morphology. Many English verbs whose Spanish counterparts are reflexive, tend to include the term *get* in English (*to get up, washed, bathed, shaved, (un)dressed,* etc.). It must be noted that almost any verb in Spanish can be turned into a reflexive verb by employing the appropriate pronoun. Some additional verbs that can be added to the list provided in the text include: **cepillarse el pelo, desvestirse, pintarse las uñas, pararse, sentarse.**

¡OJO! In many regions of Latin America, the term for *brushing one's teeth* is **lavarse los dientes,** rather than **cepillarse los dientes.**

¡A PRACTICAR! (pages 145–146)

Either prior to or after completing activities **5-5, 5-6,** and **5-7** for homework, students can complete the following simple activity where they must put the verbs in the appropriate order in which they occur in a their normal daily routine.

Pon los verbos en el orden correcto según tu rutina diaria (empieza con lo que haces por la mañana).

1. dormirse, levantarse, acostarse
2. peinarse, cepillarse/lavarse los dientes, maquillarse
3. secarse el cuerpo, ducharse, despertarse
4. quitarse la ropa, vestirse, bañarse
5. afeitarse, bañarse, pintarse

Here is another activity students can do either in written format or by asking a partner and having her/him respond. If done as a partnered oral routine, it can be part of the **En voz alta** section.

¿Qué debo hacer? / ¿Qué hago?

1. Tengo la barba larga. (Me afeito.)
2. Es hora de ir a la oficina y estoy en la cama. (Me levanto.)
3. Es hora de salir y mi ropa está en el armario. (Me visto.)
4. Hay mucho viento y tengo el pelo desordenado. (Me peino.)
5. Tengo las manos sucias. (Me lavo las manos.)
6. No hay tina *(bathtub)* en mi apartamento y estoy sucio(a). (Me ducho.)
7. Me baño y debo vestirme. (Me seco.)
8. Llego a casa después de trabajar todo el día. Estoy cansada. (Me quito la ropa. Me acuesto. Me siento en la silla.)

EN VOZ ALTA (page 147)

The following activity, in which students describe the daily routine that some well-known people go through as they get ready to face the world, can be done in addition to or instead of activities **5-8, 5-9,** and **5-10.**

1. Ricky Martin, el día de un concierto en Madison Square Garden
2. Gloria Estéfan, durante el fin de semana con su familia
3. El rey Juan Carlos y la reina Sofía, antes de una cena formal
4. Don Quijote, después de conocer a Dulcinea
5. Salma Hayek, el día del estreno *(premiere)* de su película
6. «El Duque», antes de un partido de béisbol importante
7. El Ballet Folklórico de México, después de una función
8. José María Aznar, antes de dar un discurso al público

ASÍ SE DICE Talking about things you have just finished doing: *acabar de* + infinitive (page 148)

Point out to students that the English phrase requires a present perfect construction (the auxiliary verb *have* and the past participle of the action verb *said, done, eaten*), while the Spanish structure requires **acabar** in the present tense and the action verb in the infinitive instead of its past participle.

Since this is quite a simple structure once the concept is explained, activities **5-11, 5-12,** and **5-13** on page 148 should be enough practice to assure that students are able to correctly use it.

VOCABULARIO La salud (page 149)

Ask students if they have ever been inside a rural clinic or a medical care facility dedicated to people who are financially disadvantaged. Follow up by asking them if they have been to the college/university infirmary. The latter should result in an affirmative response from at least a few students even if the former elicits none. Ask them to describe the experience and the physical set-up of such a medical facility.

¡A PRACTICAR! (page 150)

Have students complete **5-14** and **5-15** for homework, and continue with the following short activities if you feel students need more practice.

¿Qué haces...

1. cuando tienes fiebre?
2. si comienzas a toser?
3. cuando tienes náuseas?
4. si tienes escalofríos?
5. si te duele la garganta?

Aquí están las soluciones, ¿cuál es el problema?

1. Me acuesto y guardo cama por unos tres o cuatro días.
2. Me tomo la temperatura y tomo dos aspirinas.
3. Voy a la oficina del doctor y me da una receta.
4. El doctor me da un jarabe.
5. El doctor me pone una inyección de antibióticos.

EN VOZ ALTA (page 151)

Have students pair up to do activities **5-16, 5-17,** and **5-18.** The activities can be done orally in pairs if you think this a more effective and applicable way to do them.

ESTRUCTURA II Describing people, things, and conditions: *ser* versus *estar* (page 152)

Point out to your students that each of the verbs has its roots in a different Latin verb. **Ser** comes from the verb *essere* from which English also gets words such as *essence* and *essential.* If you keep these connections in mind, you can connect **ser** to essential or inherent characteristics of a noun. **Estar,** however, has its origins in the Latin verb *stare,* meaning *to rise* or *to stand up,* which indicates a change in position or state. If the connection is made to changing states, then the relationship of **estar** to health conditions or changeable characteristics is easy to remember. Using these explanations, the relationship of each verb to its use in expressing different types of information becomes evident and clear.

¡A PRACTICAR! (page 153)

Assign activities **5-19** and **5-20** for homework and follow their classroom review with the following activity:

Benjamín _____ mi hijo. Él _____ enfermo hoy. Está tosiendo y tiene fiebre. Por eso _____ necesario ir a la oficina del doctor. Su oficina _____ en la Calle Morelos. Su cita (*appointment*) _____ a las tres de la tarde y Benjamín _____ un poco nervioso. Pero, el doctor Sandoval _____ muy bueno y siempre _____ calmado.

El doctor Sandoval _____ guatemalteco. Yo también _____ de Guatemala. Los dos _____ de la capital del país. Nosotros _____ amigos por muchos años. Él _____ casado con mi amiga, Eleonor. Eleonor _____ delgada y alta. Tiene piernas largas y unos ojos azules que _____ muy grandes. Eleonor _____ del sur de los Estados Unidos y por eso (*that's why*) habla español. El doctor dice que todo _____ bien con Benjamín. Sólo (*Only*) tiene un pequeño resfriado. Va a _____ mejor (*better*) mañana después de tomar la medicina y el jarabe. Ahora Benjamín y yo _____ muy contentos y volvemos a casa. Esta tarde Benjamín _____ mirando su programa favorito de televisión. Al fin y al cabo (*All in all*) _____ un día bonito.

EN VOZ ALTA (page 154)

Assign activities **5-21** and **5-22** as homework before having students complete the following activity in pairs.

1. Explícale a tu compañero(a) cómo es y cómo/dónde está tu amigo(a) o pariente favorito.
2. Luego, tu compañero(a) va a hacerte preguntas para obtener más información.
3. Tu compañero(a) te cuenta (*tells you*) a ti sobre su amigo(a) o pariente favorito y tú haces preguntas a él (ella).

ENCUENTRO CULTURAL (page 155)

Have students read the selection and answer the following questions in addition to those provided in the text.

1. ¿Quiénes cultivaban la coca en años pasados?
2. ¿Dónde cultivaban la coca?
3. ¿Qué es la coca?
4. ¿Qué hierbas que son remedios conoces?
5. ¿Crees que son efectivos estos remedios?

Also, add the following discussion question: **El uso de la cocaína es legal en Bolivia. ¿Crees que debemos legalizar la cocaína en los Estados Unidos? Explica tu respuesta.**

ESTRUCTURA III Pointing out people and things: demonstrative adjectives and pronouns (page 156)

Demonstrative adjectives function to designate specific nouns in relation to the speaker in terms of space and time. Items that are closest (in space and time) to the speaker (and possibly also the listener) are designated as *this/these,* while items at an intermediate distance (to the speaker and possibly the listener) are designated *that/those.* Items at a great distance from both speaker and listener are designated as *over there* or *(over) yonder.*

Share the following mnemonic device with your students as a trick to remember which demonstratives designate proximity: *This* and *these* have *T's* as do the terms for them in Spanish **(este[a], estos[as]).**

¡OJO! During the fall of 1999, the **Real Academia de la lengua española** issued another determination regarding the grammar/orthography of Spanish. They declared that demonstrative pronouns no longer need to have a written accent mark and that the demonstrative adjectives and pronouns can be identified and differentiated by their grammatical context. Pedagogically speaking, it is still a good idea to use the written accent so that students are made aware of the differences and so that as their instructor, you are able to ascertain if they understand the difference between the two demonstratives and their functions. Once you are fairly sure, you can refrain from penalizing them for accent omission.

SÍNTESIS

These activities are designed for groups of three or four: the volunteer, the doctor, and one or two patients. The written assignments can be turned in for grading. The activity will recycle the vocabulary of the chapter regarding the body, health, and medical treatment, etc. All four skills and different combinations thereof are integrated in these activities: speaking, listening, writing, and reading. Cultural aspects seen in this chapter can also be included, provided the "doctor" or her/his patient(s) believe in alternative medicine. The scenario presented below can be turned into a visit to the **curandero(a)** if your students have enough knowledge to be effective. Giving them the option to do either or both will provide them with an excellent opportunity to use the language creatively while at the same time do some Internet surfing to acquire additional information.

You have just been accepted as a volunteer at the local clinic for Latin American refugees. It is your job to find out what their problems are, how long they have been suffering from the ailment, their daily habits that may contribute to their problems, etc. You are then supposed to give the doctor the information you have found out. Together with the patient and the doctor you must write up the patient's medical notes. Then, you and the doctor must write out the instructions that the patient must follow in order to get better.

6 ¿Quieres comer conmigo esta noche?: Venezuela

CHAPTER OPENER (page 166)

Have students describe the plaza and the restaurant scene shown. Then, ask them to get into pairs (or small groups) and compare the plaza in downtown Caracas to those in Spain and Bolivia. What do they have in common, what is different, how does each reflect the society of which it is a part? How does each reflect the culture of the indigenous population in Latin America and of previous historical periods in Spain? Finally, go on to compare the restaurants with those with which students are familiar or which they frequent.

VOCABULARIO La comida (page 168)

To introduce food and restaurant vocabulary, ask students to jot down key words they associate with the following questions.

1. ¿Cómo se llama tu restaurante favorito? ¿Cómo es?
2. ¿Qué tipo de comida sirven allí? ¿Cuál(es) es (son) tu(s) plato(s) favorito(s)?
3. ¿Cómo es el servicio? ¿Cómo son las personas que trabajan allí? Y ¿cómo describirías *(would you describe)* las personas que comen allí?
4. ¿Cómo son los precios? ¿Son los platos caros o baratos?
5. ¿Con qué frecuencia comes allí? ¿Quién(es) va(n) contigo?

¡A PRACTICAR! (page 169)

Have students do activities **6-1** and **6-2** as homework so that you can review them quickly in class and spend time doing oral activities. The next activities can be done in small groups or as a class activity.

When done as a small group activity, the following questions can be done as a "round-robin" so that the student who answers the first question chooses the next respondent and the question to be answered. Thus, the same questions can be asked more than once, and a variety of answers can be accommodated in order to show students that there is more than one way to appropriately respond to a given question. This last point is important because students often appear to forget that in their own language they intuitively know this, but when they move to another, they think that there is only one "correct" answer to each query. Here are some questions regarding food to get their discussion started.

1. Cuando tienes mucha hambre, ¿qué prefieres comer?
2. Si acabas de correr o hacer ejercicio, ¿qué te gusta beber?
3. A veces, ¿tienes ganas de comer algo especial? ¿Qué cosa?
4. Cuando tienes sed, ¿qué prefieres tomar?
5. Cuando estudias, ¿qué tienes ganas de comer?

This next activity can be given out to be done at home, or students can continue to work in groups. Make this a contest to see which group can finish first and come up with **el nombre del restaurante favorito del (de la) profesor(a),** which appears vertically using the first letter of each answer when they are placed directly under each other.

Un acróstico: Escribe la palabra que se describe.

L	echuga	**1.** Legumbre verde para ensaladas
A	gua	**2.** Mineral sin gas
P	apas	**3.** Patatas en Latinoamérica
L	angosta	**4.** Marisco rojo y muy caro; se come con mantequilla
A	zúcar	**5.** Café con leche y
Z	umo	**6.** Jugo en España
A	ceite	**7.** Con vinagre, para la ensalada
D	esayuno	**8.** La comida de la mañana
E	nsalada	**9.** Lechuga y tomates con salsa
L	eche	**10.** Bebida blanca para los niños
M	antequilla	**11.** Se pone en el pan
A	lmuerzo	**12.** La comida del mediodía
Y	o	**13.** Pronombre de primera persona singular
A	repas	**14.** Comida muy popular en Venezuela y Colombia; rellenas de mantequilla, carne o queso

Here is another activity that can be done in small groups or as a class. If done as a class, write the headings on the board and ask for contributions. Put each group in charge of a particular portion of the menu and have them build their own restaurant menu. An alternative comes from allowing each group to decide what kind of restaurant they want to open and to write up their own menu according to the divisions provided below. They need only select those that apply to their particular type of restaurant!

Escribe una lista de platos/comidas según su lugar (clasificación) en el menú.

Para picar: _____

Las bebidas: _____

Las legumbres: _____

Los platos fuertes: _____

Las carnes: _____

Los mariscos: _____

Los postres: _____

Ahora el grupo puede comparar su lista con la de los otros grupos.

This activity makes a good transition into the next **En voz alta** activity.

EN CONTEXTO (page 170)

Have students get into small groups and recreate the scene they have just read. First, have them remain loyal to the scene, then ask them to vary it according to: (1) the time of day; (2) where they sit; (3) what they order; (4) the house specialty; (5) the quality of the food and service; and (6) what they have for dessert and drinks.

ENCUENTRO CULTURAL (page 171)

Once you and the students have completed the **Para pensar** questions, continue with a class discussion related to the following: **¿Qué comidas latinoamericanas has probado** (have you tried)?

Describe cómo preparar tu comida favorita de Latinoamérica. At this point you can ask several students who know how to prepare a Latin American dish to instruct their classmates on the preparation of their dish(es). The classmates write down the instructions, which they can then take home and try. Then they can report back to the class on how successful they were and if they liked what they made.

ESTRUCTURA I Making comparisons: comparatives and superlatives (pages 172–174)

Point out to students that comparisons are used more frequently than we imagine and that there are two types thereof: comparisons of inequality when something is more or less than something else and those of equality, where there is no difference between the two or more items. Comparisons can be made between nouns, adjectives, verbs, and adverbs, and although most items follow the established rules, there are a few irregularities, especially among adjectives and adverbs that must be memorized. The term *superlative* by definition indicates "the (adjective) + *est*" or "the most/least + adjective."

Comparisons function exactly the same way in Spanish as they do in English once students have assimilated the formula for their formation. Ask students to recall how adjectives are compared. Then all you need to do is explain that the superlative is formed by simply inserting **el/la/los/las** immediately preceding the irregular form of the adjective **(el mejor alumno, la peor amiga)** or immediately preceding the noun in front of **más/menos (los sobrinos más inteligentes, la niña menos atlética).**

Point out to your students that there is another way of expressing superlatives. If the noun class has already been established, the noun can simply be left out, as exemplified by **el más inteligente de la familia.**

¡A PRACTICAR! (page 175)

Once you are convinced that students understand the structures to be used, assign activities **6-5** and **6-6** as homework, which can be reviewed the following day.

Assign activity **6-7** to be done outside of class. You can then go over it and give students some extra practice by having them complete the activity below either individually or with a classmate of their own choosing.

Indica tus opiniones usando el superlativo. Sigue el modelo.

> MODELO: mujer / bella / mundo
> *Madonna es la mujer más/menos bella del mundo.*

1. actor / guapo / cine americano
2. estudiante / inteligente / clase
3. atleta / bajo / de la liga de básquetbol

4. músico /talentoso / Latinoamérica
5. libro / largo / literatura
6. plato / picante / restaurante
7. postre / delicioso / mundo
8. lanzador / bueno / liga de béisbol
9. bailarín (bailarina) / mal / salsa

EN VOZ ALTA (page 176)

Pair students and have them do activities **6-8** and **6-9**. Then, paired with the same classmate, ask them to continue with the following activity.

Hazle preguntas a un(a) compañero(a). Luego contéstale sus preguntas.

1. ¿Quién es más sano, tú o tu hermano?
2. ¿Quién es más inteligente, tú o el (la) profesor(a)?
3. ¿Qué hablas mejor, español o inglés?
4. ¿Es tu mamá mayor o menor que tu papá?
5. ¿Tienes más o menos dinero que los Kennedys?
6. ¿Quién es más guapo, Ricky Martin o Francisco Franco?
7. ¿Quién es menos gorda, Gloria Estéfan o Rosie Pérez?
8. ¿Bailas mejor que Gloria Estéfan?
9. ¿Cantas tan bien como Jennifer López?
10. ¿Eres tan buen actor como Salma Hayek?
11. ¿Hablas tan rápido en español como en inglés?
12. ¿Comes tanto en el verano como en el invierno?

After completing activity **6-10,** place students in pairs or groups of three persons to carry out the following survey. To round out the activity, students can report and compare the information they have gathered.

Habla con un(a) compañero(a). Pregúntale sus opiniones sobre algunas personas famosas del mundo hispano. Por ejemplo: ¿Quién es la mejor actriz del cine mexicano? ¿Cuál es la peor película de este año? ¿Cuál es el restaurante más caro de la ciudad? ¿Cuál es el plato más sabroso de ese restaurante?, etc.

VOCABULARIO El restaurante (page 177)

Another way of saying *I'm on a diet.* is **Estoy guardando la línea (guardar la línea).**, literally meaning *I'm keeping the line.*

¡A PRACTICAR! (page 178)

After students have completed activities **6-11** and **6-12** outside the classroom, go over them to make sure that everyone understands the appropriateness of the responses given. If you feel your students need some additional practice, assign the following activity, which allows them to use the language creatively.

Completa el diálogo de manera apropiada, usando la escena en el restaurante El Criollito de guía.

EL CAMARERO: ¿Qué les apetece?

EL CLIENTE: _____

EL CAMARERO: Por supuesto. Vuelvo enseguida.

EL CLIENTE: _____

EL CAMARERO: ¡Cómo no! Siempre tenemos mariscos frescos. Hoy, el pescado está buenísimo.

EL CLIENTE: _____

EL CAMARERO: ¡Excelente selección! Es la especialidad de la casa. ¿Desean algo para beber?

EL CLIENTE: _____

EL CAMARERO: ¿Algo para picar?

EL CLIENTE: _____

EL CAMARERO: Aquí tienen.

EL CLIENTE: Gracias. ¡Está delicioso! Ud. tiene razón.

EL CAMARERO: ¿Desea algo de postre? Aquí está la lista.

EL CLIENTE: _____

Sólo la cuenta, por favor.

EL CAMARERO: _____

EL CLIENTE: El servicio es muy bueno aquí.

EL CAMARERO: Muchas gracias. Feliz día.

ENCUENTRO CULTURAL (page 179)

If you have a media center available with Internet connections, ask students to go to one of Venezuela's main cities and find a newspaper site. (Rather than having everyone go to a Venezuelan site, each can choose a country whose food they would like to try.) Then ask them to find the "Restaurant/Eating Out" section. Find a restaurant ad or menu that intrigues them, read the article, write a short report/description, and then share it with the class. This can be done as a homework assignment and both the oral presentation and written portion can be graded, either by you or classmates. These "reports" can also be used as a jumping off point for further discussions about how foods are similar and different in different places in Latin America. This makes the final stage a truly international experience!

ESTRUCTURA II Describing past events: regular verbs and verbs with spelling changes in the preterite (pages 180–181)

Emphasize to students that the **-er** and **-ir** verbs whose stem ends in a vowel change the **i** of the verb ending to a **y** in the third-person singular and plural forms; otherwise a tripthong (a series of three vowels) would be created. This is an extremely rare situation in Spanish.

creer → **cre + ió** → **creió** → **creyó**   **cre + ieron** → **creieron** → **creyeron**
huir → **hu + ió** → **huió** → **huyó**   **hu + ieron** → **huieron** → **huyeron**

Also point out to your students that the preterite tense is the only one in which the **tú** form does NOT end in the letter **s**. Many native speakers, by analogy, add a verb-final **s** to these verb forms, which pedagogically is incorrect. We strongly urge you to immediately correct any **s** additions your students make *before* they fossilize and become a permanent (and incorrect) characteristic of their Spanish.

¡A PRACTICAR! (page 182)

Assign activities **6-15, 6-16,** and **6-17** to be completed at home. Go over the activities and write the verb forms on the board while stressing the use of *required* written accent marks to make sure that all students realize the importance of correct orthography. Remind them that written accents are an integral part of written language! Once you have completed a class review of the activities, you might want to give the students some additional work. In preparation for **En voz alta,** have them complete the following activity. **Anoche saliste a cenar en tu restaurante favorito con tu novio(a). Hoy hablas con un(a) amigo(a) para contarle sobre la cita. Escribe la lista de verbos que necesitas para hacerlo.**

EN VOZ ALTA (page 183)

This is an immediate follow-up to the previous activity. Therefore, do the following activity immediately prior to having students complete those found in the text. Another option is to ignore the **¡A practicar!** activity and include it as part of this next activity. Of course, you can always choose to not use them at all.

> Ahora, usando la lista anterior, cuéntale a tu compañero(a) sobre tu cita. Algunas sugerencias de temas para incluir son: dónde comieron, qué comieron, a qué hora salieron, cómo viajaron, qué bebieron, si comieron postre, qué pasó después de la cena, etc.

As a continuation of this theme, have students write a short composition (paragraph) about their date, which can be turned in after some peer editing.

ESTRUCTURA III Giving detailed descriptions about past events: verbs with stem changes in the preterite (page 184)

Begin this section by telling students that you have some good news and some bad news. The bad news is that there is a group of verbs that are irregular because they require changes to their stem rather than using irregular endings or changing completely. The members of the group must be memorized because they carry no visible signs of their oddity. The good news is that there are only three patterns of change that they follow, so that there are only three types of changes to memorize: **e → ie, o → ue,** and **e → i.** However, also point out that there is one verb in Spanish that follows a fourth pattern: **u → ue,** with **jugar.** But even this exception to the rule follows the stress pattern.

¡OJO! Point out to students that the stems that change are those where the phonetic stress falls on the stem, which accounts for the fact that the **nosotros** and **vosotros** forms maintain the root of the infinitive. The reason for these changes can be traced back to the language's Latin roots and the type of vowel found in the stem.

¡A PRACTICAR! (page 185)

Activities **6-21** and **6-22** can be written outside of class. The next activity can either be done as a handout (in or out of class) or as an overhead.

Escoge el verbo apropiado y pon la forma correcta del pretérito en el espacio en blanco adecuado.

reír(se)   sonreír(se)   morir(se)

1. Anoche les conté un chiste *(joke)* a varios amigos. Iván _____ de risa porque pensó

   que era *(was)* muy divertido. José _____ porque le gusta cualquier chiste. Jacinto,

   ni siquiera *(not even)* _____ porque a él no le gustó. ¡No tiene sentido de humor!

conseguir   decir   despedir   pedir

2. El jefe _____ a mi amiga Laura. Ella _____ una oportunidad de

   trabajar allí otra vez pero el jefe le _____ que no. Sin embargo *(Nevertheless)*, ella

   _____ un nuevo trabajo en otra oficina.

dormir(se)   poner(se)   preferir   sugerir   vestir(se)

3. A mi hermano mayor le gusta trabajar afuera. Por eso buscó otra manera de ganar dinero.

   Anoche _____ temprano y se levantó antes de las seis. Se duchó inmediatamente y

   luego _____ jeans y camiseta. Porque yo _____ llevar algo más formal,

   él _____ otra vez. Ofrecí llevarlo a la agencia pero él _____ tomar el

   autobús.

divertir(se)   sentir(se)   servir

4. El sábado por la noche Carlota salió con su novio. Los dos _____ mucho. Cuando

   Carlota se levantó el domingo, _____ terrible. Mamá le _____ una taza

   de té con limón y varias aspirinas.

SÍNTESIS

Finish up this chapter's work by pairing students to complete this extended project, which brings together much of the material presented therein.

Escoge a un(a) compañero(a) de tu clase con quien trabajar en este proyecto según el contexto que se explica a continuación.

> Acabas de ganarte la lotería y ahora tienes 13 millones de dólares. Decides dejar la universidad y establecer tu propio restaurante porque eres un(a) magnífico(a) cocinero(a). Tu mejor amigo(a) también es un(a) excelente cocinero(a) además de *(in addition to)* ser un buen(a) hombre/mujer de negocios. Ahora ustedes están haciendo planes para el restaurante.

Paso 1: Llama a tu compañero(a) por teléfono para contarle qué pasó y la decisión que tomaste. Necesitas saber si está interesado(a).

Paso 2: Él/Ella dice que es una tremenda idea, así que deciden juntarse para discutir el proyecto. Van al café cerca de la universidad y ahora tú hablas cara a cara con él/ella para decidir qué tipo de restaurante van a establecer y su nombre, dónde van a abrir el restaurante, qué necesitan para el restaurante, etc.

Paso 3: Hagan una lista de lo que necesitan para hablar con las personas que van a contratar y escriban una carta modelo que pueden mandar a todas estas personas.

Paso 4: Decidan lo que van a servir y diseñen *(design)* el menú. Estén seguros de revisar que todo esté correctamente escrito *(written)* para luego mandarlo a la imprenta *(the printer)*.

Paso 5: Hagan una lista de la comida que necesitan para el estreno del restaurante. Escriban un anuncio para mandar al periódico para tener muchos clientes esa primera noche.

This series of activities integrates all four skills as well as the grammar structures and vocabulary found in the chapter. Some of the work can be done in class, other parts can be done as homework assignments. It is a good idea to have the students turn in their work on this type of work after a weekend so that they have plenty of time to work on it.

7 De compras: Argentina

CHAPTER OPENER (page 196)

Ask students to describe what they see in the photograph of the plaza in Buenos Aires. How does the plaza differ from those that they have already seen? What does it have in common with them? How is the culture of this particular city/country and its history reflected in the plaza?

Personalize the material by asking students what aspects of the scene are familiar to them and which ones differ from the area(s) where they generally shop. In Spanish ask such things as: **Generalmente, ¿dónde compras la ropa? ¿En qué tipo de tienda prefieres comprar los zapatos y otros accesorios? ¿Con quién te gusta ir de compras? ¿Con qué frecuencia hacen ustedes esto? ¿Cuánto dinero gastas? ¿Cómo pagas las compras? ¿Es tu dinero o el dinero de tus padres?**

VOCABULARIO La ropa (page 198)

To introduce clothing vocabulary ask students to jot down key words that they associate with fashion and the types of clothes that they wear.

¿NOS ENTENDEMOS? (page 198)

In some Latin American countries, **la cartera,** together with **la bolsa/el bolso,** refers to a woman's purse. In many Latin American areas, the word for jeans is **los vaqueros. La sombrilla** and **el paraguas** are used interchangeably by many although they technically do not mean the same thing. **La sombrilla** is the equivalent of a parasol or a beach umbrella, originating with the word **sombra** *(shadow),* which is exactly what it provides! **El paraguas,** of course, stops **(para)** water/ rain **(aguas).** In some areas of Latin America, especially Central America, rather than **la chaqueta, el saco** is used for a jacket.

¡A PRACTICAR! (page 199)

Assign all activities for homework so that class time can be devoted to oral activities. If students have any doubts or questions, they can feel free to ask them at this point.

EN VOZ ALTA (page 199)

Instead of or in addition to activities **7-3, 7-3,** and **7-5,** the following activity can be included.

Choose a classmate whom you don't know well and ask her/him the following questions about her/his wardrobe and favorite clothes. Then, change roles.

La ropa favorita: ¿Qué ropa llevas/usas/vistes cuando...

1. vas a una fiesta con un grupo de amigos?
2. vas a un baile formal?
3. trabajas en la oficina después de tus clases?
4. asistes a clases en la universidad?
5. viajas en avión *(airplane)*?
6. sales a bailar con tu novio(a) a una discoteca?

EN CONTEXTO (page 200)

With the books closed, ask students to listen to the dialog, which is followed by activity ¿**Comprendiste?** Then have them read the questions in the activity and once again, without looking at the dialog, listen for the answers to the questions asked. You can help students by making an overhead of the questions in the activity so that their books can remain closed. They can jot down key words they hear in order to be able to appropriately answer.

ASÍ SE DICE Making emphatic statements: stressed possessive adjectives and pronouns (page 202)

Take the time to review the initial presentation on possessives in **Capítulo 2,** before beginning this in-class presentation.

¡A PRACTICAR! (page 203)

Activities **7-7** and **7-8** can be assigned for homework. If you want a simple written activity to use in class, either hand out the following or put it on an overhead and do as a class activity.

MODELO: ¿Es el traje de Pedro?
Sí (No), (no) es el traje suyo.

1. los zapatos de Susana
2. mi traje de baño
3. la bufanda de nosotros
4. las faldas de ustedes
5. tus vestidos
6. las chaquetas de ustedes
7. los jeans de usted
8. los calcetines de los niños
9. el sombrero de mi papá
10. las gafas de sol de Isabel y Marta

ESTRUCTURA I Talking about singular and/or completed events in the past: verbs irregular in the preterite (page 204)

¡OJO! You might want to include one set of verbs that is not included in the group because of the small number, although the verbs are commonly used: verbs ending in **-ucir** such as **conducir** *(to drive)* and **traducir** *(to translate)* form their past tense forms by following the pattern of **decir: conduje, condujiste, condujo, condujimos, condujisteis, condujeron,** and likewise for **traducir.**

¡OJO! The change from **c** to **z** in **hizo** occurs as a phonological rule, simply to maintain consistency of sound. Remind your students that writing reflects speech, not vice versa.

¡OJO! With verbs of communication, in the preterite, **tener** means *received* as in **Tuve carta de Manuel ayer.** *(I received a letter from Manuel yesterday.).*

¡OJO! Remind students that **conocer** in the preterite means *met* not *knew* or *was acquainted with.*

¡A PRACTICAR! (page 205)

Activities **7-10** and **7-11** can be done outside of class, and the activity below can either be substituted or used in addition to them.

Contesta las siguientes preguntas en oraciones completas en el pretérito.

1. ¿Cuándo fue la última vez que fuiste de compras?
2. ¿Quién fue contigo y adónde fueron?
3. ¿Qué compraste? Y tu amigo(a), ¿qué compró?
4. ¿Gastaron mucho dinero?
5. ¿Cómo pagaste las compras *(purchases)*?
6. ¿Encontraste muchas gangas *(bargains)*?
7. ¿Te probaste mucha ropa?
8. ¿Por qué decidiste no comprar más?
9. ¿Qué hicieron cuando terminaron de comprar?
10. ¿Cuánto tiempo estuvieron en las tiendas?

EN VOZ ALTA (page 206)

The following activity can be done by students either after activities **7-12** and **7-13,** or can be substituted for any or both of them. Ask students to create any one or all of these dialogs (situations) with one or more classmates. Advise them that they will be presenting the scenes to their classmates.

Situaciones: Escriban un diálogo para las siguientes escenas.

1. La dependienta y una clienta que busca un suéter azul de lana para ella.
2. Un joven y su novia en busca de una camisa y una corbata, poque él va a conocer a los padres de ella por primera vez.
3. Una chica y su madre están comprando ropa para una fiesta de cumpleaños para la chica.
4. Dos amigos(as) necesitan comprar un regalo para un(a) amigo(a) de ambos, pero no tienen ni idea de lo que quieren.
5. Dos hermanos quieren comprar un regalo para el aniversario de bodas de sus padres.

VOCABULARIO De compras (page 207)

Throughout this chapter, stress the aspects about shopping that both the American and Latin/Spanish cultures have in common. Then point out how they differ, but always focusing on the *positive* aspects of both.

¡OJO! In some parts of the Spanish-speaking world **el dependiente** becomes **la dependienta** when the clerk is a female. The same applies to **el cliente (la clienta). En efectivo** and **al contado** are used when paying *(in) cash.*

¡A PRACTICAR! (page 208)

Activity **7-14** can be assigned for homework while giving students the opportunity to ask questions when they come to class. The activity that follows can also be used to practice vocabulary.

Escoge el término que no debe estar con los demás. Luego, explica por qué.

el cheque	el efectivo	el descuento	la tarjeta de crédito
el porcentaje	la talla	el número	el tamaño
ponerse	probarse	usar	llevar
el descuento	la rebaja	la ganga	el número
costar	hacer juego	pagar	gastar
quedarle a uno	probarse	hacer juego	rebajar

EN VOZ ALTA (pages 208–209)

The following activity can be used to round out activities **7-15, 7-16,** and **7-17.**

Acabas de recibir una invitación a una cena y fiesta en la embajada argentina el sábado por la noche. Es una ocasión importante y especial, y por eso visitas una boutique exclusiva donde venden todo lo necesario para festividades de este tipo. Con un(a) compañero(a) haciendo el papel del (de la) dependiente, selecciona la ropa y accesorios apropiados. Luego, cambien los papeles.

ENCUENTRO CULTURAL (page 210)

To get things started and students thinking about the subject of the **Encuentro cultural,** have students comment on: **¿Qué piensas del tango? ¿Qué sientes cuando lo escuchas o cuando ves bailar a dos personas? ¿Hay algún baile americano que sea similar? Explica tus sentimientos sobre el tema.**

ESTRUCTURA II Simplifying expressions: direct object pronouns (pages 211–212)

¡OJO! Stress to your students that when direct object nouns are replaced with pronouns, all elements of the noun phrase must be eliminated. Thus, if the noun is modified and/or is accompanied by the personal **a,** modifiers and personal **a** are subsumed under the pronoun.

¡OJO! Lo is the *neuter* direct object pronoun and also replaces abstractions.

¡A PRACTICAR! (pages 212–213)

Activities **7-18** and **7-19** should be done outside of class and reviewed in class. The activity below provides additional practice in a concept that more often than not causes great consternation and confusion.

Paso 1: Subraya el objeto (complemento) directo.

1. ¿Compraste ropa la semana pasada?
2. ¿Dónde compraste los zapatos de tenis?
3. ¿Hubo rebajas?
4. ¿Cómo pagaste las gangas?
5. ¿Por qué no pagaste las compras con tu propio (*own*) cheque?
6. ¿Quién te manejó el carro al centro?
7. ¿Quién invitó a ti y a tu amigo(a) a comer?
8. ¿Escogiste un regalo para tu mamá o para algún otro pariente?

Paso 2: Contesta las preguntas cambiando el sustantivo de complemento directo al pronombre correcto.

Paso 3: Haz las preguntas oralmente a un(a) compañero(a) y luego, contéstale, usando pronombres de complemento directo.

Use **Paso 3** as an activity for the **En voz alta** portion of the chapter, either in addition to or instead of activity **7-20.**

ESTRUCTURA III Describing ongoing and habitual actions in the past: the imperfect tense (pages 214–215)

The imperfect tense focuses on the center of the action expressed, rather than on the beginning or end points of the action.

¡A PRACTICAR! (page 216)

Activities **7-21, 7-22,** and **7-23,** can be supplemented by the activity below.

Contesta las siguientes preguntas, empleando el pretérito o el imperfecto según convenga.

1. ¿Dónde vivías antes de asistir a la universidad?
2. ¿Te gustaron las clases en la secundaria?
3. ¿Estudiabas mucho y salías a jugar con tus amigos?
4. ¿Cómo se divertían ustedes?
5. ¿Qué hacía tu familia los sábados por la tarde?
6. ¿Adónde iban de compras?
7. ¿Quién pagó la ropa que compraste para tu graduación?
8. ¿Trabajaste por algún tiempo para ahorrar *(save)* dinero por alguna razón?
9. ¿Qué hiciste? ¿Dónde trabajaste?
10. ¿Te pagaron bien? ¿Cómo gastabas el dinero que te pagaban?

EN VOZ ALTA (page 217)

In addition to or instead of activities **7-24, 7-25,** and **7-26** found in the text, the following is offered for oral-aural practice.

Tú eres un(a) reportero(a) para una revista que publica entrevistas con personas de fama internacional acerca de su niñez y cómo llegaron a ser famosas. Con un(a) compañero(a), haz la entrevista, luego cambien de papel. Pueden escoger a personas latinas, ya sean del mundo del cine, del arte, de la música o de la política. Algunas sugerencias: Jennifer López, Enrique Iglesias, la reina Sofía de España, Ricky Martin, Carlos Santana, el Duque, Sammy Sosa, etc.

SÍNTESIS

Have students complete the following as a final synthesizing activity to finish the chapter.

Tú y tu prima de seis años y sus dos hermanos están hablando de tu niñez y de lo que hacías cuando tú eras de su edad. Por eso les cuentas cómo tú y tu mamá iban de compras a las diferentes boutiques. Puedes también contarles de las excursiones al centro comercial con tus amigo(a)s. Debes contestar todas las preguntas que te hacen tus primitos sobre las modas de aquel tiempo.

Place students in groups of three or four to work on the dialogs.

Paso 1: Compartir pareceres y organizar el orden de los temas. Escribir palabras y frases clave *(key)*.

Paso 2: Practicar el diálogo. Volver a escribirlo para hacerlo mejor. Puede ser chistoso *(humorous)*, extraño *(strange)* o «normal».

Paso 3: Cambiar de papel y volver a escribir las partes que necesiten cambios.

Paso 4: Decidir cuál versión es mejor y presentar la escena a la clase.

Paso 5: Pedirles sugerencias a los compañeros. Volver a escribir la escena, incorporando los cambios.

Paso 6: Entregar para recibir una nota.

8 Fiestas y vacaciones: Guatemala y El Salvador

CHAPTER OPENER (pages 224–225)

Start class discussion by asking students: **¿Qué asocias con procesiones y desfiles? ¿Los asocias con festivales y fiestas religiosas? ¿En qué piensas cuando ves gente con disfraces? ¿Con qué o con quiénes los asocias?**

VOCABULARIO Fiestas y celebraciones (page 226)

To introduce celebration and festival vocabulary, ask students to jot down words that the opening pictures bring to mind and to describe what experiences they have had with various types of festivities.

¡OJO! You might point out to the class that many people simply eliminate **día** from **el día feriado** to refer to holidays. Another word for **¡Felicitaciones!** is **¡Enhorabuena!** when congratulating someone.

¿NOS ENTENDEMOS? (page 226)

Point out to your students that **las velas** means **las candelas** and **los entremeses** means **las boquitas** in Central America. Also, **los cohetes** not only means fireworks, but firecrackers as well. A synonym for **pasarlo bien** is **divertirse**.

¡A PRACTICAR! (page 227)

Activities **8-1** and **8-2** can be assigned for homework and supplemented with the activity presented below.

Selecciona la definición o sinónimo de la Columna B que corresponda a la palabra o frase de la Columna A.

Columna A	Columna B
el día del santo	**a.** la procesión
pasarlo bien	**b.** un segundo cumpleaños
el desfile	**c.** tener miedo
disfrazarse	**d.** las personas que vienen a una fiesta
los invitados	**e.** divertirse
el anfitrión	**f.** festejar
gritar	**g.** ponerse ropa diferente para que no lo puedan reconocer
los regalos	**h.** cosas que los invitados llevan a una fiesta de cumpleaños
celebrar	**i.** la persona que da o hace la fiesta
asustarse	**j.** hablar en voz alta y fuerte

EN VOZ ALTA (page 228)

Activities **8-3** and **8-4** may be replaced, mixed with, and/or supplemented by the following activity.

El día de tu cumpleaños Pregúntale a tu compañero(a) y luego cuéntale a la clase la información.

1. ¿Cuándo es tu cumpleaños?
2. ¿Cómo lo celebraste este año o el año pasado?
3. ¿Cómo celebra tu familia los cumpleaños de los niños y los adultos? ¿Hacen algo especial con lo que se identifiquen los miembros de la familia?
4. ¿Qué hay de especial en la manera como tu familia celebra ocasiones religiosas o fiestas nacionales?
5. ¿Cómo han cambiado (*have changed*) estas celebraciones desde tu niñez?
6. ¿Celebran tus amigos los cumpleaños, o las fiestas religiosas o seculares de una manera distinta a la de tu familia? Favor dar ejemplos para explicar.
7. ¿Cómo difieren las celebraciones de los Estados Unidos a las de Centro América? Explica.
8. ¿Qué opinas de las fiestas sorpresas?

EN CONTEXTO (page 229)

Have students look at the questions below and take notes that apply as they listen to the Student Text Audio CD. Ask them to keep their books closed.

1. ¿Sabían Tomás y Marta que Bienvenida iba a visitarlos?
2. ¿Cómo llegó la madre a Chichicastenango?
3. Más o menos, ¿cuándo llegó Bienvenida a Chichi?
4. ¿Por qué no fue Tomás a la estación a buscar a su mamá?
5. ¿Qué tiempo hacía ese día?
6. ¿Qué hacían los jóvenes cuando telefoneó la madre?
7. ¿Por qué fue de visita la madre?
8. ¿Qué ocurrió en el camino a la casa de Tomás? ¿Cuál fue la causa del evento?
9. ¿Cuánto tiempo llevó el viaje a la casa de Tomás y Marta?
10. ¿Cómo se saludaron los familiares?

ENCUENTRO CULTURAL (page 230)

The *Popol Vuh* is considered the Bible of the Maya people, wherein the birth of their civilization is described. It also enumerates their many gods, always based on nature and its varied aspects. Together with the *Chilam B'alam,* a collection of children's stories and songs, they are the only books that the Spanish clergy were not able to completely destroy.

In addition to the questions provided in **Para discutir,** add: **¿Por qué es importante el monasterio de Santo Domingo? ¿Dónde se encuentra el monasterio? Explica lo que es el *Popol Vuh*.**

You can also add the following to the questions posed in the **Para pensar** section: **¿Qué opinas de la mezcla del catolicismo con el paganismo maya? ¿Por qué crees que ocurrió eso tan fácilmente? ¿Por qué no pasó lo mismo con los indígenas de los Estados Unidos? Explica.**

ASÍ SE DICE Inquiring and providing information about people and events: interrogative words (page 231)

Introduce this section by recycling the interrogative words that were learned in the previous chapters. Have students use the words to ask their classmates questions with five different interrogatives. If you assign five of them to each group of three or four students, you should be able to cover all of those presented and their various forms. Students should be encouraged not to employ the same questions as those in the text but to create their own.

¡A PRACTICAR! (page 232)

Activities **8-6** and **8-7** can be assigned for completion outside class. Ask students to complete the Jeopardy-like activities presented below. This can be given out as a handout, copied onto an overhead, or even be done orally. If the last option is chosen, it can be done as part of the next section, **En voz alta.**

La respuesta es la pregunta, y la pregunta es la respuesta.

1. Prefiero las montañas a la playa.
2. Fui a la costa pacífica de El Salvador.
3. Chichicastenango está al noroeste de la Ciudad de Guatemala.
4. No somos de Chichicastenango. Somos de la capital.
5. El santo patrón de El Salvador es el salvador del mundo.
6. Las Fiestas Agostinas se celebran del 1 al 6 de agosto.
7. La capital de El Salvador es San Salvador.
8. Una pupusa es una arepa salvadoreña.
9. Los indígenas queman incienso enfrente de la catedral.
10. El *Popol Vuh* es el libro sagrado de los mayas.
11. La pesca, el buceo y la natación son deportes acuáticos.
12. Eso es una cámara.
13. Los juegos artificiales empiezan a las nueve.
14. Mi lago favorito de Guatemala es el Lago de Atitlán.
15. Mi bebida favorita guatemalteca es el atol de elote.

ESTRUCTURA I Narrating in the past: the preterite vs. the imperfect (pages 233–234)

Begin this section by writing two simple sentences on the board in the present tense whose context specifies which past tense you will employ when transferred into the past. Here are some examples:

Mi abuelo **viene** a vernos en junio.	*My grandfather comes to see us in June.*
Mi abuelo todavía **tiene** pulmonía.	*My grandfather still has pneumonia.*
Mi abuelo **vino** a vernos en junio.	*My grandfather came to see us in June.*
Mi abuelo todavía **tenía** pulmonía.	*My grandfather still had pneumonia.*

Point out to your students that the first sentence shows an action that is being reported—*grandfather comes to see us*—while the second describes his state of health—*he has pneumonia.* Thus, when moved to the past, the first sentence takes the preterite tense since he came and went (the action began and ended in the past) while the second tells us that he remains ill since it includes the adverb *still* **(todavía).** This means that the action that began in the past continues into the present and cannot be considered completed.

¡OJO! Help your students remember the essential differences between the two tenses under study by informing them that the preterite is the tense for reporting and the imperfect the tense for describing.

When you get to the section dealing with the use of both tenses within the same sentence, you can use the following as another way of explaining the combination of tenses: Coordinated actions in complex sentences (a main clause and a dependent clause) appear in the same tense *if* both actions began and ended concurrently. Examples:

Reporting: **Pablo estudió mientras (que) su novia preparó la comida.**
Describing: **Pablo hablaba mientras (que) su novia preparaba la comida.**

When the actions do not last the same amount of time, the action that began before the other (was in progress when the other began) uses the imperfect tense while the action that interrupts it (cuts across it) uses the preterite tense. Rather than employing **mientras** as above, these sentences employ **cuando.**

Pablo preparaba la cena cuando sonó el teléfono.

Point out to your students that native speakers tend to invert the order of the subject and verb in the dependent clause (following **cuando**).

¡A PRACTICAR! (page 235)

Do activity **8-9** as a class so that you can make sure the students understand the functional difference(s) between the two past tenses. However, once you've started them off by doing the first few examples of activity **8-10**, the remainder of **8-10** and **8-11** can be completed for homework. If you find that your students need additional practice, try the next activity.

_____ (Ser) el 24 de diciembre y Sara _____ (ir) a visitar a sus parientes en

Cobán, un pequeño pueblo en las montañas de Guatemala. Ella _____ (decidir) ir

porque también _____ (ser) el cumpleaños de su abuela, que _____ (cumplir)

92 años. El año pasado _____ (haber) una gran fiesta y toda la familia _____

(estar) presente. Todos _____ (divertirse) inmensamente. _____ (Comer)

chuchitos, paches y tamales, y los niños _____ (beber) agua de canela y atol(e) de elote

mientras los adultos _____ (tomar) unos tragos para brindar por la abuelita. Sara

_____ (bailar) con su amigo Sergio toda la noche. Ella _____ (darse) cuenta

que Sergio la _____ (amar), pero para ella él sólo _____ (poder) ser amigo.

Poco después, ella _____ (conocer) a Ramón, y los dos _____ (enamorarse)

en el momento que _____ (verse). Los dos _____ (pasar) todo su tiempo libre

juntos. Sara _____ (ir) a contarle la buena noticia a la familia: ella y Ramón _____ (ir) a

casarse en febrero. ¡Qué regalo tan bueno para la abuelita!

EN VOZ ALTA (page 236)

Follow up activities **8-12, 8-13,** and **8-14** with an activity called **Chismes.** Ask one of your students to begin telling a story by telling her/his classmates the opening sentence of the narration while you write it on the board or on an overhead. Then, the chosen individual selects the person to compose and say aloud the next sentence. Continue this same procedure until the story is completed or time runs out. There are only two rules: (1) the story must have a holiday or celebration theme, and (2) it must be recounted in the past tense. Once the story is written, the group can go about correcting it. As an alternative, the proceedings can be recorded rather than written down and then played back for the class. This can be quite entertaining as well as enlightening!

VOCABULARIO La playa y el campo (page 237)

Begin your introduction to the vocabulary presented in this section by asking students a few questions about their likes and dislikes. For example:

1. ¿Te gusta nadar? (Si te gusta nadar debes ir al mar durante el verano. Allí puedes bucear y hasta pasear en velero si quieres. Pues, debes ir al campo a la finca de mi tío Raúl. Hay varios lagos allí.) (Si te gusta nadar, pues si vas al campo, en la finca de mi tío Raúl puedes pescar en sus lagos o en el río. También puedes montar a caballo o pasear por el bosque y respirar aire puro.)
2. ¿Prefieres tomar el sol a pasear en canoa o caminar por las montañas? (Pues, si te gusta broncearte y tomar el sol, debes pasar el fin de semana en las lindas playas de arena negra en las costas de Guatemala. La arena no es blanca como en los Estados Unidos. Es arena volcánica, ¡por eso es negra!) (Si quieres pasear en canoa o caminar por las montañas, El Salvador tiene ríos muy navegables y muchos picos que son la envidia de muchos países europeos.)

¡A PRACTICAR! (pages 237–238)

Activities **8-15** and **8-16** can be assigned as homework and followed by answering these questions in writing.

1. Escribe cinco actividades que hicieron los turistas el año pasado en la playa.
2. Escribe cinco actividades que muchas personas hicieron durante las vacaciones en las montañas.
3. ¿En cuáles de esas actividades participaste durante las vacaciones que tomaste durante los últimos dos o tres años? ¿Por qué?

EN VOZ ALTA (page 238)

Activities **8-17** and **8-18** can be continued with or replaced by:

Tu amigo(a) sabe que fuiste de vacaciones a Guatemala y El Salvador el año pasado.

Ahora él (ella) quiere visitar los mismos sitios. Ustedes se reúnen en un café para compartir la información. Él (Ella) te hace las preguntas y tú le respondes. Luego cambien de papel y, tú le haces las preguntas a tu amigo(a).

ESTRUCTURA II Stating indefinite ideas and quantities: affirmative and negative expressions (pages 240–241)

Ask students to read over this section before presenting it in class. Since everyone employs indefinite and negative expressions in her/his everyday life, a successful technique for presenting the material is a question-and-answer activity such as the following. Ask **¿Hay algo en mi mano?** as you show the class your empty hand. Students will probably respond with **No** or a similar negative answer. This is your cue to inform them that, **No, no hay** *nada* **en mi mano,** as you write the negative word on the board across from **algo,** which you have also placed on the board, each under a suitable heading such as **expresiones indefinidas** and **expresiones negativas.**

Continue with **¿Hay alguien en la silla?** as you point to an empty chair. Again, students should respond negatively. Again, you explain, **No hay** *nadie* **en la silla,** placing the appropriate indefinite and negative words under the headings on the board. Continue cueing your students as you progress through the list of expressions. If they have looked at the list prior to their arrival in class, things should go smoothly.

¡OJO! Inform students that there is another word for *never:* **jamás.**

¡OJO! Impress upon your students the fact that in Spanish double negatives are not only perfectly acceptable, but required. There must be one negative word *before* the *conjugated* verb and another *after* it. *No* **hay** *nadie* **en casa hoy.**

¡OJO! **Ninguno(a)** can also be used as a pronoun by omitting the noun: **No quiere ninguna fruta. No quiere ninguna.**

¡A PRACTICAR! (page 242)

Activities **8-19, 8-20,** and **8-21** can be done for homework, followed by the following activity.

Tu amigo Paco siempre les contradice a todos. Completa el diálogo con los comentarios de Paco, que siempre son lo opuesto a lo que tú dices.

TÚ: Siempre comemos pupusas cuando estamos en El Salvador.

PACO: _____

TÚ: Cuando estuve allí hace un mes, no hice nada emocionante.

PACO: _____

TÚ: Tampoco pude ir al balneario con mis amigos.

PACO: _____

TÚ: Pero logré (pude) escuchar algunas bandas típicas en San Salvador.

PACO: _____

TÚ: Había alguien a mi lado que me acompañó a todas partes.

PACO: _____

TÚ: No tuve ni tiempo para ir al mercado ni para ir a la feria.

PACO: _____

EN VOZ ALTA (page 243)

Begin with activities **8-22** and **8-23** and finish up with the prompts below.

1. ¿Qué fiesta te gusta mucho?
2. ¿A qué festivales te gusta asistir siempre?
3. ¿Pruebas comidas o bebidas latinoamericanas cuando tienes la oportunidad?
4. ¿A qué músico latino guapo (cantante latina bonita) que deseas conocer?
5. ¿Te gusta la música latina? ¿Te gustan los bailes latinos también? Explica.

ASÍ SE DICE Talking about periods of time since an event took place: *hace* and *hace que* (page 244)

The phrase **hace** + time period + **que** has two functions when translated into English. When the verb appears in the present tense **(Hace cinco años que Carolina estudia flamenco.)**, it indicates that Carolina has been studying flamenco dance for five years. Yet when the tense of the main verb is changed to the preterite **(Hace cinco años que Carolina estudió flamenco.),** the indication is that Carolina studied flamenco dance five years *ago* or that it has been five years *since* Carolina studied flamenco dance.

¡OJO! Note that the English equivalent of the base structure **hace** + time period + **que** uses the present perfect tense while the Spanish phrasing employs the simple present.

¡OJO! When **hacer** appears in the imperfect tense (**hacía** + **time period** + **que**), the time period moves backwards and the main verb must also appear in the imperfect tense. Thus, **Hacía cinco años que Carolina estudiaba flamenco** is translated as *Carolina had studied/had been studying flamenco dance for five years.*

SÍNTESIS

In order to bring together the four skills, the grammar points presented in the chapter, and the cultural material, we suggest the following project for small groups of students to work on together in and out of class. If they are given some class time during which to get organized and divide the project as they deem appropriate, they will find the activity both enjoyable and illuminating.

It will also allow them to see how much they are able to do with the Spanish they have learned!

Cuatro profesores de español desean llevar a un grupo de estudiantes a Guatemala y El Salvador durante las celebraciones de Semana Santa. Desean observar los festivales en Chichicastenango y en otra ciudad guatemalteca, así como también en San Salvador y en algún otro sitio salvadoreño.

En grupos de tres a cinco personas, sigan los pasos descritos a continuación. Deben incluir lo que van a hacer en cada lugar durante este viaje cultural y educativo.

Paso 1: Entren a la Red y busquen información sobre los dos sitios mencionados y dos otros que ustedes escojan *(may choose)*.

Paso 2: Organicen la información que encontraron en la Red para preparar un folleto *(pamphlet)* para informar a los estudiantes y a sus padres.

Paso 3: Discutan cómo van a escribir el folleto, porque cada miembro del grupo debe escribir una parte de él. Decidan quién va a escribir qué parte del folleto.

Paso 4: Escriban las partes individuales del folleto.

Paso 5: Revisen la escritura de los otros compañeros para sugerir cambios necesarios y corregir los errores.

Paso 6: Vuelvan a escribir el trabajo para entregarlo para recibir una nota.

De viaje por el Caribe: La República Dominicana, Cuba y Puerto Rico

VOCABULARIO Viajar en avión (page 256)

You might want to add the following verbs, which are synonyms for two already on the page but which allow students to vary their communication. **Subir a** means **abordar** and **empacar** means **hacer las maletas.** Also share with students that **viajar** *por* **avión** is used in some countries rather than **viajar** *en* **avión.** Ask students personal questions employing the vocabulary illustrated in the pictures so that they can relate it directly to their own lives and see its applicability outside the classroom environment. If this chapter falls just before or after a holiday, vacation, or long weekend, so much the better as they can talk about what they did or plan to do.

¡A PRACTICAR! (page 257)

Assign activities **9-1, 9-2,** and **9-3** for homework and only review those items on which they have questions. Or, place students in pairs or groups and have them review each other's work, consulting you only when (and if) there is disagreement or doubt. The activity that follows is suggested as a transition between ¡**A practicar!** and **En voz alta.**

Contesta las siguientes preguntas según la última vez que viajaste.

1. ¿Adónde fuiste y con quién viajaste?
2. ¿Dónde abordaste el (te subiste al) avión?
3. ¿A qué hora despegó el avión?
4. ¿Cuánto tiempo duró el vuelo? ¿Hubo escalas? ¿Cuántas?
5. ¿Dónde te sentaste, en un asiento de ventanilla o de pasillo?
6. ¿Qué sirvió la (el) asistente de vuelo para comer y beber? ¿Cómo estuvo la comida?
7. ¿A qué hora aterrizó el avión? ¿Llegó a tiempo o llegó atrasado?
8. ¿Pasaste por la aduana? ¿Qué pasó allí?
9. ¿Cómo te gustó el vuelo?

EN VOZ ALTA (page 258)

Here is an opportunity for role-playing. It requires three people, one for each of the roles, and presents a situation to really stretch!

> La famosa actriz de cine internacional, Lucía Moreno, y su esposo, el guapo cantante Benny Arias, acaban de llegar al aeropuerto de San Juan, Puerto Rico, ciudad nativa de la pareja. La agencia profesional te mandó a encontrarlos y llevarlos al hotel donde se van a quedar en un suite de lujo. Preséntate *(Introduce yourself)* y, mientras esperan las maletas y se preparan para el viaje en limusina, pregúntales acerca de su viaje por Europa y los Estados Unidos. Con dos compañeros(as), cada uno debe de hacer el papel de la actriz, el cantante y el agente personal.

EN CONTEXTO (page 259)

To check comprehension of the paragraphs presented, have students complete the following activity where they must decide whether each statement is true or false and correct those that are false.

1. Sharon y Kate son estudiantes en Santo Domingo.
2. Sharon escribe en su diario todos los días.
3. Las dos chicas visitan la Ciudad Colonial.
4. Las chicas compraron tarjetas postales para sus amigos.
5. Kate compró un anillo y aretes para Sharon.
6. Sharon sacó una foto de Kate.
7. Conocieron a una pareja *(couple)* y a sus dos hijos.
8. Kate y Sharon tomaron un café con dos chicos.
9. Uno de los chicos las invitó a una discoteca para bailar.
10. Kate cree que los dominicanos son amables.

ESTRUCTURA I Simplifying expressions: indirect object pronouns (pages 261–262)

¡OJO! Direct object pronouns show gender in the third person, singular and plural (**lo, los, la, las**), whereas indirect object pronouns show no gender, only number (**le, les**). Indirect objects and their pronouns tend to refer only to people or personalized animals and objects while direct objects and their pronouns refer both to people as well as to animals, items, and concepts. See the following examples.

1. Complementos directos (personas, objetos y conceptos):

   Veo **a mi mamá.** → **La** veo.   Veo **a los chicos.** → **Los** veo.
   Veo **la ventana.** → **La** veo.   Veo **los libros.** → **Los** veo.

2. Complementos indirectos (personas):

   Le doy el libro **a Juan.**   **Les** doy el libro **a ellos.**
   Le doy el libro **a María.**   **Les** doy el libro **a ellas.**

¡OJO! Verbs of communication are the only ones in Spanish that allow an indirect object without also requiring a direct object. All other verbs **must** have a direct object in order to have an indirect object.

¡OJO! There is a required redundancy in Spanish sentences that have an indirect object: When the noun is present, the pronoun must also be present. See the examples that follow.

Le doy el libro **a Juan.**   **Nos** presta el carro **a mi hermano y a mí.**
*Doy el libro **a Juan.**   *Presta el carro **a mi hermano y a mí.**

[The * indicates that the sentence that follows is incorrect.]

¡A PRACTICAR! (pages 263–264)

Assign activities **9-7** and **9-8** for homework. Students can work in pairs to check their answers and consult with you on those they cannot agree on or about which they have doubts. If you want to expand the practice activities or want a substitute for **9-7, 9-8,** or **9-9,** try the following two-step activity in class.

Paso 1: Por favor subraya los sustantivos que sean el complemento indirecto en cada una de las siguientes oraciones.

Paso 2: Escribe las oraciones de nuevo, reemplazando los sustantivos con el pronombre de complemento indirecto que corresponde.

1. Manny quiere dar una sorpresa a sus padres.
2. Por eso él compra a ellos unos boletos a Santo Domingo para su aniversario.
3. Ellos agradecen el viaje a su hijo.
4. Van al aeropuerto en taxi donde pagan el costo del viaje al chofer.
5. El portero recoge las maletas y ellos dan una propina a él.
6. La pareja *(couple)* va a la sala de espera donde preguntan al agente cuándo sale el avión.
7. De pronto anuncian la salida del avión y los pasajeros abordan y entregan los boletos y las maletas de mano a los asistentes de vuelo.
8. Los padres de Manny toman sus asientos y piden unas cervezas a la asistente que ofrece bebidas a ellos.
9. Los señores López están contentos y saben que su hijo dio a ellos un magnífico **regalo.**
10. También van a traer una sorpresa a mí porque yo soy su nieta favorita.

EN VOZ ALTA (page 264)

Here is an option that you might want to use to personalize the **En voz alta** activities enhancing the oral proficiency of your students.

Mi viaje Have you ever taken a trip outside the U.S.? Get together with a classmate and talk about your trip(s). To avoid repetition, be sure to use indirect and direct object pronouns when necessary or appropriate to make the conversation sound natural as you tell each other about your travels! Use the following questions as a guide for getting information.

1. Where did you go?
2. With whom did you travel?
3. What did you tell her/him to bring along?
4. What advice did your travel agent give you?
5. Did your friends give you any advice? If so, what was it?
6. Did you buy souvenirs for your family and friends?
7. What did you bring back for them?
8. Did they like the gifts?
9. Did they thank you for them? What did they say to you?
10. Do any of them bring you gifts back from their trips abroad?

Feel free to add any other questions that allow you to ask for information you want!

ESTRUCTURA II Simplifying expressions: double object pronouns (page 266)

¡OJO! The order of the direct and indirect objects shows the relationship between the verb and its object(s). The direct object has a closer connection to the verb than the indirect object does, and must, therefore, be in closer proximity. When nouns are involved, they follow the verb:

Le doy	**el libro**	**a mi hijo.**
Verb	DO	IO

When pronouns appear, they precede the conjugated verb, and the direct object must remain closest to the verb. Thus,

Se	**lo**	**doy.**
IO	DO	Verb

When attached to either the infinitive or present participle (gerund), the order remains the same, but it is moved from in front to behind the verb form.

(Se lo estoy dando.) Estoy dándoselo.

¡OJO! The accent mark is always placed before the last vowel of the infinitive or present participle.

¡A PRACTICAR! (page 267)

Assign activities **9-13** and **9-14** for homework. Review only those questions about which the students have doubts.

VOCABULARIO El hotel (page 268)

You might want to tell the students that **hacer una reserva (reservar)** means *to make a reservation at a hotel.* You might also want to indicate that **registrarse** (the reflexive form) means *to register* while **registrar** means *to search through* (as your luggage).

¡OJO! A hotel guest is called **un huésped (los huéspedes)** whereas a guest for dinner or at a party is referred to as **un invitado. Un huésped** implies an overnight guest.

Practice the vocabulary in this section by beginning with the following questions as a starting point and expanding on them.

1. Cuando viajas, ¿en qué clase de hotel te quedas?
2. ¿Qué tipo de cuarto pides?
3. ¿Con cuánta anticipación haces la reserva?
4. ¿Cómo pagas la cuenta?
5. ¿Qué tamaño de cama pides?
6. ¿En qué condición esperas encontrar tu habitación? ¿Por qué?
7. Compara tu(s) situación (situaciones) con la luna de miel de Manny y Teri.

¡A PRACTICAR! and EN VOZ ALTA (page 269)

Assign activities **9-17** and **9-18** for homework and ask students to prepare both sides of the conversation in activity **9-19,** so that you can choose any two individuals and have them perform the dialog, without the book or notes! Activity **9-20** can be prepared in class with assigned partners, or the following activity can be used in addition to or instead of it.

Cuéntale a un(a) compañero(a) alguna aventura que tuviste mientras viajabas. Puede ser algún problema y su solución, o alguna situación inesperada, tu reacción a ella y su resultado. Puedes usar las siguientes sugerencias como puntos de partida.

1. Llegaste al hotel y no había reserva en tu nombre. Tampoco había cuartos disponibles *(available)* en ese hotel. Además, los otros hoteles tampoco tenían cuartos para esa noche o para el resto de la semana. ¿Qué hiciste?
2. Tenías un boleto para viajar a _____. Al momento de abordar, la aerolínea ofreció pagarles a tres viajeros $600 y una noche en el hotel del aeropuerto por dejar *(give up)* su pasaje y volar el próximo día. Tu novia te estaba esperando en el aeropuerto al fin del viaje, pero ustedes podrían usar *(could use)* el dinero. ¿Qué hiciste?

ASÍ SE DICE Giving directions: prepositions of location, adverbs, and relevant expressions (pages 270–271)

¡OJO! La manzana generally refers to a *square block* (especially in Latin America) while **la cuadra** indicates a *linear block.* Point out to students that **derecho** means *straight ahead* while **a la derecha** means *at/to the right.* It is important that they note the gender change!

Knowing how to ask for directions so that you can get from one place to another and then following them is one of the most important communicative skills for travelers! Providing the same type of information is likewise important. Therefore, it is useful and germane to the outside world to provide students with numerous opportunities to practice these skills. To begin with, ask them to write out directions instructing how to get from one point to another using first the map on page 270 and then, their knowledge of their town or city or campus. Students should also include the method of transportation to be used, for example: **Puedes ir a pie, si prefieres caminar, o en autobús. Si tienes bastante dinero, puedes ir en taxi.** They can begin by using the following suggestions if nothing comes to mind.

1. Indicaciones de los muelles de barcos de crucero a la Plaza del Quinto Centenario.
2. De la Iglesia de San Francisco a La Fortaleza y, luego a la Droguería Ponce de León.
3. De la librería universitaria a las residencias estudiantiles.
4. De la Facultad de Humanidades al edificio de Administración.
5. De la policía a las cortes (el jurado) al correo.
6. Del hotel principal a a Facultad de Educación.

After writing out these directions, pair students and have them take turns asking for directions. The combination of the two activities practices all linguistic skills as well as gives students the opportunity to review and recycle the vocabulary.

¿NOS ENTENDEMOS? (page 272)

You might want to add the term **las camionetas,** the term used in Guatemala and other Central American countries to refer to *buses.* The term **el camión** means *truck* or *station wagon,* not *bus* in this same region.

¡A PRACTICAR! (page 272)

Assign activities **9-21, 9-22,** and **9-23** to be done outside of class. There should be little reason to go over these activities in class as they are quite straightforward.

EN VOZ ALTA (page 272)

Follow up activity **9-24** with the following **preguntas personales,** which you can ask the students and use as a springboard for discussions and comparisons.

1. ¿Cómo prefieres viajar cuando vas de vacaciones? ¿Por qué? Y tus padres y amigos, ¿están de acuerdo contigo?
2. Para mejor ver los sitios turísticos, ¿qué medios de transporte usas? ¿Por qué?
3. ¿Te gusta explorar lugares desconocidos *(unknown, unfamiliar)* a pie? ¿Les pides direcciones a los nativos si te pierdes?
4. ¿Hay una estación de trenes en tu pueblo o ciudad? ¿Una terminal de autobuses? ¿Cómo van de un lugar a otro las personas que visitan allí?

A variation to the previous written activity, done orally is **Señas / Instrucciones:**

> Dile a tu compañero(a) cómo llegar del aeropuerto / la estación de trenes / la terminal de autobuses a tu casa o al mejor hotel del barrio. Luego, cambien de papel. Cada uno debe escribir las señas / intrucciones que recibe para luego dibujar el mapa de lo que dijo el (la) compañero(a) y, después enséñaselo para verificar si él (ella) ha comprendido *(have understood).*

ENCUENTRO CULTURAL (page 273)

As a transition activity, ask students if they've ever visited a colonial city—either in the U.S. or elsewhere. What are the characteristics that identify these places as "colonial"? How do these cities differ from the places where they live? Do Spanish colonial cities differ from those in other countries, even in Latin America? From what you know about the Spaniards in the New World, what would you expect to see if you visited Old San Juan? You might wish to incorporate some Internet/Web work and send students out to sites to see or get pictures of Old San Juan as well as to download information about the city.

ESTRUCTURA III Giving directions and expressing desires: formal and negative *tú* commands (pages 274–275)

Before introducing these forms, recycle informal commands, their meaning, and formation! Provide students with extra written practice with the following activity.

Paco, que es muy negativo y siempre le contradice a todo el mundo, ha llegado el mismo día en que tú estás aconsejando a tu sobrino, Carlitos. Sin embargo, Paco insiste en decirle a Carlitos todo lo contrario de lo que tú le dices. Aquí está lo que dice Paco. Escribe lo que tú le aconsejas.

PACO: Come muchos dulces.

TÚ: _____

PACO: Juega en la calle.

TÚ: _____

PACO: Levántate tarde todos los días.

TÚ: _____

PACO: Pídeles dinero a tus padres.

TÚ: _____

PACO: Gasta todo el dinero que te regalan.

TÚ: _____

PACO: Sé antipático con todos.

TÚ: _____

Write a variety of verbs that are found in this chapter's vocabulary on the board. Then, ask students to write an appropriate affirmative informal command. They then exchange papers with a classmate and review them orally as a class. Now, move on to formal commands.

¡OJO! Point out to your students that the spelling changes experienced in writing these formal commands are just like those already seen when learning the preterite! Also point out that the singular forms correspond to the same person as those in the preterite, minus the written accent mark. This is an excellent opportunity to remind them of the importance of written accent marks and proper pronunciation if one is to avoid misunderstandings. The above explanations are worth the time as they serve a threefold purpose: they draw on previous knowledge and show that there is continuity between seemingly isolated language components as well as showing students that language is a rule-governed system in which the rules are not arbitrary!

¡A PRACTICAR! (pages 276–277)

Assign activities **9-26, 9-27,** and **9-28** to be worked on at home. Add or substitute the following activity to practice the forms.

> Tú y tu compañero(a) están en la agencia de viajes hablando con el agente. Ustedes le hacen una serie de preguntas al agente porque es el primer viaje a Puerto Rico que ustedes hacen. Escribe la respuesta que corresponde a cada pregunta con un mandato formal, ya sea singular o plural, según lo indica la pregunta.

1. ¿Cuál es la mejor manera de viajar a Puerto Rico si no tenemos mucho tiempo?
2. ¿Dónde podemos comprar los boletos para el viaje?
3. ¿Cómo debemos pagar los boletos?
4. ¿Qué debemos empacar?
5. ¿Necesitamos llevar mucha ropa?
6. ¿Cuál es el mejor lugar para quedarnos?
7. ¿Hacemos nuestras propias (*own*) reservaciones para el hotel?
8. ¿Cuándo podemos recoger los boletos?
9. ¿A qué hora debemos llegar al aeropuerto?
10. ¿Cuánto tiempo cree que debemos quedarnos allí?
11. ¿Cuál es el mejor vuelo que debemos tomar para volver?
12. ¿Cómo vamos a llegar a nuestra casa del aeropuerto?

EN VOZ ALTA (page 277)

Set up the following context for your students so that they have yet another opportunity to hone their oral skills and practice both vocabulary and grammar presented in this chapter. This is another paired activity. It is also an opportunity to recycle previously acquired knowledge. This activity is a bit more complicated than those of the book, so first assign your students one of the simpler activities **(9-29, 9-30)** if you feel they are not yet ready for this one.

> You have just returned from a trip to the Caribbean and your boss informs you that she/he is planning a vacation to the same region. She/he has many questions as it is a first for her/him! Answer the questions by telling her/him what to take, what not to take, where to go and what places to avoid, what to do and what activities are a waste of time or too expensive, which tourist locations are a "must" and which can be left out if time runs out, etc.

Be sure to use affirmative and negative formal commands to answer her/his questions. Reverse roles so that each individual has the chance to practice both structures.

SÍNTESIS: ¡A ESCRIBIR! (page 281)

You may wish to supply the following additional vocabulary to students to aid them in better expressing themselves in their written work: **la colina = el cerro/el cerrito; el cruce de caminos = la bocacalle; el letrero = el cartel; el camino = la carretera** (although the latter really means *highway* rather than *road,* it is used interchangeably in many places since roads and highways tend to be one and the same).

SÍNTESIS: ¡A CONVERSAR! (page 282)

Use the following situation in addition to or in lieu of the activity in the text.

In groups of three or four, set up a situation that represents **El viajar debe ser una aventura.**

Phase 1: Brainstorm about what your scene is going to show to represent the topic.

Phase 2: Start writing down definite ideas to incorporate.

Phase 3: Decide on the characters that are involved and write the appropriate dialog and stage directions.

Phase 4: Review what you've written, making sure that each individual reviews a portion that someone else composed. Remember, two heads are better than one and four eyes are better than two!

Phase 5: Make any necessary revisions and begin memorizing your lines.

Phase 6: Present your adventure to the class and teacher!

You must incorporate *some* of the following structures and vocabulary:

1. Scene setting: the airport, travel agent's office, customs and immigration, the hotel, or any combination thereof.
2. Incorporate the appropriate vocabulary that deals with the situation at the location.
3. Incorporate direct, indirect, and double object pronouns so that the dialog sounds "real," and directions or formal commands.
4. Make sure that the scene(s) presents some sort of resolution to the "problem"/adventure.

Don't leave your audience hanging unless the situation is a **"misterio"** in the Bermuda Triangle!

10 Las relaciones sentimentales: Honduras y Nicaragua

CHAPTER OPENER (page 288)

Start class discussion by asking students:

1. ¿Has asistido a alguna boda latinoamericana o española? ¿o quizás a una quinceañera mexicana o un bautizo hispano?
2. ¿Qué deben hacer los jóvenes cuando comienzan a salir en pareja? ¿Deben de hablar con sus padres sobre ello?
3. ¿Crees que un noviazgo debe ser largo o corto?
4. En general, ¿cómo son las fiestas de compromiso y las bodas en los Estados Unidos?
5. ¿Qué pasa cuando una pareja se compromete?
6. ¿Qué opinas de las lunas de miel? ¿Cómo deben ser?

VOCABULARIO Las relaciones sentimentales (page 290)

To begin this section, a good activity to get students **en la onda** is to ask them to look at the various frames shown and interpret what is going on. Offer a few sentences explaining how the individuals got to that point in their relationship. Continue with the vocabulary itself, expanding as necessary.

¡OJO! Teach verbs with the preposition with which they generally subcategorize. Point out to your students that unlike English *to fall in love **with**,* Spanish **enamorarse** is followed by **de,** and *to get married **to,*** is **casarse *con.***

¡OJO! Tell your students that **los novios** has several meanings. In the context of a wedding ceremony, they are *the bride* and *groom.* However, in the context of interpersonal relationships, it takes on the meaning of *the engaged couple* or *a courting couple* with serious ends in mind. **El (La) novio(a)** carries much more emotional significance and is not simply *girlfriend* or *boyfriend.*

Here you might also want to add that **el casamiento** is a synonym for **la boda.**

Sustantivos   Add **el afecto** as a synonym for **el cariño.**

Verbos   Point out that **amar** and **querer** can both be made reflexive in order to show reciprocity. **Amar** means *to love* while **amarse** means *to love each other* as is the case with **querer** and **quererse.** At this point you might want to also add the verb **comprometerse** *(to become engaged).* **Estimar a alguien** is also a way of saying that you care for them, that you have affection for them. The word *esteem* in English does not carry the emotional connotation that **estimar** carries in Spanish.

¡A PRACTICAR! (page 291)

In addition to the activities **10-1, 10-2,** and **10-3** provided in the text, here are two short exercises, which can be incorporated into the lesson.

¿Cuál no corresponde? Escoge cuál de las palabras no corresponde.

1. la amistad	el divorcio	el noviazgo	el compromiso
2. la separación	el ramo	la novia	el arroz
3. salir con	amar a	romper con	querer a
4. el divorcio	la separación	el matrimonio	romper la relación

¿Sinónimos o antónimos? Explica si los pares significan lo mismo o lo opuesto.

1. amar   querer
2. casarse con   divorciarse de
3. romper con   separarse de
4. la boda   el divorcio
5. el cariño   el amor

EN VOZ ALTA (page 292)

After activities **10-4, 10-5,** and **10-6,** add the following activity.

Una de las bodas más famosas del siglo XX fue el casamiento del Príncipe Carlos de Inglaterra con Diana, su prometida, que era una persona muy popular. ¿Qué recuerdas de ese día? Muchísimas personas vieron todos los acontecimientos en la tele. Describe lo que se vio ese inolvidable día.

EN CONTEXTO (page 293)

The following comprehension questions can be added to those in the text and all of them can be placed on an overhead so that students can listen to the tape, read the questions, and jot down information that pertains to them.

1. ¿Qué relación hay entre Munci y Jorge? ¿Y entre Marisol y Felipe?
2. ¿Cuál es la relación que tienen Munci y Felipe?
3. ¿Cuándo se va a casar la pareja?
4. ¿Qué información comparte *(shares)* Jorge con Munci? ¿Te parece eso algo extraño? ¿Qué opinas de la falta de experiencia de Jorge?

ENCUENTRO CULTURAL (page 294)

Add these additional points for your students to ponder in the **Para discutir** section.

1. ¿Qué es una unión libre? ¿Es eso preferible a un matrimonio? ¿Por qué sí o por qué no?
2. ¿Crees tú que el automóvil cambió las tradiciones de salir y del noviazgo en los Estados Unidos? ¿Y en Latinoamérica?

ESTRUCTURA I Describing recent actions, events, and conditions: the present perfect tense (pages 295–296)

¡OJO! Note that the present perfect tense, in both English and Spanish, is an indicator that the action took place sometime before *now* (that is, the speech act). The exact time at which it took place is unimportant, but its relation to the present is of the utmost relevance.

¡OJO! Point out to your students that the verbs that employ **í** in their past participles are those whose stem ends in a vowel.

¡OJO! Explain to your students that there is no option but to memorize the irregular past participles. Any verbs, formed with these as their base, follow the same pattern, so that once the base verb is memorized, they all fall into place.

escribir → **escrito**	*describir* → **descrito**
poner → **puesto**	com*poner* → **compuesto**
volver → **vuelto**	re*volver* → **revuelto**

¡OJO! Reflexive verbs: Be sure to point out that the reflexive pronoun is always placed before both the auxiliary verb and the past participle. *Nos* **hemos casado.**

Also point out that negative words precede the reflexive pronouns. *No* **me he enamorado de ella.**

¡A PRACTICAR! (pages 296–297)

The following is an optional activity for placement after activity **10-9.**

Escribe oraciones lógicas con un elemento de cada columna y no te olvides de conjugar el verbo.

Columna A	Columna B	Columna C
mi novio(a)	conocer	los planes para la luna de miel
nuestros padres	hacer	por muchos años
yo	completar	a todos los amigos
mi mejor amigo(a)	escribir	a su hermano
tú	tirar	las invitaciones
mi novio(a) y yo	traer	los arreglos para la boda
ustedes	mandar	muchos regalos bonitos
los invitados	invitar	arroz y flores

EN VOZ ALTA (page 297)

After activities **10-10, 10-11,** and **10-12,** use the following as a wrap-up activity.

¿Qué has hecho recientemente? Tú eres el (la) reportero(a) social para el periódico local. Estás entrevistando a algunos jóvenes para un artículo sobre las costumbres sociales de la juventud. Entrevista a tres o cuatro compañeros(as) para luego escribir un artículo, incorporando los resultados de la entrevista. Puedes emplear las preguntas a continuación o inventar tus propias preguntas.

1. ¿Prefieres salir en grupo o en pareja? ¿Por qué?
2. ¿Quién es el (la) amigo(a) especial con quien te gusta salir? ¿Tienes novio(a)?
3. ¿Con quién(es) has salido recientemente?
4. ¿Adónde han ido ustedes?
5. ¿Se han encontrado con otras parejas o con amigos?
6. ¿A qué hora acostumbran volver a casa?

ASÍ SE DICE Describing reciprocal actions: reciprocal constructions with *se, nos,* and *os* (page 298)

In English, reciprocal actions are identified by the use of the phrase "each other" in situations such as: "Upon meeting on the street Susan and Martha hugged each other." Sometimes, the "each other" is implicit in the verb: "When Harry and Daniel saw each other at the party, the first thing they did was shake hands." In other words, they each shook the other's hand. Spanish uses the plural forms of reflexive verbs to accomplish this function. Sometimes, for emphasis, the phrase **el uno al otro** (or the gender and number appropriate to the context) is tacked on at the end of the sentence. Thus, we have: (1) **Al verse, Susana y Marta se abrazaron (la una a la otra).** and (2) **Cuando Harry y Daniel se vieron en la fiesta, lo primero que hicieron fue darse la mano (el uno al otro).** Here is a short activity which can be used to practice reciprocal actions.

No has visto a tu tía Graciela en dos años. Tú estás de vacaciones con un amigo que no se conoce con la tía. ¿Qué hacen ustedes al encontrarse en Tegucigalpa, la capital de Honduras?

1. Primero, tía Graciela y yo _____ (verse).

2. Luego, nosotros _____ (abrazarse).

3. Le presento a mi amigo Alan a mi tía y los dos _____ (saludarse) y _____ (darse) la mano.

4. Mi tía entonces nos presenta a su nuevo esposo Arturo. Él y yo _____ (abrazarse), pero Alan y él sólo _____ (decirse) unas cuantas palabras.

5. No entiendo lo que pasa, pero poco después, Alan y yo _____ (hablarse) en voz baja y él me cuenta que él y Arturo ya _____ (conocerse) y no _____ (llevarse) muy bien.

6. Esta noche todos vamos a cenar juntos y espero que los dos hombres _____ (tratarse) un poco mejor para no arruinar las vacaciones.

¡A PRACTICAR! (page 298)

Upon finishing activities **10-13** and **10-14,** incorporate the following: **Escribe una serie de preguntas para hacerle a un(a) compañero(a) sobre qué deben hacer los individuos de una pareja perfecta. Debes usar los verbos en forma recíproca.**

EN VOZ ALTA (page 298)

The additional activity suggested in the **¡A practicar!** section provides the perfect lead-in for the oral activities that form an essential part of second-language acquisition. Since students have already composed questions in their previous activity, have them choose a classmate of whom they can ask the questions and for whom they can answer questions. They may also use questions from **10-15.**

Usando las preguntas del ejercicio opcional de la sección de **¡A practicar!,** pregúntaselas a un(a) compañero(a). Luego tu compañero(a) va a hacerte sus preguntas a ti. ¿Están ustedes de acuerdo? ¿En qué sí y en qué no?

VOCABULARIO La recepción (page 299)

Be sure to point out who Rubén Darío was and the place he holds in the world, in Latin America, and in the heart of all Nicaraguans.

¡A PRACTICAR! (page 300)

In addition to activities **10-16** and **10-17,** you can conclude written practice of the vocabulary, asking students to answer the questions provided below, which they will organize to describe a wedding reception they have attended.

1. ¿Cuál fue la ocasión de la recepción? ¿Qué se celebraba?
2. ¿Con quién fuiste a ella? ¿Cómo se vestían ustedes?
3. ¿Qué hicieron al llegar?
4. ¿Qué comida se sirvió durante la cena? ¿Qué bebidas hubo para los invitados?
5. ¿Qué música tocó la banda o la orquesta? ¿Bailó mucha gente?
6. ¿Qué hicieron los invitados para pasarlo bien?
7. ¿A qué hora se terminó la fiesta?
8. ¿Has asistido a otra recepción desde entonces (since then)?

EN VOZ ALTA (page 300)

After activities **10-18** and **10-19,** conclude this section with the oral activity indicated below.

1. Cuéntale a un(a) compañero(a) sobre la última recepción o fiesta excepcional a la que asististe y de la que todavía no has hablado.
2. Tu compañero(a) va a hacerte preguntas para saber más del asunto *(the matter).*
3. Luego él (ella) va a contarte a ti y tú vas a hacerle preguntas también.

ENCUENTRO CULTURAL (page 301)

¡OJO! Add **acordar en** as a synonym for **estar de acuerdo** as well as the verb **juzgar** *(to judge)* since **el (la) juez** is included in the vocabulary presented. In the first paragraph of the reading, **planear** appears. Point out to your students that there are two other ways of expressing the meaning: **planificar** (followed by an infinitive or a noun) and **hacer planes para** (also followed by an infinitive or a noun).

Add these questions to **Para discutir** to make sure that the students have understood what they have read.

1. ¿Cuál de las dos ceremonias es más importante para los novios y sus familias?
2. ¿Qué hace el novio antes de que las dos familias puedan comenzar a hacer los planes para la boda?
3. ¿Quién casa a los novios durante la primera ceremonia? ¿Quiénes están presentes?
4. ¿Cómo termina esa ceremonia?

ASÍ SE DICE Qualifying actions: adverbs and adverbial expressions of time and sequencing of events (page 302)

Point out to students that if the adjective ends in a consonant (regardless of which one), simply add **-mente,** as in **leal** *(loyal)* → **lealmente** and **feroz** *(ferocious)* → **ferozmente.**

To round out the list of words useful in sequencing actions or telling how often things are done, add the expressions that follow: **una vez más** *(once more/one more time);* **de nuevo** *(again);* **frecuentemente** and **con frecuencia** *(frequently);* **sólo** *(only);* **jamás** *(never);* **todo el tiempo** *(all the time);* **al fin y al cabo** *(in the end, when all is said and done).*

¡A PRACTICAR! and EN VOZ ALTA (pages 303–304)

After completing the activities in **¡A practicar!** and **En voz alta,** have students use the following sequencing expressions to tell about the events of the reception they want to have when they get married or, if already married, that they had when they got married: **(1) primero (2) luego (3) entonces (4) más tarde (5) después (6) por fin (7) al fin.** Be sure to tell them that they can use the terms in any order they see fit, as long as it is logical.

ESTRUCTURA II Using the Spanish equivalents of *who, whom, that, and which:* relative pronouns (page 305)

Point out to students that these relative pronouns, as their name indicates, *relate* the subordinate clause to the independent clause that precedes it, and therefore, the pronoun introduces the subordinate clause, regardless of the order in which they might appear in the sentence.

¡OJO! The relative **quien** is used to refer to people not only after a preposition or the indirect object of a verb, but also when it appears in a parenthetical expression, either within parentheses or set apart by commas. In addition to the examples found in the text, share the following parenthetical expressions with students.

Vi a ese chico con mi hermana, quien lo estaba besando sin cesar.

Ese hombre gordo, a quien conocí el otro día en un bar, quiere casarse conmigo.

Aquellos jóvenes, quienes se están portando como salvajes, son los hijos de Marcos.

¡A PRACTICAR! (page 306)

Here's another practice for relative pronouns, which can be used in addition to activities **10-25** and **10-26** and, if done orally, can be included as part of **En voz alta** after activity **10-27**.

1. _____ no me gusta es bailar salsa en público.

2. Esos chicos, _____ me reconocieron inmediatamente, son los primos de Ángel.

3. La invitación _____ me mandaron llegó ayer.

4. La mujer a _____ conocí anoche se va a casar con Leopoldo.

5. ¿Es ése el chico con _____ rompió Leonor?

6. No tenía ni idea de _____ estaban hablando.

7. La madre del novio es una señora _____ tiene mucho dinero.

8. El joven de _____ está enamorada Beatriz es un tonto.

9. No sé a _____ llevar a la boda.

10. ¡ _____ hombre tan guapo! Creo que me he enamorado de él.

SÍNTESIS

In addition to the activities presented, students can also do this activity that brings together all the skills that they have acquired.

La señora Sabelotodo escribe consejos relacionados con todo tipo de relaciones sentimentales y problemas amorosos en el periódico. Su clientela se encuentra por todo el país. Durante el verano, la Sra. Sabelotodo se va de vacaciones y este año, el jefe te ha puesto a ti en su lugar. El jefe es una persona bondadosa y también te ha dado un(a) asistente que a veces te vuelve loco(a), pero a veces entiende a las personas que escriben mejor que tú. Ustedes dos tienen que leer las cartas que los individuos han mandado y responderles en el periódico.

Paso 1: Discutan el contenido que van a incluir y luego escriban una carta, explicando el problema amoroso o la situación problemática que ha ocurrido dentro de una relación sentimental.

Paso 2: Repasen el trabajo escrito para eliminar errores o hacerlo mejor. No se olviden de incluir detalles.

Paso 3: Denle su carta a otro par de compañeros(as) y tomen la carta que ellos(as) han escrito.

Paso 4: Lean la carta que acaban de recibir del otro par de estudiantes y discutan cómo contestarla en nombre de la Sra. Sabelotodo.

Paso 5: Escriban su carta, aconsejando al cliente y luego repásenla.

Paso 6: Entreguen el proyecto final y la carta a la que respondieron para recibir una nota.

11 El mundo del trabajo: Panamá

CHAPTER OPENER (page 314)

Start class discussion by asking students:

1. ¿Cuántos de ustedes trabajan además de estudiar en la universidad?
2. ¿Dónde trabajas? ¿Qué haces allí?
3. ¿Has trabajado en otros negocios o en otro tipo de empresas?
4. ¿Está relacionado el trabajo con lo que estudias en la universidad, es decir con tu carrera?
5. ¿Qué piensas hacer después de graduarte?
6. ¿Dónde quieres trabajar? ¿En qué parte de los Estados Unidos o en qué continente?
7. ¿En qué tipo de empresa prefieres trabajar?

VOCABULARIO Profesiones y oficios (page 316)

Ask students to make a list of the five professions they believe are the most prestigious or highest paying. Then ask them to make a list of the worst or worst paying jobs. Ask them to explain why they feel that way, what criteria they used to arrive at their decisions. Finally, have students compare their lists and criteria.

¡OJO! The word **el (la) maestro(a)** generally refers to an elementary school teacher; secondary school teachers and university instructors/professors are called **el (la) profesor(a).**

¿NOS ENTENDEMOS? (page 316)

Point out to your students the difference between **el policía,** the policeman, and **la policía,** the police force.

¡A PRACTICAR! (page 317)

Activities **11-1** and **11-2** should be done outside the classroom so that class time can be spent on communication. The **En voz alta** activities will help to encourage communication in the classroom.

EN CONTEXTO (page 319)

Add the following questions as a way to encourage discussion among your students and at the same time make sure that students understand what they've heard. You can make an overhead for students to look at while they listen to the Student Text Audio CD or simply write the questions on the board.

1. ¿Qué preguntas crees tú que el candidato debe hacerle al jefe o a la persona que lo entrevista?
2. ¿Qué debe ser lo más importante del puesto? ¿Por qué?

ENCUENTRO CULTURAL (page 320)

Encourage students to begin thinking about Panama and matters related to it and the canal and its importance to the world by asking the following questions before they read the passage.

1. ¿Dónde está Panamá?
2. ¿Cuál es la capital de Panamá?
3. ¿Por qué ha sido importante este país para los Estados Unidos?
4. ¿Qué sabes de la historia de este país antes de la construcción del canal que lleva su nombre?

After students read the piece on the canal, add these three questions to those already found in **Para discutir.**

1. ¿Dónde está concentrada la economía más activa?
2. ¿Por qué ha sido tan importante el canal para Panamá y para los Estados Unidos?

ESTRUCTURA I Making statements about motives, intentions, and periods of time: *por* vs. *para* (pages 321–322)

¿Por qué estudias español? *(Why do you study Spanish?)* in item 5 under *Uses of **para*** on page 322, could also be phrased as **¿Para qué estudias español?** *(For what purpose do you study Spanish?).* Both questions ask the same basic question, and we encourage you to point out the options to your students.

¡A PRACTICAR! (page 323)

In addition to activities **11-6** and **11-7,** which should be assigned for homework, have students complete either **11-8** or the following activity for additional practice. Students can consult each other in order to discuss the appropriateness of the preposition chosen in the activity below.

Escribe la preposición **por** o **para** según el contexto.

La familia Orosco salió _____ Panamá ayer. Todos van _____ avión, claro, pero

después de unos días piensan viajar en coche _____ todo el país _____ ver toda la

naturaleza y los sitios turísticos. Se van a quedar allí _____ seis meses. Todos creen que va

a ser una experiencia extraordinaria _____ la familia, especialmente para los niños.

Mi prima María Sara quiere estudiar _____ ser geóloga. Trabaja _____ un profesor

universitario de geología durante sus horas libres _____ la mañana _____ ganar

dinero _____ continuar sus estudios. _____ la tarde asiste a sus clases y

_____ la noche estudia _____ sus clases del próximo día. Durante los fines de

semana, ella y su amigo Esteban pasean _____ las orillas del río, buscando piedras *(rocks)*

interesantes _____ llevar al laboratorio y estudiar bajo el microscopio. Sé que María Sara

va a ser una magnífica geóloga y profesora.

VOCABULARIO La oficina, el trabajo y la búsqueda de un puesto (page 325)

Ask students to think about what items are found in an office. Then, ask them to reflect on what is necessary for a successful interview. Finally, ask them the following questions.

1. ¿Qué máquinas hay en una oficina? ¿Para qué sirven?
2. ¿Qué debe hacer el candidato exitoso *(successful)* durante una entrevista?
3. ¿Cuándo debe un empleado pedir un aumento?

¡A PRACTICAR! (pages 326–327)

Assign activities **11-10, 11-11,** and **11-12** to be done for homework. In addition, have students determine which item in the following sets doesn't belong and why.

¿Cuál no pertenece al grupo y por qué?

1. dejar	renunciar	jubilarse	contratar
2. el puesto	la empresa	la compañía	el negocio
3. llenar	solicitar un puesto	entrevistar	despedir
4. el sueldo	la solicitud	el salario	los beneficios
5. el fax	la fotocopiadora	la computadora	el coreo electrónico
6. el proyecto	la computadora	la impresora	el correo electrónico
7. el candidato	la solicitud	el currículum	el informe
8. la reunión	el proyecto	el currículum	la sala de conferencia
9. la oficina	el trabajo	el puesto	la colocación

EN VOZ ALTA (pages 327–328)

After completing activities **11-13** and **11-14,** but prior to activity **11-15,** have students complete the following situation so they can practice using the vocabulary in a real-life situation.

Tú quieres conseguir *(to acquire)* un buen trabajo. Por eso, has ido a una agencia de empleos. El (La) consejero(a) habla contigo para saber lo que buscas. A un(a) compañero(a), cuéntale lo que deseas, después que él (ella) te hace algunas preguntas.

Luego, cambien de papel. Para concluir el ejercicio, le pueden contar lo que cada uno de ustedes desea al resto de la clase.

ENCUENTRO CULTURAL (page 329)

Add these questions to the four found in the text in **Para discutir** and put all of them on an overhead so that students have them available to look at while they read the four paragraphs presented.

1. ¿Qué indica una falta de respeto en el mundo hispanohablante de los negocios?
2. ¿Qué trato se le otorga (dar) a un colega? ¿Qué nombre se usa al hablarle?

Add these topics for discussion and the sharing of opinions in the **Para pensar** section: **¿Qué opinas de la manera como que se tratan los hispanos en los negocios y en la oficina? ¿Podrías** *(Could you)* **integrarte en ese ambiente?**

ESTRUCTURA II Expressing subjectivity and uncertainty: the subjunctive mood (page 330)

Activities **11-16** and **11-17** will serve as adequate preparation for the more detailed explanation in **Estructura III.**

VOCABULARIO Las finanzas personales (page 331)

Ask students what terms they associate with personal finances and banking. Begin with a few simple questions such as:

1. ¿Tienes una cuenta en el banco? ¿Es una cuenta corriente o de ahorros?
2. ¿Tienes la costumbre de depositar semanalmente?
3. ¿Depositas, o sacas dinero del banco con más frecuencia?
4. ¿A quién le pides prestado dinero? ¿Te lo prestan fácilmente?
5. ¿Has ido a un banco a pedir un préstamo? ¿Para qué lo pediste?
6. ¿Has pagado a plazos por algo o pagas en efectivo siempre?

¡A PRACTICAR! (page 332)

Have students complete activities **11-18** and **11-19** as homework and ask them to answer the set of questions presented below either as a class activity or as part of their assignment.

Contesta las preguntas con una palabra o una frase de la lista de vocabulario.

1. ¿Dónde pones tu salario cuando te dan un cheque?
2. Si no quieres gastar tu dinero, ¿dónde lo pones?
3. Si deseas comprar un carro, ¿qué le pides al banco?
4. ¿Qué pagas al comienzo de cada mes?
5. Cuando no tienes efectivo, ¿cómo pagas cuando vas de compras al centro comercial?
6. Para sacar dinero cuando vas al banco y lo encuentras cerrado, ¿cómo consigues dinero en efectivo?
7. ¿Qué haces cada mes para saber cuánto puedes gastar después de pagar las cuentas?
8. Cuando pagas un poco de lo que debes cada mes, ¿cómo pagas las cuentas?
9. ¿Qué pasa cuando escribes un cheque sin tener suficiente dinero en tu cuenta?
10. ¿Qué debes hacer con parte de tu salario si deseas comprar una casa algún día?

EN VOZ ALTA (page 333)

In addition to activities **11-20** and **11-21** presented in the text, have students complete their oral practice by getting together in groups of three and putting together the scene described below.

Tú y tu novio(a) han ahorrado unos $10.000 para poder comprar una casa después de la boda. Tú eres dentista pero tu prometido(a) sólo tiene un trabajo de tiempo parcial en la oficina de un abogado mientras termina sus estudios universitarios. En este momento, ustedes están en la oficina de uno de los vicepresidentes del banco. En grupos de tres personas, hagan la conversación necesaria para negociar el préstamo para poder construir la casa de sus sueños.

ESTRUCTURA III Expressing desires and intentions: the present subjunctive with statements of volition (pages 334–337)

A mnemonic device used by many to learn and remember the types of verbs considered triggers for the subjunctive is:

Wishing, willing, wanting
Emotions
Doubt
Denial
Indefinite antecedents
Nonexistent antecedents
Generalizations

Stress that the subjunctive always appears in the subordinate clause of complex sentences where the three conditions specified below are satisfied. This can be explained by using **Carlos quiere que su madre vaya al banco con él,** as a model.

1. You must have a complex sentence: a main clause followed by a subordinate clause.

    Carlos quiere   **(que) su madre vaya al banco con él.**
    (clause 1)   (clause 2)

2. There must be a change in subject from the main clause to the subordinate clause.

    Subject 1 = **Carlos**   Subject 2 = **su madre**

3. There must be a trigger verb in the main clause: **quiere.**

¡OJO! Insistir and **decir** can take both the indicative and the subjunctive mood in the subordinate clause, according to the function being performed. Both verbs have an informative and a volitional function. When the informative function is employed, the subordinate clause appears in the indicative; when the volitional function is involved, the subjunctive mood is used. See the next two examples:

> **Informative function: Mamá dice que tío Raúl *viene* hoy.**
> **Mamá** is simply informing that **tío Raúl** is coming today.
> **Volitional function: Mamá dice que tío Raúl *venga* hoy.**
> **Mamá** is saying that **tío Raúl** should come today.

¡A PRACTICAR! (page 338)

Have students prepare activities **11-22, 11-23,** and **11-24** at home, together with the additional activity provided below.

Contesta las preguntas en oraciones completas usando el subjuntivo cuando sea necesario.

1. ¿Por qué te piden tus padres que estudies mucho?
2. ¿Les recomiendas a tus compañeros que trabajen tanto como tú?
3. Después de graduarte, ¿qué trabajo quieren tus padres que consigas?
4. ¿Qué les vas a pedir a tus padres que te den como regalo de graduación?
5. ¿Qué tipo de trabajo prohíben tus padres que hagas?
6. Si tienes una entrevista, ¿cuánto dinero deseas que te ofrezcan?
7. ¿Dónde recomienda tu consejero que busques trabajo?
8. ¿Prefieres que den muchos beneficios, o un sueldo alto?
9. Después de casarte, ¿quieres que tu esposa siga trabajando o se quede en casa?
10. ¿Quieres que tus hijos sean iguales a ti?

EN VOZ ALTA (page 339)

Begin with activities **11-25, 11-26,** and **11-27.** If more oral practice is needed, use the situation below.

Tú vas a la oficina de tu consejero(a) universitario(a) porque no estás seguro de lo que quieres hacer después de graduarte. A un(a) compañero(a) que hace el papel de consejero(a), pídele consejos con respecto a tu futuro. Haz una lista de las preguntas que quieres que el (la) consejero(a) conteste y con las que quieres que te ayude. Después, cambien de papel.

SÍNTESIS

In addition to the activites in the book, here is another set of activities designed to use all the skills that students have acquired.

Tú y tu(s) colega(s) son los jefes de una empresa dedicada a la preservación de la ecología latinoamericana. Ustedes buscan dos o tres empleados nuevos, así que han decidido contratar una agencia de personal para que haga los arreglos necesarios y les mande candidatos cualificados. Por eso ustedes deben seguir una serie de pasos para completar el proceso.

Paso 1: Tú y tu(s) colega(s) deben decidir qué puestos están disponibles, el salario, las horas de trabajo, lo que esperan que se haga, etc.

Paso 2: Escriban los requisitos para el anuncio que van a mandar a la agencia de personal.

Paso 3: Hablen con el (la) agente y explíquenle sus necesidades.

Paso 4: Entrevisten a los dos o tres candidatos que manda la agencia.

Paso 5: Los candidatos deben escribir un currículum corto para presentárselo a los jefes que los van a entrevistar.

Paso 6: Decidan cuál de los candidatos van a contratar y por qué.

12 El medio ambiente: Costa Rica

CHAPTER OPENER (page 346)

To motivate the class discussion, ask students:

1. ¿Qué saben ustedes de Costa Rica?
2. ¿Qué saben del medio ambiente costarricense?
3. ¿Por qué creen ustedes que es importante conservar los bosques y las selvas del mundo?
4. ¿Hay beneficios que se asocien con la preservación del medio ambiente? ¿Cuáles son?
5. ¿Qué problemas ha causado el desperdicio (*waste*) de los recursos naturales?
6. ¿Has trabajado en algún proyecto ecológico?

VOCABULARIO La geografía rural y urbana (page 348)

Have students get into a rural versus urban mind-set by asking them to consider the two environments while they answer the questions below.

1. ¿Has pasado tiempo viviendo en un pueblo pequeño o en otro sitio rural que no se haya desarrollado? Si lo has hecho, ¿dónde fue?
2. ¿Prefieres la vida urbana o la rural? ¿Por qué? ¿Qué (des)ventajas ves en cada ambiente?

¡A PRACTICAR! (page 349)

Ask students to complete activities **12-1, 12-2,** and **12-3** for homework. Then, in the following activity, all can work to provide the necessary vocabulary terms without using their books.

1. _____ es un arroyo grande.

2. El agua que corre muy rápidamente y cae repentinamente es _____.

3. _____ es una montaña pequeña.

4. Al estado de tener demasiada gente en un lugar se le llama _____.

5. Un sinónimo de *muy bonita* es _____.

6. Una persona que cultiva la tierra es _____.

7. Un edificio muy alto es _____.

8. El lugar donde se manufacturan productos es _____.

9. El acto de darle agua a las tierras cultivadas es _____.

10. Al conjunto de muchos carros en la carretera se le da el nombre de _____.

11. Otra palabra para *el mar* es _____.

12. La orilla del mar donde hay arena es _____.

13. La frontera donde la tierra llega al mar es _____.

14. El agua que está completamente rodeada de tierra es _____.

15. Un bosque tropical muy denso es _____.

¿NOS ENTENDEMOS? (page 349)

Ask students if they remember what Guatemalans, Salvadorans, and Nicaraguans call themselves.

If not, here they are again: **guatemaltecos = chapines; salvadoreños = guanacos; nicaragüenses = nicas.**

EN VOZ ALTA (page 350)

After completing activities **12-4, 12-5,** and **12-6,** have students continue with the following activity.

Tú y tu equipo científico acaban de volver de un viaje a Costa Rica donde exploraron la selva tropical. Ahora la revista *Medio Ambiente* ha mandado a un reportero para entrevistarlos a ti y a tu asistente. En grupos de tres o cuatro personas, «graben» la entrevista para que el reportero pueda escribir su artículo.

EN CONTEXTO (page 351)

Have students listen to the Student Text Audio CD. After the questions in **¿Comprendiste?** are completed, have them tell whether or not they agree or disagree with the following statements and why.

1. La vida rural es mejor porque hay más tranquilidad y menos estrés.
2. La vida urbana ofrece más cosas que hacer que son más emocionantes de las que hay en el campo.
3. No hay nada mejor que vivir en un apartamento lujoso en un rascacielos y salir a comer a un restaurante diferente todas las noches.
4. No hay mejor satisfacción que cultivar la tierra para luego cosechar *(harvest)* y preparar la comida en la cocina de la finca.

ENCUENTRO CULTURAL (page 352)

Add a few questions to **Para discutir** to make sure that the students understood what they read.

1. ¿De qué tamaño es Costa Rica?
2. ¿Cómo es la geografía del país?
3. ¿Por qué es tan especial este país tan pequeño?

Add the following questions in addition to those presented in the **Para pensar** section of the text.

1. ¿Por qué es importante proteger todas las criaturas naturales?
2. ¿Es un buen plan económico conservar la biodiversidad? ¿Por qué?
3. ¿Cómo podemos conservar el medio ambiente y a la vez dar de comer a todas las personas que necesitan comer?

¡OJO! El quetzal is the national symbol of Guatemala. It is said that it is also a symbol of liberty because it cannot live in a cage; it requires freedom to survive!

ESTRUCTURA I Expressing emotion and opinions: subjunctive following verbs of emotion, impersonal expressions, and *ojalá* (page 353)

¡OJO! The impersonal expressions are also referred to as *generalizations*. Regardless of which terms are used to identify them, they require the subjunctive in the subordinate clause when they are personalized.

¡OJO! Remind students that the subjunctive always appears in the subordinate clause of complex sentences where the three conditions specified below must be present. If any one of them is missing, the subjunctive cannot be employed. In this case, two out of three is bad! Use an example such as **Mi mamá tiene miedo que papá no vuelva a tiempo para la fiesta.**, which contains the verb of emotion **tener miedo,** as a model.

1. You must have a complex sentence: a main clause followed by a subordinate clause.

   Mi mamá tiene miedo   **(que) papá no vuelva a tiempo para la fiesta.**
   (clause 1)   (clause 2)

2. There must be a change in subject from the main clause to the subordinate clause.

   Subject 1 = **Mi mamá**   Subject 2 = **papá**

3. There must be a trigger verb in the main clause: **tener miedo.**

Since the three requirements are satisfied, the verb in the dependent clause **(volver)** must appear in the subjunctive **(vuelva).**

¡OJO! Add these two related triggers to the list of verbs of emotion listed in the text: **sorprenderle (a uno)** *(to be surprised by)* and **temer** *(to fear)*. Provide students with choices in vocabulary whenever possible.

¡OJO! The impersonal expressions listed on page 353 of the text can also take the form of exclamatory phrases such as **¡Qué bueno!** and **¡Qué lástima!** They also take the subjunctive in the subordinate clause, as evidenced by the examples below.

   ¡Qué bueno que Juan esté preparado para viajar a Centro América!
   ¡Qué lástima que no puedas ir a Costa Rica con nosotros!

¡OJO! The term **ojalá** has its origin in the Arabic expression translated as *May it be Allah's (God's) will* and, thus, can be classified as an impersonal expression.

¡A PRACTICAR! (page 354)

Assign activities **12-7, 12-8,** and **12-9** as homework, which can then be gone over either in pairs or groups. This additional work can be done together.

Cambia el infinitivo a la forma apropiada del subjuntivo.

1. Es mejor que tú _____ **(apagar)** las luces al salir de viaje. Me molesta

   que nosotros _____ **(tener)** que pagar una factura muy alta. Me

   sorprende que tú _____ **(gastar)** la energía sin pensar cuando es nece-

   sario que _____ **(conservarse).**

2. Es verdad que David _____ **(ser)** inteligente, pero dudo que

   _____ **(poder)** resolver los problemas ecológicos con la computadora.

3. Es lástima que la naturaleza _____ (estar) en peligro en tantos lugares.

Ojalá que nosotros _____ (aprender) antes de que sea demasiado tarde.

A veces es difícil que la gente _____ (darse) cuenta del daño que hace.

4. Va a ser imposible que tú _____ (ir) con nosotros a Costa Rica si no sacas

buenas notas. ¿Cómo es posible que a ti no te _____ (gustar) trabajar

con la naturaleza? Además, temo que tú no _____ (saber) la importancia

de nuestro trabajo.

5. Los costarricenses esperan que todo el trabajo _____ (proteger) las

especies en peligro de extinción. Nos sorprende que más gente no _____

(querer) ayudar con el proyecto. Es posible que (la gente) _____ (tener)

miedo de vivir en la selva.

EN VOZ ALTA (page 355)

After having students complete activities **12-10, 12-11,** and **12-12,** have them continue with activity **12-13.** Add a few more topics from which they can choose so that there can be real debate among the various groups on meaningful and important topics for our world.

1. Las necesidades comerciales versus la preservación del medio ambiente
2. La contaminación del aire y la cantidad de basura versus el aire puro y el ambiente limpio
3. El reciclaje versus el aumento en los sitios donde se amontona la basura

VOCABULARIO La conservación y la explotación (page 356)

Ask students to explain what they see as the pros and cons of **la conservación** and **la explotación** of the environment and natural resources. Place them in groups of three or four to discuss the topics and their views regarding what can be done to save the planet.

¡OJO! You might want to add **la abundancia** to the list as it is the most common antonym for **la escasez.**

¡A PRACTICAR! (page 357)

Have students do the textbook activities **(12-14, 12-15,** and **12-16)** as homework and then practice the vocabulary by matching the terms with their definitions in the next activity.

Escoge de la Columna B el sinónimo o el antónimo de la palabra en la Columna A.

Columna A

1. construcción
2. conservar
3. reciclaje
4. contaminar
5. contaminado
6. desarrollar
7. reforestar
8. recoger
9. la abundancia
10. la naturaleza

Columna B

a. el desarrollo
b. destrucción
c. la escasez
d. gastar
e. desperdicio
f. proteger
g. puro
h. destruir
i. talar
j. arrojar

EN VOZ ALTA (page 358)

Place students in pairs or groups for activities **12-17, 12-18,** and **12-19.** As an added possibility, ask them to role-play based on this situation:

> Hay una conferencia sobre ecología y la protección del medio ambiente de todo el mundo.
>
> Te han invitado a participar en un panel de discusión sobre cómo solucionar los siguientes problemas ambientales: (1) la sobrepoblación (2) la falta de reciclaje (3) la contaminación (4) la escasez de recursos naturales. En grupos de cuatro personas, organicen su panel y propongan por lo menos una solución lógica para presentarles a sus compañeros(as) y a su profesor(a).

ENCUENTRO CULTURAL (page 359)

Ask students to read the narrative dealing with **La Selva** and then proceed to answering the **Para discutir** questions in the text. These additional questions can be included.

1. ¿Cuándo se estableció La Selva? ¿Quién la estableció?
2. ¿A qué está dedicada La Selva? ¿Por qué es importante?

You can add the following questions to those already presented in the **Para pensar** section of the text.

El programa de protección medioambiental costarricense ha sido muy exitoso. ¿Crees que es posible hacer lo mismo al nivel local? ¿Estás dispuesto(a) (Are you willing) **a participar en tal proyecto? ¿Por qué sí o por qué no? ¿De qué manera?**

ESTRUCTURA II Expressing doubts, uncertainty, and hypothesizing: the subjunctive with verbs, expressions of uncertainty, and adjective clauses (pages 360–361)

¡OJO! Hypothetical situations are the same as indefinite antecedents. The preceding noun, which is qualified by the adjective clause, is the antecedent.

¡A PRACTICAR! (pages 362–363)

Activities **12-20, 12-21,** and **12-22** can be assigned as homework and then reviewed by placing students in groups of three or four to compare and review their answers, leaving you available to clarify uncertainties and correct errors. For additional practice, the following activity is dedicated to the subjunctive in adjective clauses.

1. A veces encuentro flores hermosas que _____ **(estar)** a plena vista. Pero hoy estoy buscando flores que _____ **(ser)** muy raras. Hay unos animales que también _____ **(ser)** algo raros. Pedro no ha encontrado ningún animal que _____ **(estar)** en peligro de extinción.

2. ¿Dónde está ese hipopótamo que nosotros _____ **(ver)** ayer? Hay un hipopótamo que _____ **(necesitar)** ayuda. ¿Hay alguien aquí que _____ **(poder)** ayudarlo?

3. Yo conozco a un chico que _____ (**trabajar**) en la Reserva Biológica. ¿Conoces a alguien que también _____ (**hacer**) eso? No, no conozco a nadie que _____ (**querer**) hacer tal cosa. María Isabel conoce a varios jóvenes que _____ (**desear**) salvar los animales.

4. ¿Has encontrado a alguien que te _____ (**ayudar**)? No, no he encontrado a nadie que me _____ (**gustar**). Mi jefe tampoco puede encontrar a nadie que _____ (**terminar**) el trabajo que falta.

5. Sé que Rosita tiene un sombrero que _____ (**ser**) de Centroamérica. Quizás esta tarde yo _____ (**poder**) encontrar un par de aretes de Costa Rica que le _____ (**parecer**) bonitos y que no _____ (**costar**) demasiado. Quiero buscar unos regalos que _____ (**ser**) atractivos y que _____ (**apoyar**) el trabajo ecológico. Rosita también está interesada en los problemas ecológicos pero no puede encontrar ningún trabajo que le _____ (**pagar**) lo suficiente para vivir. Espero que _____ (**existir**) el puesto perfecto para ella porque ella _____ (**ser**) la mejor amiga que una persona _____ (**poder**) tener.

EN VOZ ALTA (page 363)

Put students into groups of three or four individuals to complete activities **12-23, 12-24,** and **12-25.** Then have them, still in their groups, discuss their beliefs, certainties, and doubts regarding the following subjects.

1. La escasez de agua y aire puros
2. La necesidad del reciclaje
3. Lo ilógico de la destrucción de los bosques
4. La solución del problema de la capa de ozono
5. La conservación de las especies
6. El aumento en la necesidad del transporte público

VOCABULARIO Los animales y el refugio natural (page 364)

Point out that animals play an important role in the history and folklore of the Latin American people and their native ancestors. Even present-day Catholicism in these countries is a blend of indigenous paganism and the religion brought to the New World by the Spaniards. The jaguar, the "plumed" serpent, the quetzal, and the coyote were central figures in the religions of the Aztec, Toltec, and Maya. Encourage students to share what they know about the importance of animals to the cultural roots of today's Latin American nations. If little is known, take the time to allow them to search the Internet for information relating to the topic. This might seem a bit off the mark for a chapter dealing with ecology and conservation, but the link between the native Latin Americans, their past, and the fauna and flora of the land can be used to spark and maintain the interest required if the natural resources of the area are to be saved.

¡**OJO!** Point out to the class that in Guatemala, the word for *owl* is of Mayan origin, **el tecolote** rather than **el búho.** In other countries, the term **la lechuza** is the preferred term for the animal. Also, in most Central American countries rather than **el caimán** for *alligator,* the word **el lagarto** is used.

¡A PRACTICAR! (page 365)

If students learn the vocabulary at home and prepare the activities in the text (**12-26** and **12-27**), class time can be devoted to the use of the material rather than simply to its explanation and repetition.

As an added practice, play **¿Qué animal soy?** In which you ask that students write out a description of the animals found listed in the text so that classmates can guess "who" they are!

Haz una descripción de los animales de la lista a continuación para luego presentárselas a tus compañeros(as) de clase. Puedes usar las siguientes sugerencias en tu descripción: (a) color, (b) tamaño, (c) dónde vive, (d) algo especial del animal, (e) lo que come y (f) el tipo de piel que tiene.

Los animales que debes describir incluyen:

1. el oso
2. la culebra
3. el gorila
4. un ave
5. el lobo
6. el tigre
7. el cocodrilo
8. el mono
9. el león
10. el elefante

EN VOZ ALTA (page 365)

After completing the activities in the text (**12-28** and **12-29**), have students orally present their **¿Qué animal soy?** adivinanzas. Tell them they can add other animals such as **el búho, la cebra, el ciervo, el camello,** and **la mariposa.**

SÍNTESIS

In order to give your students the opportunity to become aware of their increased knowledge of Spanish and their ability to use the language, give them the following scenario and ask them to put together the project suggested therein. Allow students class time for organization and an adequate amount of time for its completion.

Tú eres el (la) director(a) de relaciones públicas y propaganda para el Parque/La Reserva Biológica (nombre) en (lugar), Costa Rica. Tú y tus asistentes están a punto de crear una campaña para atraer a voluntarios y donaciones para el parque. Es hora de sentarse y darle vida al proyecto, porque si no tiene éxito van a tener que abandonar el buen trabajo que han hecho hasta este momento. En grupos de tres o cuatro personas:

Paso 1: Vayan a la Red electrónica y busquen información adicional sobre uno de los parques o reservas de Costa Rica.

Paso 2: Discutan la información que han encontrado.

Paso 3: Escojan un aspecto de la ecología, del medio ambiente o de los animales en peligro de extinción y qué tipo de propaganda van a promover.

Paso 4: Diseñen el anuncio que van a presentarle al público para atraer a trabajadores y a donadores para ayudar el proyecto.

Paso 5: Discutan y luego arreglen o cambien el anuncio.

Paso 6: Preséntenselo a la clase y entréguenselo a su profesor(a).

13 El mundo del espectáculo: Perú y Ecuador

CHAPTER OPENER (page 378)

To motivate the class discussion, ask students:

1. ¿Has visto alguna película hecha en Latinoamérica o España?
2. ¿Has tenido la oportunidad de mirar algún programa en español en la televisión? ¿Qué programa? ¿Te gustó? ¿Por qué sí (o no)?
3. ¿Quién crees que es el (la) mejor artista hispano(a) de cine? ¿Y el (la) mejor cantante hispano(a)?
4. ¿Tienes alguna obra de arte preferida? ¿Quién es tu pintor(a) o escultor(a) hispano(a) favorito(a)?

VOCABULARIO Programas y películas (page 380)

¡OJO! You might want to add a few associated terms to the list provided in the textbook. A recently accepted term for *movie* is **el film.** A synonym for **poner** when it means *to turn on (an appliance)* is **prender** and when it means *to show (a movie)* is **pasar.**

Have students think about their TV viewing habits and the types of programs they generally watch. They should also think about how much time they devote to their viewing activities. Their movie-going habits and preferences should also be considered when preparing them for this portion of the chapter. Some of the questions presented below can be used to move them in the right direction.

1. ¿Cuánto tiempo pasas enfrente del televisor? ¿Qué tipo de programas miras generalmente? ¿Tienes un horario fijo *(set)*? ¿Miras los mismos programas todas las semanas o prefieres ver distintos programas, según como te sientas?
2. ¿Vas al cine con frecuencia? ¿Con quién vas al cine? ¿Qué películas prefieres ir a ver? ¿Hay algún tipo de película que te moleste ver? Explica por qué.

¡A PRACTICAR! (page 381)

Have students complete activities **13-1** and **13-2** for homework. Then, as a class activity, all can cooperate on providing the necessary answers to the questions provided below.

Responde a las preguntas según la lista de vocabulario del capítulo.

1. ¿Hay un anuncio que te guste en la televisión? ¿Cuál es? Descríbelo.
2. ¿Qué canales de televisión miras con frecuencia? ¿Por qué?
3. ¿Cuál fue la última película que fuiste a ver en el cine? ¿Qué tipo de película era? ¿Cuál era su título? ¿Quiénes eran los actores?
4. ¿Te molesta la violencia en los programas de televisión o en las películas?
5. ¿Crees que hay demasiado sexo en el cine y también en los programas de televisión?
6. ¿Escuchas las noticias en la radio o prefieres mirarlas en la tele? ¿Cuál canal ofrece el mejor reportaje?
7. ¿Qué piensas de las películas extranjeras? ¿Lees los subtítulos o prefieres tratar de comprender el diálogo? ¿Prefieres las películas dobladas *(dubbed)*?
8. ¿Qué opinas de las telenovelas? ¿A qué personas asocias con este tipo de programa? ¿Por qué? ¿Crees que es malo mirar telenovelas? ¿Por qué sí (o no)?

EN VOZ ALTA (page 382)

After completing activities **13-3, 13-4,** and **13-5,** have students continue with the following activity, but this time in set pairs.

Después de escoger a un(a) compañero(a), decidan juntos cuál de los dos temas va a describir cada uno.

A. Cuéntale a tu compañero(a) sobre tu programa favorito de televisión. Debes incluir la siguiente información:

1. El nombre del programa
2. Los actores principales (si los hay)
3. El tipo de programa
4. El día que se televisa
5. El tema
6. El episodio especial que te llamó la atención o te afectó
7. Por qué te gusta tanto el programa

B. Cuéntale a tu compañero(a) cúal es tu película favorita, entre todas las que has visto. Debes incluir la siguiente información:

1. El nombre de la película
2. Cuándo la fuiste a ver y con quién
3. Cuánto tiempo duró
4. Las estrellas (actores conocidos)
5. El tipo de película
6. La historia o el tema
7. Tu reacción a la película
8. Por qué te gustó tanto

EN CONTEXTO (page 383)

Have students listen to the Student Text Audio CD with books closed. After the questions of **¿Comprendiste?** are completed, have them answer the following questions related to the content of the text they have heard. These questions can be placed on an overhead so students can jot down the pertinent information as they listen to the CD a second time.

1. ¿Dónde ocurre la exposición de arte?
2. ¿De dónde son todos los artistas?
3. ¿Quién ganó el concurso?
4. ¿Qué son «las obras espontáneas»? ¿Cómo las explica la artista?
5. ¿Qué es *Manchas de café*? ¿A qué grupo de obras pertenece?
6. ¿Cuál es la obra favorita de Rosario?
7. ¿Cómo clasifica ella a esa obra de arte?
8. ¿Por qué necesita esta última obra la ayuda del espectador?

ENCUENTRO CULTURAL (page 384)

The following questions are provided to stimulate further conversation and discussion of some of the topics treated in the reading. Do them after **Para discutir** as they are intended to broaden students' knowledge regarding the topics. Some information has been provided in the footnotes below, but if more is wanted or needed, students can use the Internet to locate additional data.

The movies mentioned in questions 1 and 3 are easily found in video stores with a foreign films section.

1. ¿Has visto alguna película de Pedro Almodóvar? ¿Cuál de ellas has visto? ¿Qué piensas de sus obras? ¿Te gustan o no? ¿Crees que son fáciles de entender?[1]
2. ¿Sabes quién es (era) Cantinflas?[2] ¿Cómo se puede comparar con Jerry Lewis? ¿Crees que son parecidos en cuanto a su manera de actuar?
3. *Como agua para chocolate* fue una película muy popular aquí en los Estados Unidos. ¿La has visto o quizás has leído la novela de Laura Esquivel en la que está basada? ¿Qué opinas del «realismo mágico» que se emplea en ambas obras?[3]

ESTRUCTURA I Talking about anticipated actions: subjunctive with purpose and time clauses (page 385)

¡OJO! Tell your students that purpose and time clauses are *adverb clauses* since they perform the same function as an adverb.

¡OJO! Add **a fin de que,** meaning *so (that),* to the list of conjunctions of purpose.

¡OJO! A mnemonic device for remembering the six conjunctions *always* requiring the subjunctive in the subordinate clause is **A SPACE.**

Afin de que
Sin que
Para que
A menos que
Con tal (de) que
En caso (de) que

¡OJO! Explain to your students that even though **aunque** is considered to be a conjunction of purpose due to its ability to take either the subjunctive or the indicative in the subordinate clause, it is oftentimes placed with expressions of doubt.

¡OJO! Here is another mnemonic device to help students learn and remember the six conjunctions that take the subjunctive mood when the dependent clause refers to a pending action, condition, or event and that takes the indicative mood when the action, condition, or event is either habitual or completed: **DETACH.**

Después (de) que
En cuanto
Tan pronto como
Antes (de) que
Cuando
Hasta que

¡OJO! The meaning of the adverbial expression **antes (de) que** automatically forces the action of the clause that follows to take the subjunctive mood, inasmuch as the action must be pending.

[1] Algunas de las películas de Almodóvar llevan los títulos en inglés, *Women on the Verge of a Nervous Breakdown* y *Tie Me Up, Tie Me Down* y son muy populares en los Estados Unidos.
[2] Cantinflas era un actor de comedias mexicanas que hacía papeles muy parecidos a los que hace Jerry Lewis en muchas de sus películas. También actuó en la película *Around the World in 80 Days* con el actor inglés David Niven. Cantinflas murió hace muchos años pero continúa siendo muy popular en el mundo latinoamericano.
[3] Laura Esquivel, así como Jorge Luis Borges, Miguel Ángel Asturias e Isabel Allende, mezcla lo real con lo fantástico en sus escritos. Esta mezcla también se aprecia muy bien en la película.

¡A PRACTICAR! (pages 386–387)

Activities **13-6, 13-7,** and **13-8** should be assigned for homework and followed up with the activity below, if more practice is needed.

Completa las oraciones siguientes con la forma apropiada del infinitivo.

Todos los años invito a mis padres para que _____ (**venir**) de México a verme.

No tengo tiempo para verlos a menos que me _____ (**visitar**). Piensan visitar las galerías de arte la próxima vez que _____ (**estar**) aquí. Puesto que yo

_____ (**tener**) vacaciones, vamos a poder salir en cuanto ellos _____

(**llegar**). Por lo general compramos algunas obras de arte después de que (nosotros)

_____ (**ir**) a todas las exhibiciones. Mamá no nos deja descansar hasta que

_____ (**ver**) todo lo que hay que ver. Siempre me ayuda a decorar sin que (yo)

_____ (**tener**) que pedírselo. He esperado más de dos semanas para que ella

_____ (**decidir**) cuál cuadro debo comprar. No ha dicho nada aunque (yo) le

_____ (**preguntar**) todo el día. La tengo que llevar a otra galería a fin de que

_____ (**estar**) satisfecha al ver que no hay más gangas. Me va a regalar varias piezas

de arte para que (yo) _____ (**poder**) ahorrar mi dinero. Mi abuelo también me dice

que me va a prestar la estatua que tiene en su oficina con tal de que se la _____ (**de-**

volver) después de seis meses. Le voy a devolver la estatua en cuanto _____ (**encon-**

trar) otra que me _____ (**gustar**). Mis tíos también me dan dinero para que yo

_____ (**comprar**) música y literatura en español. Tengo un apartamento muy ele-

gante, pero gano muy poco sin que lo _____ (**saber**) mis amigos.

Ahora escribe cinco oraciones que continúen el tema con las siguientes conjunciones y expresiones adverbiales:

    aunque   a menos que   hasta que   tan pronto como   después de que

EN VOZ ALTA (page 387)

Have students complete activities **13-9, 13-10,** and **13-11** before reading aloud the sentences they created for the narrative presented above.

VOCABULARIO Las artes (page 388)

Begin this section by asking students if they think of themselves as creative artists.

1. ¿Te consideras como algún tipo de artista? ¿Qué clase de arte haces?
2. ¿Qué tipo de pintura o escultura te llama la atención?
3. ¿Te gusta asistir al teatro? ¿Prefieres ver representaciones de obras clásicas o modernas?
4. ¿Qué tipo de arquitectura te fascina? ¿Has visto algún edificio del famoso arquitecto Gaudí? ¿Qué piensas de sus diseños?
5. ¿Has asistido a una exposición de algún fotógrafo conocido? ¿Prefieres las fotografías a los cuadros pintados? ¿Crees que requiere menos talento fotografiar que pintar?
6. ¿Qué carrera artística crees que es la más difícil?

¡OJO! Remind students that **sacar fotos (fotografías)** means *to take pictures* but also has a synonym in **fotografiar**. Another useful verb is **actuar** defined as *to act*. Inform your students that although the word **poeta** is employed for both men and women poets indicating their sex by the gender of the article, **la poetisa** is another word for *poetess*. The case is the same for the term **actor,** although the term **la actriz** is also employed.

¡A PRACTICAR! (page 389)

Ask students to complete activities **13-12** and **13-13** at home. Then, complete **13-14** and supplement it with the activity below to practice the vocabulary from a different angle.

La lista de la Columna A contiene la clasificación de las obras que producen diferentes artistas. Bajo la Columna B, escribe el oficio de la persona que produce la obra, y en la Columna C, pon el nombre de otro(a) artista hispano(a) que pertenezca a esa categoría. Si tienes algún problema, consulta con el Internet y/o con tu instructor(a).

Columna A	Columna B	Columna C
1. un concierto	_____	_____
2. una fotografía	_____	_____
3. una canción	_____	_____
4. un cuadro	_____	_____
5. un poema	_____	_____
6. una estatua	_____	_____
7. un drama	_____	_____
8. una novela	_____	_____
9. una ópera	_____	_____
10. una danza	_____	_____

EN VOZ ALTA (page 390)

Ask students to work on activities **13-15, 13-16,** and **13-17** before working on the next three suggestions.

1. In groups of three or four, have students choose a Hispanic artist they have heard of or in whom they are interested and use the Web to find information about him or her. Then, have them report to the class what they have found out:

    1. ¿Quién es?
    2. ¿De dónde es?
    3. Su campo *(field)* de arte
    4. Sus obras famosas
    5. ¿Innovaciones a su campo artístico?

2. **¿Quién soy?** Have students pick a Hispanic artist and give a description to classmates using information similar to that found in items 1 to 5 above while the classmates attempt to figure out who the artist is.

3. **Las 20 preguntas** One student chooses an artist. Classmates take turns asking questions in order to determine the artist's identity.

ENCUENTRO CULTURAL (page 391)

After reading the information on Oswaldo Guayasamín and answering the **Para discutir** questions that follow, have students continue with the questions below to make sure that they have understood the reading.

1. ¿Dónde nació este pintor?
2. ¿Cuándo comenzó su carrera de pintor?
3. ¿Cuándo tuvo lugar su primera exhibición?
4. ¿Qué es el título de su primera gran obra?
5. ¿Cuánto tiempo le lleva a Guayasamín para pintar uno de sus cuadros? ¿Con qué material pinta?
6. ¿Qué pintaba él al fin de su vida?

ESTRUCTURA II Talking about unplanned or accidental occurrences: no-fault *se* construction (page 392)

The most important point to remember is that the construction is similar to that of verbs such as **gustar,** where the syntactic subject and the semantic subject differ; the semantic subject is actually the indirect object of the verb and what appears to be the surface direct object is really the deep structure subject. The function of this construction is to place responsibility for the action or behavior on the "object," similar to saying *The glass fell* rather than stating *I dropped the glass.* There is no construction in English similar to that of the Spanish ergative verbs.

¡A PRACTICAR! (pages 392–393)

Have students complete activities **13-18** and **13-19** for homework and finalize the practice with these skeleton phrases.

Escribe oraciones completas con las frases esqueletas que siguen sin cambiar el orden de los elementos. Sigan el modelo.

> MODELO: artistas / olvidar / muchas cosas
> *A los artistas se les olvidan muchas cosas.*

1. Carmela / olvidar / currículum / en el carro
2. maestro / perder / llaves / ayer
3. asistente / caer / pintura / al suelo
4. maestro y Beto / quedar / cuadros / en casa
5. maestro / nunca / acabar / entusiasmo / por el arte
6. Carmela y Beto / quebrar *(break)* / pinceles
7. Beto / pasar / fecha *(it escaped his memory)*
8. todos / olvidar / traer / dinero a la tienda

EN VOZ ALTA (page 393)

Have students begin with activity **13-20,** followed by activity **13-21.** After the first student has finished answering the questions in **13-21,** have the second student share his (her) experiences and then have them report on each other to the class.

ASÍ SE DICE Describing completed actions and resulting conditions: use of the past participle as adjective (page 394)

¡OJO! When the emphasis is on the action itself and is followed with a "by phrase" to indicate the "perpetrator" of the action, this is known as the *passive voice*.

¡A PRACTICAR! (pages 394–395)

Ask students to complete activities **13-22, 13-23,** and **13-24** as homework. Then ask them to complete the paragraph below.

Escribe la forma correcta del participio pasado de los verbos entre paréntesis.

Todos los problemas con la exhibición fueron _____ **(resolver)** por Isabela y su supervisor. Los cuadros que están _____ **(colgar)** en las paredes de la primera sala fueron _____ **(pintar)** por artistas peruanos, mientras que las estatuas _____ **(hacer)** de mármol están en la sala a la derecha. Cuando las cajas fueron _____ **(abrir)** por Isabel, ella notó que varias obras de arte estaban _____ **(romper),** pero los artistas pudieron arreglarlas. Ahora que están _____ **(poner)** en su lugar, van a ser _____ **(ver)** por millones de espectadores. Las puertas de la exposición van a estar _____ **(abrir)** a partir de mañana al mediodía. ¡Estén _____ **(preparar)** para pasarlo bien y para asombrarse por la belleza que presentamos!

EN VOZ ALTA (page 395)

Have students complete activities **13-25** and **13-26** in pairs. Then have them change roles so that each one has an opportunity to both ask and answer the questions in fhe first activity and to tell her/his version of the three accidents requested.

SÍNTESIS

This activity may serve as a replacement or a supplement. Place students in groups of three or four to take part in the following multi-part project.

Tú eres el (la) dueño(a) de una galería de arte que se especializa en todo tipo de arte latinoamericano contemporáneo. Por eso, tú y tu(s) asistente(s) están haciendo los planes para la próxima exposición.

Paso 1: Decidan en qué se va a enfocar esta exposición: cierta región geográfica (Centro América, el Caribe), cierto país (Ecuador, Perú), cierto tipo de arte (pintura al óleo, acuarelas, escultura) o en una combinación de todos.

Paso 2: Salgan a surfear en la Red electrónica y busquen información sobre una variedad de artistas que caigan bajo la categoría que Uds. hayan escogido.

Paso 3: Discutan la información que van a incluir en el folleto que necesitan publicar para el público que va a asistir al estreno de la exhibición.

Paso 4: Preparen el folleto anunciando y describiendo la exposición. Incluyan una lista de los artistas que vayan a participar en ella con una minibiografía de cada uno, las obras que se vayan a presentar, etc.

Paso 5: Repasen su folleto para asegurarse de que han incluido toda la información necesaria e importante y de que no haya ningún error para poder mandarlo a la imprenta.

Paso 6: Entréguenle el folleto a su instructor(a).

14 La vida pública: Chile

CHAPTER OPENER (page 402)

To motivate the class discussion, ask students:

1. ¿Cuánto interés tienes en la política local de tu pueblo o ciudad? ¿Y en cuanto a la política nacional?
2. ¿Votas en todas las elecciones? ¿Por qué sí o por qué no?
3. ¿Crees que el derecho a votar y la libertad política son importantes? Explica.
4. ¿Participas activamente en la vida política de tu país? ¿Cómo? ¿Por qué sí o por qué no?

VOCABULARIO La política y el voto (page 404)

To get the students thinking about the vocabulary included in this chapter, have them pair up and write as many political terms as they can. Ask them if they know the term in Spanish for each. Then, go over the vocabulary list and assign the activities for homework.

¡A PRACTICAR! (page 405)

Have students write out activities **14-1, 14-2, 14-3,** and **14-4** for homework and then go over them in class to make sure that students are using the vocabulary correctly.

EN VOZ ALTA (page 406)

After students have completed activities **14-5, 14-6,** and **14-7,** complete the following activity.

Tú eres el (la) reportero(a) principal del Canal 92 y tus jefes te han dado la oportunidad de entrevistar a uno de los más conocidos políticos de los siglos XIX y XX. Puedes hablar con Jacobo Arbenz (dictador Guatemalteco), Simón Bolívar (libertador suramericano), Manuel Noriega (dictador y narcotraficante panameño), Fidel Castro (líder cubano) o Augusto Pinochet (dictador chileno). Hazle a uno de ellos las preguntas apropiadas para saber por qué y cómo llegó al poder y a la posición en la historia mundial y de su país, cuándo se interesó en la política, si logró todo lo que quería, qué piensa de lo que hizo o no pudo hacer durante su tiempo en el poder. Si necesitas información, pídesela a tu profesor(a) o búscale en el Internet.

EN CONTEXTO (page 407)

Have students read the four questions presented in the text together with the ones below before listening to the Student Text Audio CD. Then have them listen while looking for the information to answer the questions provided. If necessary, play the Student Text Audio CD a second time so that the students can gather the appropriate information.

1. ¿En qué hotel está hospedada Marina?
2. ¿Por qué reconoce Marina a Óscar?
3. ¿Qué es una manifestación? ¿Por qué hay una manifestación ese día?
4. ¿Por qué no sabe Marina lo que está ocurriendo?
5. ¿Qué le explica Marina a Óscar sobre filosofía y política?
6. ¿Qué es el deber cívico de cada ciudadano?
7. ¿Qué acuerdo hacen los dos jóvenes?
8. ¿Con cuál de ellos te identificas? ¿Por qué?

ENCUENTRO CULTURAL (page 408)

After reading the selection, have students answer the **Para discutir** questions provided in the text as well as the following.

1. ¿Qué puesto ocupaba Pinochet cuando Allende era presidente?
2. ¿Qué hacía Pinochet en Inglaterra cuando fue detenido por los ingleses?
3. ¿Cuál fue el resultado de la lucha legal en Gran Bretaña?

Then, add the following questions to the discussion.

1. ¿Qué piensas de los gobiernos que violan los derechos humanos, tales como los de China y los de Europa oriental?
2. ¿Crees que hay violaciones de los derechos humanos en los Estados Unidos?
3. ¿Cómo se puede evitar este tipo de violación?

ESTRUCTURA I Talking about future events: the future tense (pages 409–410)

¡OJO! In some Latin American countries, especially in Central America and the Andean region, there is a difference in meaning and purpose between the periphrastic future (**ir** + **a** + infinitive) and the simple future tense. The former shows less certainty of occurrence than the latter, which shows purpose, thereby increasing the likelihood that the situation will occur.

¡OJO! Be sure to point out that there is only one set of personal endings for all verbs regardless of the conjugation to which they belong. There are no irregular verbs in the future tense, only those that have irregular stems.

¡A PRACTICAR! (page 411)

Have students complete activities **14-8, 14-9,** and **14-10** for homework, then have them do the following if more practice is needed.

Cambie los verbos subrayados *(underlined)* del párrafo al tiempo futuro.

Mañana <u>visitamos</u> varios sitios de la ciudad de Santiago. El autobús <u>llega</u> al hotel a las ocho y media de la mañana. <u>Salimos</u> para la Plaza de las Armas a las nueve menos cuarto. Nadie <u>puede</u> perder el autobús. También <u>vamos</u> a la universidad. Algunos <u>prefieren</u> un restaurante con comida americana, mientras otros <u>quieren</u> comer comida típica de la región. <u>Volvemos</u> al hotel después de las siete de la tarde. Luego <u>tenemos que</u> acostarnos porque <u>estamos</u> cansados. <u>Es</u> un día precioso, en el que <u>experimentamos</u> muchas aventuras. Al día siguiente todos <u>ponen</u> los regalos que compraron en sus maletas y <u>continuamos</u> a la próxima ciudad donde <u>hay</u> una función de baile folclórico. Todos <u>nos acordamos</u> con felicidad de nuestro viaje a Sur América.

EN VOZ ALTA (page 412)

Have students complete activities **14-11, 14-12,** and **14-13** and, if necessary, continue with the next discussion in pairs.

A un(a) compañero(a), pregúntale sobre sus planes para viajar durante los próximos cinco años. Debes incluir adónde y por cuánto tiempo, qué hará allí, con quién, por qué escogió ese lugar (o esos lugares), etc. Luego cambien de papel y deja que tu compañero(a) te pregunte sobre tus planes.

VOCABULARIO Las preocupaciones cívicas y los medios de comunicación (page 413)

¡OJO! Add the term **el narcotráfico** to the list of **preocupaciones cívicas** and **la Red electrónica** and **el correo electrónico** to the section on **medios de comunicación** in order to round out the vocabulary of this section.

¡A PRACTICAR! (page 414)

After completing activities **14-14, 14-15,** and **14-16** for homework, ask students to answer the following questions.

Completa las siguientes oraciones con una palabra o expresión de la lista de vocabulario.

1. Muchos países latinoamericanos tienen un alto nivel de _____ porque muchas personas no saben leer. (analfabetismo)

2. Cuando los trabajadores desean mejores condiciones y se niegan trabajar, decimos que están en _____. (huelga)

3. El Brasil es el país suramericano con la tasa más alta de _____. (inflación)

4. Uno de los derechos protegidos por la Constitución de los Estados Unidos es _____. (la libertad de prensa)

5. Para muchas personas religiosas es un pecado matar un embrión y por eso están en contra del _____. (aborto)

6. En los Estados Unidos hay mucha _____ de los países hispanos, especialmente de México y Cuba. (inmigración)

7. _____ es un método rápido y fácil de buscar información. (el Internet)

8. Todos los días, muchas personas escuchan _____ en la radio mientras que otras lo miran en la tele. (el noticiero)

9. Una de las prioridades de la organización de Doctores sin fronteras es _____ las enfermedades y curar a la gente pobre. (eliminar/reducir)

10. Para evitar los golpes de estado, es necesario _____ al pueblo y _____ contra los males de la sociedad. (informar, protestar)

EN VOZ ALTA (page 415)

Have students complete activities **14-17, 14-18,** and **14-19.** Then have them choose a partner with whom to work on the next activity.

Uno(a) de ustedes es candidato(a) para presidente. El (La) otro(a) es el líder de los inmigrantes que están protestando contra la violación de los derechos de Elián González. Uds., los inmigrantes, creen que este chico debe permanecer en los Estados Unidos, mientras que muchos miembros del gobierno estadounidense piensan que debe volver a Cuba con su padre. Cuando terminen, cambien de papel y vuelvan a discutir la situación.

¿NOS ENTENDEMOS? (page 415)

It is considered a lack of respect to refer to older people as **viejos**. In Central America, the term **la (gente) grande** is used to refer to older people.

ENCUENTRO CULTURAL (page 416)

Have students read the narrative presented and then answer the **Para discutir** questions in complete Spanish sentences. Then have them discuss the questions posed under **Para pensar.** Have students consider the topics below in addition to those already in the text.

1. ¿Es importante proteger los derechos de aquéllos que tienen ideas que no sean populares o que estén en contra de las ideas de la mayoría? ¿Por qué?
2. ¿Es necesario que la democracia los proteja a todos? ¿Por qué sí o por qué no?

ESTRUCTURA II Expressing conjecture or probability: the conditional (pages 417–418)

¡OJO! Point out to your students that to form the conditional tense they need to know only one set of personal endings, whether the verb is regular or irregular. Remind them that the stem for the conditional tense is the entire infinitive, as it is for the future tense. In addition, the stems employed are identical to those employed in the formation of the future. Once again, there are no irregular endings.

¡A PRACTICAR! (page 419)

After completion of activities **14-20, 14-21, 14-22,** and **14-23,** have students continue with the activity below.

Tú sueñas con poder ayudar a la población mundial por medios pacíficos. Completa las siguientes oraciones, explicando lo que harías para lograr tus metas.

1. yo / darles / dinero / a los pobres

   _____

2. todos los niños del mundo / poder / asistir a la escuela

   _____

3. doctores / curar / a todos lo enfermos del mundo

   _____

4. siempre / haber / lo suficiente de todo

   _____

5. nosotros / salir / a informarle / al público sobre los derechos humanos

   _____

6. la prensa / les decir / la verdad a todos

   _____

7. la cantidad de comida disponible / aumentar / en el tercer mundo

   _____

8. haber / paz / y la guerra / terminar

   _____

EN VOZ ALTA (page 420)

Have students work on activities **14-24, 14-25, 14-26,** and **14-27.** If more oral practice is needed, ask them what they would do if they awoke one morning to find themselves in a body of the opposite sex.

Una mañana te despiertas y te encuentras dentro de un cuerpo del sexo opuesto. ¿Qué harías en esta situación?

ESTRUCTURA III Making references to the present: the present perfect subjunctive (page 421)

¡OJO! Remind students that the **haber** in the formation of this tense/mood is the *personal* or *auxiliary* verb rather than the *expletive* (impersonal) **haber** from which **hay** is conjugated. The present subjunctive forms of **haber** are **haya, hayas, haya, hayamos, hayáis, hayan.**

¡A PRACTICAR! (page 422)

Have students work in pairs on activities **14-28** and **14-29.** Then have them change partners or get into small groups to review the activities. You may also go over the activities as a class so that all questions are answered and any confusion is clarified before going on to do more complex activities. The following activity can be done in addition to or in lieu of the activities in the book.

El señor Sandoval busca un(a) asistente para su negocio de consulta. Completa las oraciones con la forma correcta de los verbos indicados para ver qué tipo de asistente busca.

1. Quiere que el(la) asistente *(has had)...*
2. Prefiere que esta persona *(has worked)...*
3. Hoy desea entrevistar a una joven que *(has lived)...*
4. Teme que los otros aspirantes no *(have not been able to)...*

EN VOZ ALTA (page 423)

Pair your students to complete activities **14-30** and **14-31.** Then choose a few pairs to demonstrate each of the activities to the rest of the class.

SÍNTESIS

This activity may serve as a replacement or as a supplement. In groups of three or four individuals, consider yourselves the executive council of a group of social and political activists. Choose a political or social problem that requires action and do the following:

Paso 1: Discuss what can be done to ameliorate the situation or eradicate the problem without violence. Also, determine what short- and long-term goals the group has.

Paso 2: Make a list of actions/activities that the group can organize or sponsor and mention why they are important to the organization's goals. (This is crucial in order to motivate your members!)

Paso 3: Write a letter or narrative explaining the group's position to release to the news media in order to attract more individuals to join you.

Paso 4: Review what you have written and edit it as necessary. Then rewrite it in its final form.

Paso 5: Present your position at a news conference (to your classmates).

Paso 6: Turn the final draft in to your instructor so that she/he can evaluate it.

Los avances tecnológicos: Uruguay

15

CHAPTER OPENER (page 430)

To put students in the right mind-set and to motivate class discussion, ask them to first think about and then answer the following set of queries.

1. ¿Qué opinas de los avances tecnológicos?
2. ¿Crees que valen la pena *(they're worth it)* o piensas que son demasiado costosos y que dependemos demasiado de ellos?
3. ¿Qué máquinas tienes en tu casa que consideres necesidades (y no lujos) y que muestren los avances de la tecnología?

VOCABULARIO Los avances tecnológicos (page 432)

Advances in technology and the results thereof have come to be a part of everyday life.

Therefore, it is important that students learn the vocabulary associated with business and communication technology as well as the different innovations on which we have come to rely in our homes. Because many of these machines were designed and developed in the United States or in other countries not part of the Spanish-speaking world, many words are easily recognized cognates adapted to Spanish phonology and morphology.

¡OJO! One term that you should consider adding to this list of home appliances is **la grabadora,** especially since the verb **grabar** is included in the vocabulary provided.

¿NOS ENTENDEMOS? (page 432)

Many Spanish speakers shorten the term for *remote control* to **el remoto**, just as in English *(the remote).*

¡A PRACTICAR! (pages 432–433)

Have students complete activities **15-1** and **15-2** as homework. Then go over any of the items that may have caused students trouble before going on to work on the activity below as a class.

Contesta las preguntas con una palabra o frase de la lista de vocabulario.

1. ¿Qué equipo tecnológico o electrónico tienes en casa?
2. ¿Alquilas películas para verlas con tu videocasetera?
3. ¿Compras discos compactos o cintas *(tapes)* con música?
4. ¿Tienes un contestador automático? ¿Por qué?
5. ¿Qué opinas de los teléfonos celulares? ¿Tienes uno? ¿Lo usas con frecuencia? ¿Para qué sirven?
6. ¿Te acuerdas de desconectar o apagar todo tu equipo cuando sales de tu casa? ¿Por qué es importante hacerlo?
7. ¿A veces te duermes con la tele o el estéreo prendidos?
8. En tu casa, ¿quién controla el remoto?

EN VOZ ALTA (page 433)

After completing activities **15-3**, **15-4**, and **15-5** as homework assignments or, time permitting, ask students to get into groups of three and prepare the scene that is described below.

> Tú y tu novio(a) van de compras a una tienda de equipos electrónicos tal como Circuit City o Best Buy porque has ganado la lotería y has comprado un nuevo condominio. Ahora necesitas comprar aparatos con todos los más modernos avances tecnológicos. Al entrar, uno(a) de los (las) vendedores(as) de la tienda se ofrece a ayudarte. Tú y tu compañero(a) les explican lo que desean comprar, cuánto tienen para gastar y por qué quieren lo que han pedido. El (La) vendedor(a) por su parte trata de convencerlos de que gasten más dinero y compren equipo adicional. Después de practicar la escena, el (la) profesor(a) les pedirá que se la presenten a los (las) compañeros(as) de clase.

EN CONTEXTO (page 434)

Have students read the questions that follow before listening to the Student Text Audio CD so that they can listen for the appropriate information. Then play the Student Text Audio CD a second time so that they are able to verify the correctness of their responses. Allow students to discuss the answers as a large group activity. The sequence should begin with **¿Comprendiste?** and continue with the additional questions provided here.

1. ¿Qué han hecho los padres de Alejandra por su hija y su yerno?
2. ¿Cómo difieren las personalidades de los jóvenes?
3. ¿Por qué cree Federico que es una ocasión perfecta para abrir la tienda?
4. ¿Por qué no tiene fe Alejandra en lo que le dice Federico?

ENCUENTRO CULTURAL (page 435)

Rather than limiting the questions to those listed in the text, you may add these four to make sure that the students have understood the reading.

1. ¿Qué es muy importante en el comercio global? ¿Por qué?
2. ¿Qué les faltaba a los países latinoamericanos en años pasados?
3. ¿Por qué se creía antes que era peligroso invertir dinero en Uruguay?
4. ¿Qué es Antel?

Add the next two sets of questions for students to think about and then discuss in **Para pensar.**

1. ¿Tienes interés en trabajar en Uruguay o en otro país de Sur América? ¿Por qué sí o por qué no?
2. ¿Sabes lo que es NAFTA? Explícaselo a tus compañeros de clase. ¿Crees que MERCOSUR es menos, tan o más necesario que NAFTA? Explica por qué piensas así.

ESTRUCTURA I Making statements in the past: past (imperfect) subjunctive (pages 436–437)

¡OJO! Remind students that impersonal expressions are identical to personalized generalizations, such as *Era interesante* **que mi trabajo** *resultara* **en un negocio exitoso.**

¡A PRACTICAR! (page 438)

Assign activities **15-6**, **15-7**, and **15-8** to be completed outside of class so you can review during class and clear up any problems. The following is presented as an alternative/additional activity.

¿Bajo qué condiciones vivirías en Uruguay? Completa las siguientes oraciones para contestar esta pregunta, usando los verbos indicados.

1. Viviría en Uruguay hasta que (ser)...
2. Preferiría vivir en Montevideo en caso de que (estar)...
3. Me gustaría vivir en una casa allí si no (costar)...
4. Necesitaría un buen empleo que (tener)...
5. Llevaría todas mis cosas para que nosotros (poder)...

EN VOZ ALTA (page 439)

Add the activity below after students complete activities **15-9** and **15-10.**

Cuéntale a un(a) compañero(a) los consejos que tus padres y otros parientes te dieron cuando comenzaste tus estudios universitarios. Luego, pregúntale a ese(a) mismo(a) compañero(a) lo que le aconsejaron a él (ella) sus padres y otros parientes en cuanto a la universidad. Túrnense para hacer la actividad.

VOCABULARIO La computadora (page 440)

This section of vocabulary stresses terms related to computers, word processing, the World Wide Web, and cyberspace. Again, point out the many terms that have become part of Spanish by simply applying Spanish phonological and morphological rules to the English words.

¡OJO! Be sure to inform your students that in Spain, people refer to a computer as **el ordenador** rather than as **la computadora.**

¡A PRACTICAR! (pages 441–442)

Assign activities **15-11, 15-12,** and **15-13** as homework before going on to the next activity. Then, review them all as a class to make sure that everyone understands how to use the vocabulary.

Identifica la palabra que se define.

1. El lugar donde guardo la información dentro de la computadora (el archivo)
2. Los mensajes que recibo de mis amigos en la computadora (el correo electrónico)
3. La máquina que uso para convertir documentos e imágenes de manera que la computadora los pueda leer (el escáner)
4. Otro nombre para la Red electrónica (el Internet)
5. El lugar en el ciberespacio donde las personas se reúnen (la sala de charla)
6. Los aparatos por donde salen la música y otros sonidos de la computadora (los altavoces)
7. El instrumento necesario para hacerle click (el ratón)
8. El medio magnético para grabar la información de la computadora (el disquete)
9. El sitio donde se puede ver lo que se escribe o lo que hay en la Red electrónica (la pantalla)
10. Lo que haces con la información cuando terminas un trabajo en la computadora (archivar)

EN VOZ ALTA (page 442)

After completing activities **15-14** and **15-15,** ask students to continue with the following activity.

Con un(a) compañero(a) de clase, hagan la escena siguiente. Explícale a tu amigo(a), que nunca ha usado una computadora, lo que debe hacer para buscar, y luego archivar la información que necesita para su tarea sobre la zona turística uruguaya. También explícale cómo se usa su nuevo programa de redacción *(word processing)* para escribir su trabajo final y después, imprimirlo. Luego cambia de papel con tu compañero(a) y deja que él (ella) te explique a ti cómo obtener *(gather)* información, usando tu computadora.

ENCUENTRO CULTURAL (page 443)

Have students read the cultural information in the textbook so that they can answer the **Para discutir** questions that immediately follow it. Then add these two questions to those in the text.

1. ¿Qué avances pueden resultar de la alianza de los fabricantes de los PDA y las operadoras telefónicas?
2. ¿Hay versiones más avanzadas de los PDA en otros países? ¿Cómo son?

ESTRUCTURA II Talking about hypothetical situations: *if* clauses (page 444)

¡OJO! Be sure to explain to your students what hypothetical statements are and under what circumstances they are used. You might also explain to them that they use the subjunctive because they are considered "contrary to fact" and similar to those adjective clauses dealing with nonexistent antecedents.

¡A PRACTICAR! (pages 444–445)

Ask students to do activities **15-16** and **15-17** at home so that you can go over them in class. Then review them and continue with this short activity.

La ciudad necesita para la biblioteca un nuevo jefe que sepa integrar las computadoras y navegar el Internet. Quieres el puesto porque crees que eres la persona ideal para el puesto porque has hecho lo mismo en tu último empleo. Ahora te toca explicarle al supervisor de la ciudad por qué eres el (la) mejor candidato(a) y qué planes tienes para modernizar la biblioteca si te seleccionaran. Escribe la forma correcta del verbo en paréntesis según el contexto.

Pienso que la biblioteca _____ (funcionar) mejor si yo _____ (ser) el bibliotecario y _____ (poder) instalar varias computadoras allí. Además, me parece que todos los empleados _____ (trabajar) más y _____ (estar) más contentos si nosotros les _____ (dar) un aumento de sueldo. Si todos _____ (tener) más dinero y beneficios, entonces _____ (poner) más interés en el trabajo de ahora en adelante. Si yo _____ (poder), les _____ (dar) a mis empleados más oportunidades de tomar decisiones y ellos _____ (sentirse) más importantes y como parte del proceso. Pues, si ellos _____ (participar) en el manejo de la biblioteca, _____ (haber) menos problemas en el futuro y todo _____ (funcionar) mucho mejor. Creo que todo _____ (comenzar) con un contrato para mí y una media docena de computadoras conectadas a la Red electrónica.

EN VOZ ALTA (page 445)

Have students work together on activities **15-18** and **15-19** before going on to interview Bill Gates in the next activity.

Tu jefe en la revista *El mundo cibernético* te ha mandado a entrevistar a Bill Gates sobre su compañía, su éxito y sus problemas con el gobierno estadounidense. Tu compañero(a) hará el papel de Bill Gates, mientras que tú haces el papel del (de la) reportero(a). Tú debes decidir qué preguntas quieres hacerle al multimillonario para poder escribir tu artículo.

SÍNTESIS

This activity may serve as a replacement or a supplement.

Tres de tus amigos te han invitado a hacerte miembro de un consorcio que desea invertir fondos en varios locales de Sur América. Has decidido asociarte con ellos, puesto que tu abuelo murió recientemente y te dejó un millón de dólares de herencia.

Paso 1: Discutan el tipo de negocio en que desean invertir dinero y establecer una empresa internacional.

Paso 2: Hagan un plan financiero y decidan el equipo que necesitan, tanto para abrir la empresa, como para establecer y mantener comunicación a través del mundo con socios y clientes.

Paso 3: Repasen su plan y la lista de mercancía *(merchandise)*.

Paso 4: Arréglenlo para presentárselo al banco local.

Paso 5: Háganle la presentación oral del plan a los oficiales bancarios (sus compañeros de clase) y al (a la) profesor(a).

Paso 6: Entréguenle el proyecto a su profesor(a).